Pitt Latin American Series
Pitt Series in Policy and Institutional Studies

The Brazilian Voter

Mass Politics in Democratic Transition 1974–1986

Kurt von Mettenheim

University of Pittsburgh Press
Pittsburgh and London

Published by the University of Pittsburgh Press, Pittsburgh, Pa., 15260
Copyright © 1995, University of Pittsburgh Press
All rights reserved
Manufactured in the United States of America
Printed on acid-free paper

Designed by Jane Tenenbaum

Library of Congress Cataloging-in-Publication Data

Von Mettenheim, Kurt, 1957–
    The Brazilian voter : mass politics in democratic transition,
1974–1986 / Kurt von Mettenheim.
        p.   cm.
    Includes bibliographical references (p. 273–290) and index.
    ISBN 0-8229-3838-3
    1. Political participation—Brazil.   2. Voting—Brazil.
3. Elections—Brazil.   4. Brazil—Politics and
government—1964–1985.   5. Brazil—Politics and government—1985–
I. Title.
JL2492.M47   1995
324.981'063—dc20   94-39781
                                                                        CIP

A CIP catalogue record for this book is available from the British Library.
Eurospan, London

Contents

List of Tables and Figures

Acknowledgments

This manuscript began at Columbia University in 1984 with the patient orientations of Douglas Chalmers. Alfred Stepan, Maria do Carmo Campello de Souza, Robert Shapiro, Margaret Keck, Kenneth Erickson, Joan Dassin, and many colleagues at the Institute for Latin American and Iberian Studies provided insightful suggestions early on. The Inter-American Foundation provided support for field research during 1984–1985 through its doctoral fellowship program. David Collier, Fabio Wanderley Reis, and other members of the Inter-American Foundation review committee offered generous, constructive, and substantive comments about the original field research project.

During the following rather inexplicable five years in São Paulo, comments by Jose Arthur Giannotti, Bolivar Lamounier, Guillermo O'Donnell, Celia Quirino dos Santos, and Jose Francisco dos Santos brought me closer to the democratic realities and liberal tragedies of Brazilian politics. During this time, the Centro Brasileiro de Analise e Planejamento (CEBRAP) and the Instituto de Estudos Economicos, Sociais, e Politicos de São Paulo (IDESP) provided both institutional base and intellectual inspiration. Special thanks are in order to Ruth Cardoso, Francisco de Oliveira, Tereza Caldeira, and the "young economists" at CEBRAP, as well as Elizabeth Balbechevsky and Marcus Figueiredo for help organizing electoral surveys at IDESP. Many ideas about Brazilian voters and politicians in this manuscript are indebted to Fernando Henrique Cardoso, who generously permitted close observation of both his 1985 campaign for Mayor of São Paulo and 1986 campaign for reelection to the Senate.

I also would like to thank Jonathan Hurwitz, Jeffrey Mondak, Bert Rockman, and Wen Fang Tang, for their advice and collegiality in the University of Pittsburgh's Department of Political Science. Special thanks are in order to Mitchell Seligson for his patient reading and careful comments, as well as Julio Carrion for extensive assistance

with statistical matters. Ernesto Cabrera, Robert Chisholm, Yasuhiko Matsuda, Jorge Papadopolous, Jamie Jacobs Anderson, and Andrew Stein must also be thanked for their help in clarifying arguments during a graduate seminar on Brazilian politics, co-taught with James Malloy. Special thanks are in order to James Malloy, whose intellectual acumen and editorial vision shaped this manuscript in more ways that he recognizes.

I fear the manuscript does little justice to the intellectual debts incurred along the way.

The Brazilian Voter

Introduction

How rational are voters? Can politics within the rules of liberal democracy deepen social and economic justice? Does the expansion of suffrage and political participation generate instability and ungovernability? Do highly efficient mass party organizations tend to monopolize elections and exclude new social movements and issues? While these questions have occupied political philosophers for some time, studies of electoral behavior and party development remained at the forefront of social science inquiry in the twentieth century by analyzing not only the American experience, but also substantive cross-national phenomena. These subfields were built on a sequence of ground-breaking analyses of new political problems, such as voters embracing fascism in Europe during the 1930s, the reorganization of democracies after World War II, the subsequent decline of modern, class-based voting in the 1960s, the emergence of new social movements and postmaterialist values in the 1970s, and the turn toward conservative parties in advanced democracies in the 1980s.[1]

The unprecedented number of transitions from authoritarian rule to democracy in recent years raise both classic questions and new substantive problems that challenge conventional theories of electoral behavior, party development, and democratic politics in the 1990s. The Brazilian experience has been at the forefront of scientific and political debates on authoritarianism, political instability, and the transition to democracy in southern Europe, Latin America, Asia, Eastern Europe, and the new republics of the former Soviet Union. Eleven years of gradual, nonviolent political change and institutional reform under military rule culminated in a transfer of power to civilian rule in 1985. After 1974, increasingly contested elections were central mechanisms of the Brazilian transition, with over 82 million Brazilians voting for president by 1989.[2] This book presents three interrelated and mutually reinforcing arguments that attempt to understand Brazilian voters and mass politics in democratic transition and to place their experience

before analysts of electoral behavior, party development, and democratic theory.

Brazilian Voters and Theories of Electoral Behavior

The first argument is that party politics in contested elections after 1973 caused a rapid alignment from the weak and unstructured voting patterns of authoritarian Brazil to new patterns of public opinion and voter alignment—some resembling those in advanced democracies, others typically Brazilian. Scholars agree that the most important political factors that organize public opinion and determine voter choice are (1) party identification, (2) positions on issues, (3) perceptions of government performance, (4) campaign participation, and (5) attitudes toward democratic institutions.[3] This book presents substantial evidence from survey data collected just before the 1974, 1978, and 1982 national elections, that these same factors (individually, collectively, and often in quite different ways) rapidly organized Brazilian public opinion and voter choice during this initial phase of the transition from military rule to democracy.

In broader terms, the pace of change in Brazilian popular beliefs during a democratic transition is consistent with recent studies of electoral behavior that emphasize complexity, rationality, and change in contemporary public opinion.[4] Many analysts now reject the traditional view that political change is inhibited by voters' ignorance—or, as Campbell, Converse, and Stokes wrote in *The American Voter* (1960), "Whatever the depths of a person's political involvement, there are rather basic limitations on cognitive capacities which are likely to make certain of the most sophisticated types of content remain inaccessible to the poorly endowed observer."[5] The rapid changes that occurred among Brazilian voters after 1974 also suggest that what scholars had seen as uninformed public opinion under authoritarian rule was not ignorance, lack of education, or lack of political socialization, but rather proof of the depoliticizing effects of military control.[6]

Traditional measures of political sophistication—how individuals think about politics—used in studies of electoral behavior would miss many of the recent changes in the Brazilian electorate because they are designed to tap European ideologies or U.S. notions of group interest rather than capturing the specific ideas, concepts, and political

context that have influenced Brazilian voters. As set up by Campbell and colleagues in *The American Voter* and by Converse's groundbreaking work of 1964, "The Nature of Belief Systems in Mass Publics,"[7] the conventional scale of conceptualization is as follows: (1) ideologue, (2) near ideologue, (3) perceptions of group interest, and (4) general notions about the nature of the times. According to these (widely debated) measures of political sophistication, the cognitive content of many responses to survey questions in Brazil can be classified only in residual categories such as "nature of the times" or "no content." This book unpacks from these latter categories two conceptions of politics that are typical among Brazilian voters—which we will call "immediate" and "personalistic"—to examine how they inform political beliefs and choices.

A central argument of this book is that immediate and personalistic conceptions of politics are both cause and consequence of the direct plebiscitarian appeals, patronage machines, and state-centered populist-nationalist tradition, which have prevailed in Brazilian mass politics since the 1930 revolution.

This is an open-ended study of emerging characteristics among Brazilian voters in democratic transition during the 1970s and early 1980s. While it employs statistical methods and survey techniques that can provide causal descriptions of electoral behavior, this study recognizes that emphasis on method and technique often conceals fundamental weaknesses in social science models of voter choice.[8] Formal models of democratic electorates often fail to recognize that voter choice is unpredictable. Only voters determine final causes, and they do so anew in every election. Indeterminacy, unpredictability, and surprise are intrinsic features of democratic elections.[9] This analysis of Brazilian voters does not seek to confirm any single model nor derive definitive causal factors from survey data gathered during the transition period. The claim and hope of this book is that voters' choices may in the future be determined by diverse perceptions of economic, social, and political justice in the context of an empowered pluralistic society, open and competitive elections, and democratic institutions.

The data for analysis of Brazilian voters in democratic transition are drawn from sequential surveys conducted by major universities and social science institutes before the 1974, 1978, and 1982 national elections in state capitals and two rural areas.[10] In 1974, surveys were applied in the southeastern cites of Belo Horizonte, São Paulo, and

Porto Alegre by their respective federal universities and by the Centro Brasileiro de Analise e Planejamento (CEBRAP) in São Paulo. In 1978, surveys were applied in these same cities as well as in Rio de Janeiro. For the 1982 election, identical questionnaires were applied in these same four southeast capitals, in three additional capital cities in the less developed northeast region (Salvador, Bahia, Fortaleza, Ceara, and Recife, Pernambuco), as well as in two rural municipalities.

The electoral surveys are not national samples. Surveys were not conducted in the sparsely populated northern states of the Amazon basin or the new agricultural states of the center-west; and the rural samples were limited to two areas in southeastern Brazil. Nonetheless, they enable us to make significant observations about the uneven development of mass belief systems and mass politics in Brazil because researchers applied the 1982 survey in four major capitals of the advanced southeast region, three capitals in the less developed northeast, and two rural areas. Furthermore, by recoding the 1974 and 1978 surveys according to the 1982 questionnaire, we can arrive at substantive conclusions about stability and change among Brazilian voters over time during the transition to democracy. In sum, the data permit comparison of Brazilian public opinion across significant blocks of time and space, enabling us to examine core questions of electoral behavior, party development, and democratic theory and practice in Latin America.

Brazilian Voters and Democratic Theory

The second major argument of this book focuses on the implications for democratic theory of the rapid changes that have occurred among Brazilian voters. The causal logic, cognitive content, and political context of public opinion during the period of transition to democracy in Brazil reveal unmediated, direct democratic patterns of state-led representation that are at considerable odds with liberal theories of electoral representation and mass democracy. New concepts of *direct democracy* and *state-led representation* are required to understand Brazilian public opinion and to challenge traditional liberal assumptions about the unidirectional, bottom-up articulation of voters' preferences.

The complex reciprocal effects, top-down appeals, and feedback mechanisms of power emphasized in recent studies of mass belief

systems appear to have been critical during Brazil's recent transition; yet they are not fully recognized by the traditional model of voter choice or current accounts of Brazilian public opinion.[11] The traditional model of public opinion and voter choice in advanced democracies is that long-term factors such as political socialization, class-based identity, and party identification moderate short-term shifts in public opinion caused by current economic factors, candidates' personalities, and new political issues.[12] However, the concept of direct democracy implies a fundamentally new causal sequence: voters choose on the basis of their perceptions of executive performance and national issues of the day, and they ground their choices in ideas about substantive justice rather than being determined by long-term factors such as political socialization, class identity, or party identification.

New concepts of direct democracy and state-led representation are necessary because traditional conceptions of electoral representation from the advanced democracies are seriously flawed. Classic ideas such as *mandate, authorization, accountability,* and *virtual representation* fail to describe adequately how representation works in mass democracies today.[13] Theories of geographical and demographic representation are also insufficient because public perceptions now cut across traditional cleavages of class and region.[14] Political parties no longer retain the near monopoly on representation that was typical of competitive party systems for much of the postwar period.[15] And while liberal theory still views representative government as bottom-up and voter-driven, current studies of mass belief systems emphasize the fragmentation of public opinion into a complex mosaic of many identities, perspectives, and concerns that are formed but not fully determined by elite discourse and media coverage.[16]

Instead of recognizing direct democratic impulses in public opinion, those who study advanced democratic electorates tend to explain influences from above by referring to elite leadership, voters' irrational psychological processes, or the manipulation of public opinion by skillful marketing, public relations, and polling. Competitive theories of democracy are accurately labeled *elite theories* because scholars believe that leaders must form public opinion and influence voter alignment.[17] Landmark studies by Theodore Adorno (1950), Robert Lane (1962), and Elizabeth Noelle-Neumann (1984) suggest that voters succumb to irrational appeals because of low ego-strength, repression, displacement, or other psychological mechanisms.[18] Several recent ac-

counts of public opinion argue that party officials in centralized campaign organizations are increasingly able to manipulate voters through improved political marketing techniques.[19] While these perspectives provide insights about Brazilian public opinion, emphasizing elite leadership, mass psychology, and technologies of manipulation fails to acknowledge the force of direct, unmediated, personality-based conceptions of politics among Brazilian voters and the importance of direct, plebisicitarian appeals and patronage machines in Brazilian party politics. The concepts of *direct democracy* and *state-led representation* capture the realities of direct, unmediated, complex, and constantly changing links between state and society in Brazil. These concepts also suggest that perceptions and preferences among Brazilian voters are direct, unmediated, complex, changing, populist, and responsive to candidates' personalities; yet nevertheless they are linked to matters traditionally associated with direct democracy such as seeing elections as plebiscites and voting on one's convictions about social and economic justice. The concept of direct democracy, as developed herein, refers neither to romantic visions of a perfectly united state and society, nor the institutional use of referenda, nor smaller models such as New England town meetings or Rousseau's Geneva. (Indeed, the idea of direct democracy may also be relevant to the electorates of advanced democracies, given the changes that have occurred in recent decades.) In sum, the concept of direct democracy suggests that Brazilian voters bring direct, short-term perceptions to their judgments of parties, national issues, and executive performance even without the moderating influences of civic culture, long-term political socialization, deep class identities and ideologies, and party identification.

Brazilian Voters and Party-Electoral Politics

The third major argument of this book shifts to the level of party and electoral politics to clarify the political context of Brazilian public opinion. It has been widely asserted that Brazilian parties remain underdeveloped. To the contrary, significant evidence suggests that the executive-centered presidential and federal system of authoritarian Brazil facilitated the nomination of party professionals to executive posts and administrative offices during the period of liberalization, and

that this produced a rapid, sweeping reorganization of mass parties through alliances with local and state patronage machines. This process is not without precedent. Party-electoral politics during Brazil's transition display characteristics strikingly similar to those of U.S. parties in the late nineteenth century—this despite military rule, the lack of direct presidential elections between 1960 and 1989, the close interconnections between the Brazilian state and society, and the new role of contemporary mass media.

Theories based on the ideological parties and disciplined parliamentary politics found in Europe fail to capture the concrete practices, systemic function, and representative role of political parties and elections in Brazil.[20] The United States' experience (especially before Progressive-era legislation weakened parties) is a more adequate reference because it deflects attention away from the *organizational structures* of parties and toward their *electoral practices.* W. D. Burnham argues: "The term [party system] relates primarily to what might be called voting systems or electoral-politics systems rather than to organizational structures."[21] From the acute observations of Max Weber and James Bryce to the "new political historians" of today,[22] what has made the U.S. experience exceptional is its sequence of party systems; the early emergence of mass parties; the predominance of pragmatism, patronage, and a spoils system over ideology; the effect of having a presidential instead of parliamentary system; and the importance of federalism in a new and large country.[23]

Mass parties arose early in nineteenth-century America because presidential elections encouraged direct popular campaign styles and because the president's ability to nominate party professionals to administrative posts permitted alliances, through the spoils system, among elected officials, party machines, and patronage systems.[24] Parliamentary politics and disciplined, well-organized parties were not behind mass inclusion in the United States. As noted, scholars like Burnham, Converse, Jensen, and Kleppner have extensively debated the cultural, historical, social, and political meaning of these characteristics of U.S. parties. But a shift has occurred: debate now rages within a new paradigm for understanding U.S. party development that rejects traditional theories based on European parliaments and well-organized, ideologically based political parties.

Three aspects of U.S. party development offer a fundamentally new perspective on electoral politics in Brazil: (1) the importance of

populism and the plebiscitarian quality of presidential elections; (2) the capacity of presidents and other executives to nominate party loyalists to administrative posts; and (3) the autonomy of local and regional patronage machines under federalism. If one shifts the comparison from Europe to nineteenth-century America, both the place of parties in Brazilian political history and their causal role in forming public opinion appear very different. Instead of focusing on the weak and fleeting character of formal party organizations, their incoherence in terms of European ideologies, and their corruption as a threat to technocratic visions of economic reform, one can see party machines as critical not only to state building and policy formation throughout Brazilian history, but also to the rapid organization of mass politics during the recent transition to democracy.

To clarify the similarities and differences between party development in the nineteenth-century United States and in Brazil, this book reviews the course of party-electoral politics in each major period of Brazilian history. Following an accepted practice of U.S political historians, Brazil's political history can be divided into a succession of party systems. After a period of postindependence conflict (1822–1836), Brazil's first party system emerged during the regency of Dom Pedro II, who later became emperor. The liberal and conservative parties dominated imperial politics thereafter (1836–1889) by forming electoral alliances between the central imperial government and the diverse provincial and county machines, which Oliveira Vianna calls "political clans."[25] The second Brazilian party system during the Old Republic (1889–1930) devolved state power to provincial presidents, single-state parties, and oligarchs through an executive-centered federalism modeled on the U.S. system.

After the 1930 revolution and Getulio Vargas's Estado Novo reconstituted centralized state power and organized inclusionary corporatist institutions, the third Brazilian party system (1945–1964) at last embodied all three elements of precocious party development found in the U.S. experience. After 1945, direct executive elections and the capability of presidents, governors, and mayors to directly appoint party politicians to administrative posts permitted the rapid reorganization of corporatist and patronage-based political machines into mass patronage parties (PSD, PTB, UDN). Finally, during the recent transition from military to civilian rule, one can discern the emerging characteristics of a fourth Brazilian party system by focusing

on the same pattern: how the plebiscitarian nature of executive elections—eliciting either opposition to or support of the military government—was linked to electoral alliances with party patronage machines through administrative appointments of professional politicians.

Can these links between candidates exploiting the plebiscitarian quality of direct elections for executive office and patronage machines be called democratization? Debates about populism, patronage, and mass inclusion reveal deeply divided views of party politics in nineteenth-century America. Given this polarization, we might return to Max Weber's classic description of U.S. party development as *passive democratization* because it distinguishes the analytic task of identifying the new and emerging characteristics of mass electoral and party politics from the equally important but distinct consideration of their normative implications.[26] Indeed, these features of party development (lamented by many in the United States) are even more problematic in Brazil. The reorganization of patronage systems into mass parties by populist candidates for executive office appeared extremely late in Brazilian history. And while political parties, public opinion, and patterns of mass participation recently emerged under military rule in an intensely state-centered society characterized by extreme disparities between rich and poor, differences do not invalidate a comparison between like patterns of political development.

This shift in perspective has significant implications for expectations about the empowerment of civilian society and the growth of parliamentary institutions in Brazil and elsewhere.[27] Theories of civil-society empowerment in Brazil not only describe how new, independent social organizations in an increasingly pluralistic society delegitimized military rule and forced a change of regime, but also how life under authoritarianism may have created new conditions for democratic politics.[28] But the tendency to see political change as driven primarily by new patterns of association and other changes in society has led to two misconceptions about Brazilian voters. At first, discussions of civil-society empowerment in Brazil understood plebiscitarian voting under military rule as primarily antiauthoritarian.[29] Later analyses of electoral results and survey research argue that opposition voting during the transition period was amorphous and confined largely to urban areas in the southeast.[30] This study extends work in Brazilian electoral sociology by suggesting that the plebiscitarian character of

elections in a two-party system under military rule generated not only broad patterns of opposition voting, but also broad patterns of support for the government party. The survey data suggest that support for military governments and the government party (ARENA, later PDS) was organized in a manner typical of mass electoral politics in presidential and federalist systems, despite the lack of direct presidential elections. Indeed, a review of the national elections under military rule shows that many authoritarian state leaders quickly learned how to compete in semicompetitive elections.

Second, the idea of civil society empowerment has led to a misconception about local politics and Brazilian voters. Political scientists, along with opposition forces such as new union movements, neighborhood-based communities, progressive Catholic clergy, and opposition party leaders, believed that organizing local demands, empowering citizens, and resisting military rule could go hand in hand. But the organization of local opposition leaders and winning elections in a mass society are two very different types of collective action. Survey data suggest that during the transition period local problems were linked to the national issues of the day not by opposition groups, but by the patronage practices of professional party politicians in rural areas.

Indeed, in Brazil, local issues and problems have always been endowed with political meanings. During the 1945–1964 period, clientelist and populist politicians constructed electoral bases in de facto districts and pursued national careers based on the symbolic state offerings of neighborhood facilities to the people. After 1964, an entire generation of professional politicians emerged on the local level during authoritarianism. They built careers either by linking local improvements to the military ideology of development, or operating within the scant (but extant) political spaces in state administration. The effectiveness of these professional *cabos eleitorais* (literally, electoral infantry) during the transition period was noted by researchers investigating the strategies of the new Partido dos Trabalhadores (Workers Party, PT) in the 1982 election.[31]

The plebiscitarian character of electoral and party politics on the national level first organized sectors of public opinion into opposition and support of the government in 1974. However, as in previous periods of competitive politics in Brazil, voter alignment was also determined by patronage systems on the local level. By 1986, the PMDB (the opposition party under military rule and member of the Demo-

cratic Alliance that brought civilian José Sarney to power in 1985) won twenty-one of twenty-two contested governorships, and majorities in the Constitutional Congress as well as virtually all state assemblies in the 1986 elections. This landslide (short-lived as it turned out to be) was not caused by a surge of opposition, but because professional politicians on the regional and local levels allied themselves with the party in expectation of the estimated 130,000 administrative nominations that it would soon control.[32]

In sum, the most important causes of electoral change during the Brazilian transition have to do with the emergence—in both a historical and theoretical sense—of mass politics. New social forces did indeed generate new discourses and new actors, and thereby helped to create a new cleavage between those who opposed and those who supported the military government. However, the consolidation of new types of politics and new political cleavages occurred not under authoritarianism, nor during dramatic moments of social mobilization typical of transition politics, but as leaders and party workers carried out the day-to-day tasks of mass politics in the transition period. In broader terms, political change during the Brazil's transition to democracy seems to confirm a classic assertion about political parties: professional politicians tend to win elections because of their superior party organizations and the work of their full-time staffs.

Shifting the comparison from Europe to the United States also suggests that advocates of parliamentary institutions may overstate their criticism of Brazilian and Latin American presidential systems.[33] Scholars of U.S. politics have long debated the origin, evolution, and problems associated with their presidency. But comparative analysts tend to describe the U.S. experience as exceptional and conceive of party development as it occurred in European nations—through parliaments, prime ministers, professional bureaucracies, and disciplined ideological parties. There was extensive debate on the relative merits of parliamentary and presidential systems in Brazil and other Latin American nations during the recent round of constitutional and institutional design after the end of military rule. Among the legislative initiatives of the 1988 Brazilian constitution was a call for a popular referendum, held on April 21, 1993, to decide whether to retain the current presidential system or adopt either parliamentary institutions or a monarchy—or presumably a combination of the two. Although 57 percent of voters embraced presidential rule, debates before the

referendum were dominated by paradigms derived European parliamentary systems largely because analysts failed to articulate the central features of presidential institutions and the separation of powers. A central contention of this book is that the U.S. experience is a more productive point of departure for analyzing voters and mass politics in Brazil.

The plan of *The Brazilian Voter* reflects these concerns about public opinion, the emergent characteristics of party-electoral politics, and broader questions of democratic theory. Chapter 1 clarifies arguments and acknowledges their origins in the work of Max Weber, the literatures on political parties, contemporary democratic theory, and empirical research on public opinion and voter alignment. Chapters 2 through 5 present a comparative historical analysis of party-electoral politics in Brazil and the nineteenth-century United States. Careful review of parties and electoral politics in Brazilian history is required to counter what can best be described as a structural dysfunctionalism [*sic*] that pervades many accounts of parties and electoral representation in Brazil.[34] While the adoption of liberal institutions rarely produced broad change in Brazil's history, a positive, not apologetic, account is needed of how political parties organized state-society relations in Brazil.

Chapters 6 through 10 turn to electoral survey data from 1974 to 1982 to directly examine Brazilian voters in the transition era. The similarities and differences between Brazilian voters and those of advanced democratic electorates are explored by reviewing the causal logic of Brazilian public opinion in each dimension of voter choice stressed by analysts of advanced democracies. Considered in turn are the development of partisan affinity, the impact of issue positions and perceptions of government performance, new patterns in social and electoral participation, and the distribution of affect for democracy among Brazilian voters from 1974 to 1982. These dimensions are analyzed and placed in the context of their normative-theoretical heritage in the liberal democratic tradition. Quantitative methods are used because they can identify the emergent characteristics of mass belief systems among Brazilian voters and mass politics in this initial period of transition to democracy. In the conclusion I address this study's implications for research on public opinion and voter alignment, democratic theory, and theories of political parties and party development.

PART I

Voters, Political Parties, and Democracy in Theory

— *Chapter 1* —

Brazilian Voters, Party Development, and Passive Democratization

This chapter attempts to solidify conceptual bridges between these arguments about the recent behavior of Brazilian voters, party-electoral politics in Brazil, and democratic theory. The first section distinguishes between minimal and descriptive definitions of democracy, hoping to avoid the recent tendency in political theory to set progressive, participatory theories of change against conservative, elite-oriented, competitive theories of stasis. The second section argues that the many subdisciplines of empirical research on electoral behavior have become so specialized that they have strayed from central questions of electoral representation and democratic theory—questions that are especially critical for analyzing new electorates during and after transitions from military rule.

The third section attempts to bridge this gap between electoral behavior research and democratic theory by exploring new concepts of *direct democracy* and *state-led representation*. These concepts are clarified by comparing heuristic path models of electoral behavior in advanced democratic electorates and in Brazil, and by obtaining statistical estimates for the latter. Far from deterministic, these models are used to introduce the similarities and differences between Brazilian

voters and those in advanced democracies that will be pursued systematically in later chapters.

The third section defines, discusses, and measures the extent of immediate and personalistic conceptions of politics among Brazilian voters. Few Brazilians justify their vote in terms of European ideologies or U.S. notions of group interest. Instead, analysis of Brazilian survey data suggests that the predominance of unmediated and personalistic ways of thinking about politics are cause and consequence of the very different context of party-electoral politics in Brazil. For an understanding of these differences, the analysis must shift away from models based on well-organized European party systems and parliamentary institutions to a comparison based on the American experience of presidential elections, patronage machines, and the spoils system.

The final section reviews Max Weber's description of the precocious development of political parties in the United States as an example of *passive democratization*, a concept that combines analytic precision and a sober outlook on the implications of these new trends in mass politics for the liberal democratic tradition. Instead of political development, popular empowerment, and democratization, Max Weber suggests that mass parties may not level social differences but simply articulate new, perhaps quite autocratic, political elites.

Minimal and Descriptive Definitions of Democracy

After thirty years of polarization between competitive and participatory theories of democracy in political science, new perspectives are urgently needed for empirical analysis of Brazil and other nations attempting to complete a transition from military and authoritarian rule. Since the work of Joseph Schumpeter, theories labeled *competitive*, *empirical*, or simply *mainstream* focus on the selection of leaders through competitive elections as the core characteristic of mass democracy.[1] On the other hand, those who propose *participatory* theories of democracy criticize competitive theorists for omitting broader values that are central to the liberal democratic tradition and explore diverse mechanisms of change and democratization in contemporary societies.[2] While *democracy* is clearly an example of what William Connolly calls an essentially contested concept, the distance between

mainstream theories of stasis and participatory theories of change has been overstated.[3]

Competitive theories of democracy need not, as critics charge, usurp the normative questions posed by classic democratic thinkers, *if* they are linked to theories of party and electoral change. The contribution of Schumpeter and other theorists was to clarify the implications of politics in mass society for those interested in the viability of classic democratic values.[4] Schumpeter's oft-cited definition concisely interprets these implications: "Democracy is a political method, that is to say, a certain type of institutional arrangement for arriving at political, legislative, and administrative decisions"; later he wrote, "The democratic method is that institutional arrangement for arriving at political decisions in which individuals acquire the power to decide by means of a competitive struggle for the people's vote."[5] Schumpeter and others argue that because popular inclusion and participation are unworkable in modern times, mass democracies can function better if elected officials have broad discretion to formulate and implement policy. From this perspective, leaders should be held responsible for their performance only at election time.[6]

While Schumpeter's rejection of the broader norms and ideals associated with democracy may be unacceptable, those who see a simple dichotomy between participatory theories of change and competitive theories of stasis overlook a crucial point: Schumpeter's later assertions about the constraints on change and democratization do not necessarily follow from his core insight. Instead, his definition is best understood, in methodological terms, as *minimal*. Minimal definitions are helpful because, as Giovanni Sartori notes: "As many attributes or properties as possible are dropped from the definition, *with the understanding* that attributes that formerly appeared as definitional properties are restated as hypothetical or variable properties."[7]

Given these distinctions, Schumpeter clarifies the new organizational and social context for democracy by limiting its meaning and pursuing a minimal definition strategy. However, as Sartori suggests, the norms and expectations central to theories of democracy must be restated as hypothetical or variable properties. Whereas Schumpeter's work lacks such normatively based, empirically oriented research questions about democracy in mass society, others differ.[8]

For example, Weber's definition of democracy in *Economy and Society* offers the same clarity and realism as Schumpeter's. Weber also

recognizes that mass society and large nation-states provide contexts for democratic politics quite different from ancient polities. But unlike Schumpeter, Weber restates classic norms and meanings of democracy as variable properties and considers several political mechanisms that may give contemporary politics attributes that are in some sense functionally equivalent to democracy in classic Athens.

> The *demos* itself, in the sense of a shapeless mass, never "governs" larger associations but rather is governed. What changes is only the way in which the executive leaders are selected and the measure of influence that the *demos*, or better, that social circles from its midst are able to exert upon the content and direction of administrative activities by means of "public opinion." . . .
>
> The political concept of democracy, deduced from the "equal rights" of the governed, includes these further postulates: (1) prevention of the development of a closed status group of officials in the interest of a universal accessibility of office, and (2) minimization of the authority of officialdom in the interest of expanding the sphere of influence of "public opinion" as far as practicable.[9]

Weber's descriptive definition contains two critical elements that Schumpeter's minimal definition does not. First, for Weber, further postulates deduced from the equal rights of the governed are central to the political concept of democracy. Weber mentions universal access to office and expanding the sphere of influence of public opinion as two mechanisms that may produce outcomes in mass society that are consistent with the core values of democracy. But note that these additional elements in Weber's definition are *descriptive*. That is, despite being deduced from a normative conception of democracy (the equal rights of the governed), they are concrete institutional procedures that are eminently viable in mass society and the large nation-states of today.

The second element that distinguishes Weber's descriptive definition from Schumpeter's minimal definition is his concept of public opinion. Weber insists that the concept of democracy requires expanding the sphere of influence of public opinion as far as is practical. However, by placing the term "public opinion" in quotation marks, and referring to the ways in which social circles can influence it, Weber seems to suggest that popular opinion is not a given, but the product

of public expectations, political organization, and the dynamics of discourse in mass society. Decades after he formulated this view, political scientists still view public opinion not as given but as formed by diverse factors amenable to scientific inquiry.

Democratic Theory and Research on Public Opinion and Voter Alignment

Given the new context of electoral politics in mass society, can public opinion still realize the postulates of classic democratic theory such as popular participation, personal realization, and efficient decision making by collectivities? How far should the importance of elite authority be minimized? How far can the influence of public opinion be maximized? Over the last decades, research has provided widely different responses to these questions. But analysts of public opinion and electoral behavior appear further from answering core questions of democratic theory today than when they began. Scholars rarely synthesize empirical findings from the many subfields of empirical research into broader theories of public opinion in mass democracies.[10] This gap between theory and research makes it difficult to examine new electorates during and after democratic transitions because broad concepts and theories about public opinion and electoral representation are lacking. A few comments about both the history and the current impasse in electoral behavior studies are in order.

The first full-scale surveys of public opinion and voter alignment conducted in the 1940s and 1950s by social scientists presented a dismal outlook for achieving democratic ideals in mass society.[11] Early survey evidence suggested that the vast majority of American voters, instead of being active, interested, and informed citizens, remained passive, uninterested, and politically ignorant. Voters' choices appeared to be determined primarily by extremely long-term identifications with political parties that reflected political socialization through the family over several generations.[12] This emphasis on long-term political socialization and party identification is understandable, given the experience of this generation of scholars with flash parties, democratic breakdown, and the rise of fascism earlier in the twentieth century. But their conclusions about public opinion and democratic

breakdown were not merely justified by a sociology of knowledge; they were also supported by new survey data.

Indeed, a lasting virtue of earlier public opinion analysis is the effort to link broad questions of democratic theory directly to empirical research. For example, the authors of *The American Voter* developed the levels-of-conceptualization scale to describe the types of mass beliefs (ideological and group-interest perceptions of politics) that would permit, in Max Weber's terms, maximizing the influence of public opinion without generating the radicalization and polarization that led to fascism and a breakdown of democracy. But results from surveys conducted during the 1950s suggested that few Americans conceived of political matters as their leaders did. Instead, researchers found that voters in postwar America were relatively satisfied with government, rarely participated in politics, and rarely voted on the basis of substantive political issues. In sum, since very few voters thought in terms of ideology or group interest and found most political issues irrelevant, and since party identification and political socialization took generations to solidify, theorists appeared to have found compelling evidence to support Schumpeter's theory of democracy.[13]

This picture of American voters came under sustained attack in the 1970s.[14] For example, the authors of *The Changing American Voter* argued that widespread civic apathy, satisfaction, and trust in political leaders were unique features of U.S. public opinion in the 1950s. While the politicization of class and party loyalty arising from the Depression and New Deal were still influential forces at mid-century, the most compelling aspect of the Eisenhower years, with Eisenhower's personality-based leadership style and unifying foreign issues that muted political differences, was their blandness. After 1960, new political issues began to emerge. Public opinion researchers in the 1970s suggested that voters in advanced democracies were able to make voting decisions on the basis of new political issues far more rapidly than had been assumed. Survey data from the 1960s and 1970s (and secondary analysis of earlier data) suggested that change was limited less by long-term factors such as political socialization and the ignorance of "poorly endowed observers" than empirical democratic theorists had believed.[15] New findings shifted the emphasis from long-term socialization to short-term judgments.[16] By examining how political issues tended to cluster according to how they were presented

in the media, researchers argued that public opinion is constantly formed and transformed. In short, by the 1970s scholars believed that the rational politicization of mass publics was possible.

This revisionist picture of public opinion and voter alignment in advanced democracies has in turn faced criticism.[17] Indeed, since the mid-1970s, research on public opinion and voter alignment has seen much debate about research design, measurement error, levels of analysis, and other methodological and statistical problems. Even within subfields, scholars differ about how party identification, issue voting, perceptions of candidates and their personalities, postmaterialist attitudes, perceptions of economic performance, and other factors organize public opinion and determine voter choice. The theoretical, methodological, and statistical problems of the field are complex and compelling, but the cost of specialization has been high. Questions of democratic theory and electoral representation remain quite distant from most empirical work done today because of the extreme specialization and compartmentalization of pubic opinion research.

Direct Democracy and State-led Representation: A Model of Brazilian Voters

Understanding Brazilian voters requires new concepts to bridge the subdisciplines of electoral behavior and link this accumulated knowledge to central problems of democratic theory. This task is further complicated because the behavior of Brazilian voters reveals patterns quite different from existing theories of electoral representation and mass democracy in the liberal tradition. A central argument of this book is that the immediacy and personalism of political conceptions in Brazil enabled Brazilian voters to respond rapidly to the plebiscitarian appeals and patronage machines that dominated party-electoral politics during the recent transition era. Instead of reiterating classic liberal assumptions about the bottom-up articulation of preferences, new concepts of *direct democracy* and *state-led representation* are required to explain the course of rapid change in public opinion and voter alignment in Brazil.

Comparing heuristic path models of voters in advanced democracies with those of Brazilian voters may help clarify these differences. The path diagram in figure 1.1 summarizes the causal logic of voter

Figure 1.1   Path Diagram of Voter Alignment in the Advanced
Democracies

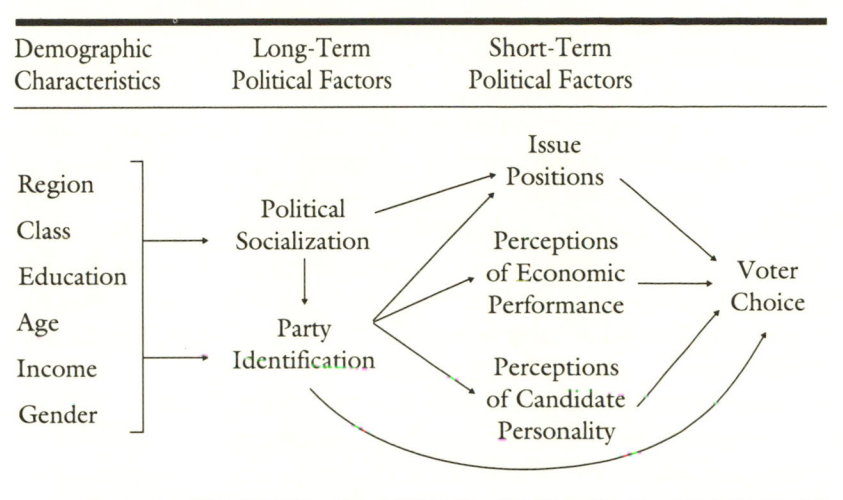

Demographic Characteristics	Long-Term Political Factors	Short-Term Political Factors

Note: This heuristic path diagram represents the central causal claims about public opinion and voter alignment among scholars of advanced democratic electorates.

choice in democratic electorates, according to recent reviews by Herbert Asher and G. Bingham Powell.[18] This model focuses on political factors that *cause* voter choice such as party identification, positions on issues, retrospective judgments of economic performance, and perceptions of candidates' personalities. Other factors that *inform* public opinion, such as political participation and political culture, are omitted.

While participation and attitudes toward democracy among Brazilian voters are examined in later chapters, they are omitted from the path diagram because, strictly speaking, they do not explain why voters choose one party over another. While demographic factors are included in the path model, they are dropped from subsequent analysis both because they are weak predictors of Brazilian voter choice and because this analysis builds on sociological studies of the Brazilian electorate to examine how *political* perceptions, beliefs, and judgments organize public opinion and voter alignment in Brazil.[19]

While the short-term judgments that determine voter choice in advanced democracies such as positions on issues, judgments of ex-

ecutive performance, and concepts of justice also informed Brazilian voters in the transition period, the causal logic, conceptual content, and political context of these dimensions of public opinion differed considerably. Neither demographic characteristics nor long-term political factors such as political socialization or party identification are enough to explain electoral behavior since 1974. Understanding Brazilian voters requires new concepts of direct democracy and state-led representation.

The concept of direct democracy means that Brazilians voted on the basis of short-term perceptions of national issues, executive performance, and the left-right dimension, without the moderating influence of European ideologies, U.S. notions of group interest, or other long-term identifications based on party or class. The concept of direct democracy more accurately describes the fundamentally different causal sequence among Brazilian voters: instead of arising from political socialization, class identity, and party loyalty, in Brazil political choices tend to be determined exclusively by voters' judgments of their leaders' performance, positions on current national issues, and conceptions of substantive justice remitting to economic and social equality.[20] Figure 1.2 presents a path diagram illustrating the concept of *direct democracy* that clarifies the similarities and differences between Brazilian voters and those of advanced democracies.

Figure 1.2   Direct Democracy and Voter Alignment in Brazil

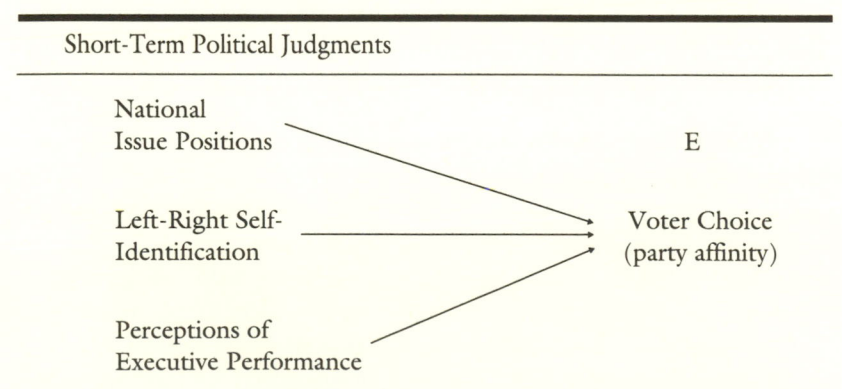

Short-Term Political Judgments

National
Issue Positions   E

Left-Right Self-   →   Voter Choice
Identification   →   (party affinity)

Perceptions of
Executive Performance

Note: This path diagram represents the most important causal factors identified in the 1982 electoral survey. For the estimation of relative and collective causal weight, see table 1.1.

The heuristic model presented in figure 1.2 can be restated in terms of the following regression equation, and estimates for this regression equation are presented in table 1.1.

$$\text{Vote} = C + b_1 \text{ National Issues} + b_2 \text{ Executive Performance} + b_3 \text{ Left/Right} + E_1$$

where:

Vote = the intent of respondents to vote for governor in the 1982 election, recoded by party from left to right

National Issues = a 4-point scale of opposition to or support for the military government that counts the number of positions taken by respondents on four current national issues

Executive Performance = a 15-point scale that sums three questions asking respondents to measure presidential, gubernatorial, and mayoral performance, each on a scale from 1 to 5

Left/Right = self-placement by respondents on a 10-point scale, from left to right, measuring their political inclination

C = constant

E = error term

Table 1.1   The Effects of Direct Judgments on Voter Choice, 1982

	Beta	T	Sig T	Added R²
Left-right self-placement	.35	7.9	.00	.24
Scale of executive performance	.19	4.4	.00	.04
Scale of national issues	.16	3.7	.00	.02
(Constant = 3.32)		5.7	.00	.00
Total adjusted R²				.32

Source: 1982 electoral survey. Unless otherwise noted, the southeast urban sample of the 1982 survey is used for data analysis. See Appendix 2 for information on scales, survey questions, and the regression analysis.

Note: Reported statistics were obtained from regressing three scales on intent to vote listwise in SPSS/PC.

Taken as a whole, how respondents placed themselves on the left-right scale, their perceptions of leaders' performance, and their positions on national issues of the day give a remarkably accurate indication of how they intended to vote for governor during the two weeks before the 1982 election. The standardized regression coefficients (Betas) obtained from regressing respondents' intention to vote by party on a left-right continuum (.35), perceptions of executive performance (.19), and the scale of national issue positions (.16) suggest that there are statistically significant relationships between these variables and voter choice. The adjusted R^2 of .32 for the entire equation means that these political dimensions of Brazilian public opinion explain 32 percent of the variation in respondents' intent to vote for governor in the 1982 election when recoded from left to right by party.

Several comments are in order. First, perceptions of other political matters and the demographic characteristics of respondents were excluded from the model because they failed to provide additional explanation for the variation in voter choice when added to the multiple regression analysis. Both a constructed scale of local issue positions (which are emphasized in theories of civil society empowerment), as well as standard measures of occupation, age, family income, and education (which are emphasized in demographic analyses of electorates) were thereby trimmed from the model. When regressed on respondent's intent to vote, these variables failed to increase adjusted R^2 for the equation as a whole or to exhibit significant Beta coefficients.

Second, although many respondents failed to answer survey questions about where they would place themselves on a left-right continuum and did not give their opinion on national issues, the model remains compelling because of the large number and wide distribution of valid cases, the primarily demographic explanations for differences between those who responded to questions and those who did not, and the experience of other analysts with low response rates to surveys conducted early in a period of transition to democratic government.[21] Of the 2,463 respondents in seven southeast capital cities, 1,755 (71.3 percent) failed to place themselves on the left-right ideological scale, and 1,128 (45.8 percent) failed to take positions on national issues. The regression analysis nonetheless remains compelling because the minimum pairwise number of 496 cases retains a large subset of cases with a broad distribution of respondents. Furthermore, demographic

attributes such as education, per-capita income, and occupation explain much of the difference between those who responded and those who did not.[22]

In surveying Spanish voters from 1978 through 1984, soon after the transition from authoritarianism to democracy, Peter Mc-Donough, Antonio López Piña, and Samuel H. Barnes also found relatively low response rates to questions about left-right self-placement. Subsequent analysis by the same researchers found a dramatic increase in the number of respondents reporting their left-right tendency.[23] The Spanish experience suggests that although some questions in the 1982 electoral survey in Brazil had few responses, this might change in the future. After all, the 1982 election was held under military rule with significant constraints on media coverage and political campaigning. Only further research will be able to determine how Brazilian public opinion evolves in subsequent elections after the transition from military rule.

While each causal dimension is analyzed with considerable care in separate chapters, this broad model permits the identification of several important similarities and differences between Brazilians voters in the period of democratic transition and voters in advanced democracies.[24] First, these patterns in the 1982 data suggest that substantial change occurred among Brazilian voters during this period. There is compelling evidence that Brazilian voters under hard-line military rule (1969–1973) were poorly informed and depoliticized, and that few people voted on the basis of their perceptions of national issues, executive performance, or left-right self-placement.[25] Nonetheless, only ten years later, in 1982, three political dimensions provide robust explanation of respondents' choice for governor. This rapid organization of voter alignment during the Brazilian transition period supports recent theories of electoral behavior that emphasize rationality, complexity, context, and change, and counters the earlier emphasis on long-term constraints such as education, political socialization, and the cognitive capacities of poorly endowed observers.

Second, the explanatory power of both voters' left-right self-placement and their direct, unmediated judgments of executive performance suggest the plebiscitarian character of Brazilian elections. Because these two variables overwhelm demographic characteristics, perceptions of specific government policies, and local concerns, regression analysis suggests that Brazilian voters choose parties and can-

didates on the basis of direct, unmediated judgments of executive performance that are related to conceptions of substantive social and economic equality. Later chapters build on this regression analysis by analyzing the causal logic, cognitive content, and political context of each of these dimensions through additional statistical techniques and comparative methods.

Third, although *party identification* is a central determinant of voter choice in theories of electoral behavior, it is placed in the heuristic path model immediately below *voter choice* (in parentheses) and excluded from the regression equation. Theoretical, conceptual, and methodological reasons are behind this. On the theoretical level, the emphasis on plebiscitarian appeals and patronage machines suggests that Brazilian parties are short-term constellations of candidates, electoral alliances, ideas, and symbols. Consequently, one would expect voters' partisan affinities in a period of transition to democratic government to be a constellation of short-term judgments made at election time rather than founded on long-term structural characteristics based on socialization in the family. While rarely coherent in terms of European-style ideologies and often ephemeral as formal organizations, Brazilian parties call upon popular sympathies in each election through plebiscitarian-populist appeals and alliances with patronage machines. The survey data does indeed suggest that Brazilian voters in the era of democratic transition had developed affinities with parties and candidates by the time of the November 1982 election. (See chapter 6.)

But because party identification was measured only two weeks preceding the 1982 election, the conceptual distinction between partisan affinity and intent to vote remains problematic. This conceptual problem is aggravated because the variable that measures party identification was coded identically to the variable that measures respondents' choices for governor and other officers in the 1982 election—that is, by party. Despite these problems of measurement, the extent to which Brazilian voters in democratic transition developed partisan affinities remains a critical theoretical problem. Hence, in the model I place the concept in parentheses and analyze it separately in a later chapter, using statistical procedures that attempt to resolve these problems of conceptualization and measurement.

The final difference between Brazilian voters and those in advanced democracies concerns the extremely uneven development of

mass belief systems between Brazil's more advanced urban areas and less developed rural areas. Unfortunately, because there were only two major parties contesting the 1982 election in northeast and rural areas, voter intent becomes a dichotomous dependent variable. Consequently, no path model similar to that reported in figure 1.1 could be devised for northeastern cities or rural areas.[26] Nonetheless, chapters 6 through 10 present extensive survey evidence to suggest that Brazilian voters in the urban areas of the advanced southeast differ fundamentally both from voters in less developed northeast capitals and especially from those in rural Brazil.

Scholars widely agree that dependent capitalism generates extremely unequal economic, social, cultural, and political development. This study focuses on the political contexts and the uneven development patterns of Brazilian mass belief systems. Electoral and party politics in Brazil exacerbate the disparities between urban and rural areas because populism and plebiscitarian impulses tend to characterize politics in the cities of the most economically advanced regions. Likewise, the patronage machines that prevail in local and legislative elections tend to be especially powerful in the vast underdeveloped rural areas of Brazil. Subsequent chapters attempt to clarify the causes and contexts for these uneven patterns of development.

Immediate and Personalistic Conceptions of Politics: Populist and Party Machine Contexts

Brazilian party politics differs from those in advanced democracies because populist and plebiscitarian appeals prevail in direct executive elections, while patronage machines predominate in local and legislative elections. Populist discourse—meaning immediate or transparent appeals to voters' senses of economic and social justice—is decisive in majoritarian elections for executive posts. Until recently, populism was seen as a nineteenth-century relic in the First and Second Worlds. However, in a country of staggering income differences and exclusive politics, this may still be the century of populism—to paraphrase Schmitter. Direct, unmediated, and often emotional relations provide powerful links between candidate and voter in Brazil. The second critical element is patronage. By demarcating *de facto* electoral districts, party patronage machines dominate the proportional

representation races for legislative office. Until this influence of populist and patronage politics on Brazilian public opinion is understood, theories of political representation, democracy, and democratization in Brazil will be amiss.

How do populism and patronage shape Brazilian public opinion? As early as 1956, Aziz Simão examined voting tendencies for labor parties (PCB and PTB) in the city of São Paulo based on a demographic analysis of the cities neighborhoods.[27] Simão's contribution lies in his recognizing the importance of *weak* correlations between living in a working-class neighborhood and voting for labor parties during the 1950s. Simão explains this weakness by noting that the decree that outlawed the Communist party in 1947 crippled a well-organized political party. Simão also suggests that class voting in São Paulo was weakened by what he described as charismatic populist candidates. In fact, the major populist politicians of the 1950s in the city of São Paulo, Adhemar de Barros and Janio Quadros, first developed their electoral bases and party machines in the working-class neighborhoods studied by Simão. In sum, an early work of Brazilian electoral sociology sees patronage and populism as central explanations of how parties organize public opinion and determine voter choice.

Unfortunately, subsequent scholarship concentrates primarily on the negative consequences of populism and patronage. For example, Oliveiros Ferreira argued that the populist disaggregation of class and group voting impeded the representativeness of pre-1964 parties. Thus, policy making before 1964 lacked the necessary rationality supplied by channels of pluralist representation.[28] From a different theoretical perspective, Francisco Weffort described populism as a new type of false class consciousness typical of countries undergoing dependent industrialization: "Populism is an extremely manipulative form of mass mobilization because it perpetuates clientelistic deference in a capitalist setting in order to avoid the political translation of class and other social cleavages."[29]

Scholars also noted that the traditional Brazilian electoral system of statewide proportional representation tended to reinforce personalistic links because voters were faced with lengthy and bewildering lists of candidates, instead of clear party choices.[30] Monographs on local party rivalries and patronage disputes became an established genre of Brazilian scholarship in the 1950s and 1960s.[31]

By emphasizing the failures of patronage and populism, scholars of Brazilian politics tend to overlook their importance as mechanisms of mass inclusion. Some authors avoid this problem. For example, Leal's classic account of Brazilian *coroneis* (powerful landowners), beyond its normative position, sees clientelism as a mechanism for organizing municipal, regional, and federal power.[32] Brazilian clientelism was neither liberal nor democratic, but it organized political power in a typically Brazilian state-led manner. Soares also argues that voters in the modern areas of Brazil responded to populist appeals and voted increasingly on ideological grounds (although not in the European sense) in the 1945–1964 period.[33] Unlike rural voters, citizens of the developing urban areas of the southeast began to judge candidates and issues by substantive democratic criteria—an important new development caused by populism and the plebiscitarian nature of the Brazilian presidential system.

Souza argues that populist discourses and patronage practices before 1964 were both cause and result of the marginal roles of party politicians and the centralized Brazilian executive. By classifying state decisions into Lowi's *distributive, regulatory*, and *redistributive* types of policies, Souza notes that parties tended to control only marginal (distributive) matters from 1945 to 1964.[34] Nonetheless, for Souza these distributive practices of party leaders generated popular expectations that were immediate and amorphous on the national level and personality-based on the local level. Public opinion on the national level remained rather unformed in the postwar period because party leaders limited political discourse to ambiguous populist promises. Popular expectations on the local level were more particular because distributive politics forced politicians to develop machines based on clientelist exchange and corporatist obligation.

The importance of populism and patronage in Brazilian electoral politics suggests that two problems must be solved before analyzing Brazilian voters. First, to measure how public opinion was organized during the transition period, we need clear criteria. However, since the original typologies established by Angus Campbell and Phillip Converse, the accepted criteria for measuring the sophistication of individual voters relies on *ideological* and *group interest* conceptions of politics derived from Europe and the United States.[35] Very few Brazilians think about politics in these terms. Instead, Brazilian voters tend to think about politics in more *personalistic* or *immediate* terms,

to be defined more fully below. Although debate continues about master-coding survey respondents into categories, the purpose remains the same.[36] Levels-of-conceptualizations scales describe the types of rationality among voters that could organize electoral representation in mass democracies while avoiding demagogic appeals, radicalization, and ungovernability. Without a more accurate description of how Brazilians think about politics, one cannot understand the impact of populist and patronage politics, nor consider the prospects for combining democratization and governability in Brazil.

This book defines immediate and personalistic types of conceptualizations to capture the differences between Brazilian voters and those in advanced democracies. *Immediate* political conceptualizations are defined as those that perceive and judge politics by referring to a substantive democratic meaning, without the mediating influences or rationales supplied by party, ideology, or group interest. On the theoretical level, immediate political beliefs are the types of public perceptions implied by Rousseau's ideal of "transparent" relations among citizens in a small state. Although immediate political conceptions retain a substantive democratic content, they are not necessarily liberal. An example of an immediate political concept in Latin America is the idea of the *people*.[37] Because mass inclusion came to Latin America through populist politics, in political discourse and individual perceptions the concept of the *people* is much closer to the idea of substantive democracy than it is in advanced democratic electorates.[38]

Personalistic political conceptualizations are defined as those that perceive and judge politics primarily by reference to the character of historical personalities, again without the mediating influence or rationale of party, ideology, or group interest. In Brazil, affinity for a particular politician—local, regional, or national—is the most common description offered for an individual's political identity. Given the complexity of party images and alliances in local, regional, and national politics in Brazil, the personal characteristics of politicians are often a more reliable public referent for making political judgments than abstract notions of ideology or group interest.

Personalistic, immediate, and ideological types of political conceptualizations among Brazilian voters can be measured by recoding open-ended responses in the 1982 electoral survey. By combining Converse's upper levels of conceptualization (ideologues, near ideologues, and perceptions of group interest) and by creating two new

categories for *immediate* and *personalistic* political conceptualizations, we can distinguish between two substantive theoretical types of responses from among Brazilians previously described as unsophisticated and/or unpoliticized and whose survey answers were once placed in miscellaneous residual categories such as "nature of the times" or "no content" (see table 1.2).

There is considerable support for this revised typology of how Brazilian voters think about politics in both the survey data and Brazilian social science.[39] Citizens developed immediate and personality-based conceptions of politics under populism and the patronage systems because they were central mechanisms of mass incorporation during both periods of democracy and authoritarianism in twentieth-century Brazil. The institutional and symbolic legacy of Getulio Vargas's populist and nationalist Estado Novo is a common theme among scholars. As noted above, Souza and others systematically explore the impact of populism and patronage on democracy before 1964. Regarding the transition period, Cardoso suggests that the immediacy and transparency of Brazilian political beliefs, far from inchoate, may have actually facilitated the rapid emergence of plebiscitarian patterns of voter alignment for and against military government after 1974.[40]

Table 1.2 Types of Political Conceptualizations Among Brazilian Voters, 1982 (percent)

Types of Conceptualization	Southeastern Cities	Northeastern Cities	Rural Areas
Ideology or group interest	6.4	4.7	10.8
Immediate	12.6	13.9	7.5
Personalistic	34.1	32.2	26.5
No response or no chosen candidate	46.7	49.2	55.2
Total	100.0	100.0	100.0
(N)	(2,463)	(1,297)	(481)

Source: 1982 electoral survey.

Note: Reported frequencies are open responses to the following question: "Why do you intend to vote for your chosen candidate for governor?" Further information about measurement is included in Appendix 3.

This study reports strong evidence in each dimension of Brazilian public opinion to support the idea that direct populist appeals on the state and national level, and party patronage on the local level, reinforced the traditional immediate and personality-based responses of Brazilian voters during the recent change of regime.

A second problem requires attention. Scholarship on Brazilian public opinion focuses primarily on individual characteristics and thereby underestimates the importance of aggregate-level rationality among Brazilian voters.[41] Studies of public opinion in Brazil tend to define the structure of mass belief systems in terms of the ideological sophistication of individuals. This methodology consists of classifying *individual* survey respondents within previously defined types of conceptualization (master codes), according to the researcher's own expert judgment.[42] While this method is used to describe how Brazilians think about politics throughout the present analysis, this approach alone is insufficient. Individual-level typologies of how voters perceive politics and vote often conceal aggregate patterns in the survey data that cannot be traced to the characteristics of individual voters.

To identify additional structures in mass publics, scholars have turned their attention from factors that influence individual voters such as ideology, group interest, class, region, and party identification, to the effect of issue positions, postmaterialist value orientations, and other less tangible determinants of public opinion and voter alignment. These latter factors often cut across existing cleavages and tend to appear in survey data only on the aggregate level as constellations of issue positions.[43] The 1982 data contain aggregate-level patterns among party images, issue positions, postmodern values, judgments of accountability, and participation that are similar to patterns of aggregate-level rationality in the advanced democracies.

In sum, understanding the actions of Brazilian voters in an era of democratic transition requires us to address two methodological matters. First, on the typological level, existing theories of mass publics are unable to capture the sophistication of Brazilian voters because they assume the wrong kinds of sophistication. In Brazil, immediate and personalistic discourses link citizens and the state, voters and parties, and set parameters for political debate within society. Second, because scholarship on Brazilian public opinion tends to define mass beliefs on an individual level, various kinds of rationality that exist in survey data exclusively on the aggregate level are overlooked. Weber's

theory of party development as passive democratization can be used to place these immediate and personality-based conceptions in broader perspective.

Brazilian Parties and Max Weber's Theory of Passive Democratization

The mass party could be described as the modern pluralist prince of political development theory because mass parties have democratized and institutionalized political power within the rules and procedures of liberal government. In the late nineteenth and early twentieth centuries, mass parties changed not only the way democratic systems functioned, but also the very meaning of liberalism and citizenship. Comparative studies of party systems are based on how parties evolved in Europe.[44] The classic pattern of democratization from in-group parliamentary parties, to out-group electoral parties, and ultimately to mass democratic parties in Europe has been well documented.[45] Mass parties increasingly dominated electoral politics because of their superior resources, permanent organization, and professional staff. The empowerment of parties in Europe occurred through two historical processes. The first was the evolution of parliamentary politics from virtual representation and responsible government to *electoral* representation and *responsive* government.[46] Second, the expansion of party control over public bureaucracies consolidated what came to be known as party government.[47]

The argument presented here about the predominance of political parties and the organization of public opinion during the Brazilian transition is based on Weber's conception of mass parties and democratization, a concept that differs substantially from both the liberal tradition and comparative analysis of party systems and public opinion.[48] Two of Weber's arguments are especially relevant for understanding the relation between party organizations and democratization in Brazil. The first is Weber's rather melancholy account of the relation between bureaucratization and democratization. The second is Weber's historical argument about precocious party development in the United States.

Weber describes passive democratization as the leveling of the governed, which is a common, although not inevitable, consequence

of bureaucratization. His most concise definition of passive democratization, in "The Leveling of Social Differences" (from *Economy and Society*), is as follows:

> The minimization of the civil servant's power in favor of the greatest possible direct rule of the *demos*, which in practice means the respective party leaders of the *demos*. The decisive aspect here—indeed it is rather exclusively so—is the leveling of the governed in face of the governing and bureaucratically articulated group, which in its turn may occupy a quite autocratic position, both in fact and in form.[49]

Furthermore, because the consequences of bureaucratization cannot be determined beforehand, the tendency of bureaucracy to produce even this passive (and from a normative viewpoint quite problematic) type of democratization is not unilateral.[50] Instead, the political consequences depend on the social, economic, and political context in which bureaucracies develop.

Although Weber uses *passive democratization* as a general category to describe processes in widely divergent contexts, he cites party development in nineteenth-century America as an example in two classic texts. Weber argues that the plebiscitarian appeals and direct nominations of professional politicians to administrative posts encouraged by the U.S. presidential system actually facilitated the rapid organization of mass parties based on alliances between presidents and the patronage networks of senators. This argument can be found earlier in the work of M. I. Ostrogorsky, later in Maurice Duverger's, and continues to inform research among political historians. But its most concise presentation can be found in "Politics as a Vocation" and *Economy and Society*.[51] Weber first reviews party development in European parliamentary systems and recognizes the importance of the new contexts in American society for party organization.[52] However, Weber's primary concern is with the impact of different institutional contexts on party development in a federal and presidential system.

> In America alone, and in the democracies influenced by America, a quite heterogeneous system was placed into opposition with [the parliamentary] system. The American system placed the directly and popularly elected leader of the victorious party at the head of the

apparatus of officials appointed by him and bound him to the consent of "parliament" only in budgetary and legislative matters.[53]

The combination of a federal republic with a presidential system is one of the central features of American exceptionalism. What were the consequences of this combination for the organization of mass politics? Weber is unequivocal: "The Germans perfected the rational, functional, and specialized bureaucratic organization of all forms of domination from factory to army and public administration. For the time being the Germans have been outdone only in the techniques of party organization, especially by the Americans."[54]

Furthermore, Weber argues that it was precisely the plebiscitarian element of presidential elections on the national level, and the patronage character of machine politics on the local level, that facilitated this rapid organization of mass parties. He notes: "That the plebiscitary 'machine' has developed so early in America is due to the fact that there, and there alone, the executive—this is what mattered—the chief office of patronage, was a president elected by plebiscite."[55] For Weber, "The creation of such machines signifies the advent of *plebiscitary democracy*."[56] Indeed, populist and machine politics challenged and often defeated oligarchic control in U.S. cities and states and created new leaders of party bureaucracies.[57] While recent debate among new political historians has been polarized between positive and negative interpretations of nineteenth-century party development in the United States, Weber's concept of passive democratization forces a reconsideration of both positions by forcefully juxtaposing passivity with democratization and by recognizing authoritarian elements among party leaders.

Weber's concept of passive democratization not only offers a fundamentally new perspective on U.S. party development; it also provides a fresh historical, conceptual, and theoretical point of departure for understanding the Brazilian experience. It recognizes that the organization of mass parties and mass democracy failed to generate the outcomes that modern liberal theory associates with parliamentary democracy, such as disciplined, well-organized parties and ideological politics. But instead of emphasizing the departures of the U.S. or Brazilian experience from the evolution of parties in Europe, the concept of passive democratization surpasses standard normative positions and focuses on concrete political changes.

Far from the distant objectivity and intellectual malaise some have found in Weber's work, the concept of passive democratization enables us to discuss specific problems in mass democracy and to make specific proposals for their resolution. Weber was not blind to the perils of patronage. For example, after noting the rapidity of party development in the young United States, Weber immediately turns to the problems of politics at the turn of the twentieth century: "A corruption and wastefulness second to none could only be tolerated by a country with as yet unlimited economic opportunities. [Yet] the system is gradually dying out. America can no longer be governed only by dilettantes."[58] This concern with corruption and administration by dilettantes is certainly relevant to Brazil: a central problem for Brazilian democracy is how to professionalize politicians who built careers through patronage and populism. Weber suggests that only stable and enduring careers in party-electoral politics can produce such balanced political leaders. Today, a balance between populist oratory and sensitivity toward international and domestic constraints on state policy is urgently needed in Brazil.

Furthermore, while calling political change during a period of party development *passive* challenges our image of an active citizenry, Weber's analysis suggests that these experiences tend to produce considerable political mobilization and mass incorporation in the political system. Perhaps the strongest evidence of mobilization during periods of party development is the extent of demobilization that followed. In the United States, the period of mass party politics described by Weber was followed by Progressive-era reforms designed to weaken parties, defeat new mass party elites, and defuse popular participation. Electoral redistricting attempted to weaken party machines by dividing the immigrant vote in urban areas. Poll taxes, literacy tests, and other restrictions on voting were imposed, especially in the southern United States. The Australian ballot was adopted to deprive parties of the right to distribute ballots. The direct primary system was introduced to weaken party-elite control over the nomination of candidates. Finally, by reducing the number of presidential appointments, civil service reform attempted to weaken the grip of parties on the bureaucracy and to depoliticize government administration.[59] Whereas popular demobilization and the disorganization of parties in America was inspired by the Progressive movement and achieved through legislation, in Brazil, such popular demobilization, weaken-

ing of parties, and the defeat of party elites occurred only after the crisis of democratic breakdown and military intervention in 1964.

In sum, scholars tend to lament the distance between the realities of Brazilian electoral and party politics and idealized models of parliamentary government, ideological party systems, and liberal patterns of interest-group representation.[60] But difference does not imply dysfunction. Prevailing views of Brazilian party and electoral politics must be replaced by theories that can more adequately account for the place of parties in the organization of democracy in Brazil. As Douglas Chalmers notes, if parties represent diffuse vertical hierarchies rather than specifically defined interests, if the role of parties in decision making is specialized and not particularly dominant, if parties act within highly interdependent state-society relations that blur the distinction between public and private, then *mass parties* and *electoral politics* mean something considerably different in Brazil.[61]

Consideration of these differences in the Brazilian case is especially urgent because parties still have the task of fully incorporating the masses into politics. Scholars tend to view the mid-twentieth century as the apogee of the consolidated modern party system, after which parties declined in importance. However, in Europe and North America, parties have been weakened and more immediate and postmodern politics have emerged in a context of dense, widely extended corporatist networks. In Brazil, corporatist networks exclude the vast majority of Brazilians. After the 1988 constitution introduced mandatory voting for all citizens over eighteen years of age (including illiterates) and permits those above sixteen to vote, political parties still seem the most likely mechanisms for organizing popular expectations in a democratic Brazil.

PART II

Brazilian Voters,
Party Systems, and
Democracy in History

Introduction to Part II

Chapters 2–5 analyze the succession of party systems in Brazilian history to clarify the similarities and differences between the early development of mass patronage parties in nineteenth-century America and the Brazilian experience. Party development in the United States and Brazil was encouraged by the plebiscitarian nature of presidential elections, the capacity of presidents and other executives to directly nominate party loyalists to administrative posts, and the formation of electoral alliances and legislative coalitions among patronage machines, which typically retain considerable local and regional autonomy under federalism. While the cumulative effect of these mechanisms appeared only once before in Brazilian history (from 1945 to 1964), Brazil's experience nonetheless confirms the exceptional character of U.S. politics and strengthens Weber's original insight about party development in the nineteenth-century United States: when the plebiscitarian appeals of presidential elections are linked to patronage machines through the distribution of administrative appointments, the result is rapid, pervasive, and (from a normative point of view) passive democratization.

Current views of Brazilian parties fail to recognize this trajectory of party development because they still adhere to the naive liberal model of a responsible party system dating from the 1950s. This model criticized U.S. parties for their lack of clear ideology and programs, poor discipline in Congress, weak central organizations, the widespread use of patronage, and corruption.[1] However, since the 1960s, scholars such as Douglas Chambers, Walter Burnham, Theodore Lowi, Samuel Hays, and others developed fundamentally new accounts of U.S. party development. They focus on the practices of party professionals rather than formal party organizations, emphasize the impact of plebiscitarian appeals in presidential elections rather than the rationality of party ideology and programs, and they suggest that patronage machines may be rapidly transformed into mass parties

when linked through the spoils system to state and national campaigns for executive office.

These new theories of party development in the United States produced fundamentally new conceptions of American democracy. Burnham, who sees V. O. Key's pathbreaking concept of critical elections as providing a broad theory of political change in American history, argues that the wave of populism and party mobilization in the late nineteenth century (reversed by Progressive-era legislation) was a lost opportunity for party building and popular inclusion.[2] Lowi contends that the peculiar combination of formal party continuity alongside substantive electoral and policy changes throughout U.S. history is based on the powerful constituent function of the nation's elections.[3] Hays notes that the classic sociological distinction between community and society was articulated within party-electoral politics in the United States. Citizens resisted northeastern liberal visions of modern capitalist society by reinforcing patronage machines in local communities.[4]

This theoretical paradigm of American party development offers enormous opportunities for reassessing Brazilian party-electoral politics. Recognizing the importance of plebiscitarian appeals in elections, the prerogative of executives to make administrative appointments, and the prevalence of patronage machines in the state-centered Brazilian polity provides a new perspective on parties and elections in Brazil, helps to explain the dominance of immediate, personalistic conceptions of politics among Brazilian voters, and permits a more realistic assessment of mass politics during the recent transition in Brazil. Perhaps the peculiar combination of monarchs, state bureaucrats, oligarchs, and party-electoral politics under the Brazilian empire seem quite distant from today's problems of mass politics and democratic transition. But closer analysis reveals underlying continuities in plebiscitarian legitimation, the predominance of patronage, the connections linking center, province, and county, and other elements that reproduce patterns of state-led electoral representation in Brazil to this day.

This analysis does not apply theories of American party development to Brazil *tout court*. Instead, the U.S. experience provides an ideal type for comparative historical analysis. Perhaps the most critical difference between party development in Brazil and the United States is that emphasized by Hans Daalder: "It was of profound significance

whether an articulated party system developed before, after, or concurrently with the rise of bureaucracy."[5] This difference is less a question of state or party strength than of timing. Mass parties developed in the United States during the nineteenth century, well before the emergence of modern government bureaucracies and federal intervention in the 1930s. In Brazil, mass parties first appeared during the 1945–1964 period of competitive politics, well after central government bureaucracies had been established, and immediately following a period of dramatic state intervention under the Estado Novo of Getulio Vargas (1937–1945).

For Daalder, the relative timing of party and bureaucratic development in Europe determined both the extent of party and parliamentary control over government bureaus, as well as broader patterns of stability and instability.[6] The structural differences between U.S. and Brazilian parties confirm the first part of Daalder's argument. Party development in America gave the parties power over government bureacracies throughout the nineteenth century (before civil service reform and other Progressive-era measures weakened their grip). In comparison, Sartori argues that Brazilian party politics lacks the subsystemic autonomy of fully consolidated party systems because Brazilian party leaders remain dependent upon state structures.[7] Souza also suggests: "One cannot speak of party system institutionalization when the power of party groups emerges or is exercised exclusively through interaction with bureaucratic agencies, without an institutional site for parties to acquire a broader collective reality."[8] In sum, the first part of Daalder's argument holds. The late development of mass parties in Brazil generated a party system with less formal control over the government bureacracy.

The relative timing of state and party development also helps to explain the exceptional character of Brazilian party politics within Latin America.[9] While other Latin American countries share similar institutional configurations of presidentialism and federalism, most Latin American political parties were organized well before the establishment of central state bureaucracies. Perhaps the clearest case is Colombia, where alliances among regional militia evolved into powerful electoral-military organizations—the Liberal and Conservative parties—that continue to divide Colombian society deeply and determine state-bureacratic politics today.[10] Chile and Argentina also developed professional party organizations and democratized com-

petitive electoral politics by the turn of the century, before the emergence of the centralized state and modern bureacuracy.[11] Although Venezuela is often presented as a model of democratic stability and party continuity, as well as a country in which mass parties developed only after central state bureacracies were built by dictators in the 1930s, the role of formal political pacts seems to be a critical intervening variable.[12]

The second part of Daalder's argument, that late party development generates political instability, requires greater attention. While Brazilian parties lack the formal organization, parliamentary discipline, and ideological clarity of some European parties, one cannot thereby infer that Brazilian parties are dysfunctional. Instead, Chalmers argues:

> The aspects of parties often identified as faults—absence of a solid, independent organizational network, presence of personalist leadership, weakness of ideological or programmatic content, rapid rise and fall of ad-hoc parties, lack of sharp identification with class or other specific interests—are clearly the product of the Latin American socio-political structure. More important is the fact that *it is these characteristics which make parties functional* within that structure.[13]

The causal link between Brazilian party-electoral politics and instability, such as the crises which led to democratic breakdown in 1964, cannot be explained by focusing on organizational discontinuity, corruption, patronage, fluid alliances, and poorly disciplined party elites.

On the contrary, late party development caused political instability in modern Brazil because centralized state bureacuracies came under the control of candidates winning office through plebiscitarian appeals. After 1945, Brazil's political leaders reorganized patronage machines into political parties by regulating complex electoral alliances between candidates for executive and legislative elections on the federal, state, and municipal levels. The ensuing breakdown of democracy in 1964 occurred because this process of late party development simultaneously threatened to *strengthen* the party system and to remove state bureaucracies from the control of other social and political actors.[14] Shifting the comparative perspective from the European to the U.S. experience of party development requires a reassessment of the causal relations between party competition, populist mobilization, and

limits on change under capitalism that produced the military intervention in 1964.[15]

Those who study U.S. parties suggest that political change occurred in the United States primarily through a sequence of critical, realigning elections that generated new policy constellations. But Brazil's powerful central bureacracies raised the stakes of electoral change. Consequently, instead of a sequence of party systems punctuated by critical elections and policy realignments, as in the United States, Brazilian party systems were reconstructed after questions of political inclusion and exclusion or policy change were resolved by other—usually military—means. From this perspective, the succession of Brazilian party systems can be seen as a sequence of *averted realignments*: refusal to include new claimants (or old) and abandoning a party system for the authoritarian reorganization of the party-electoral sphere.

Because parties developed late in Brazil, Brazilian populism also differs considerably from populist movements in the nineteenth-century United States. Unlike the U.S. and European populist movements, which had a social and agrarian character, populism emerged in Brazil as a political movement organized by state leaders geared primarily toward urban groups.[16] The vision of the state as a multiclass national front resisting the domination of foreign capital and imperialist interests is a unique feature of Latin American populism.[17] This state-centered, urban-oriented character of Brazilian and Latin American populism must be placed in the context of a dramatically expanded role of Latin American states in their dependent economies.

One may object to a comparison between such different experiences. Indeed, the differences between Brazilian and U.S. party development relates to a broader problem regarding the role of misplaced ideas and institutions from abroad in Brazilian culture and politics.[18] Brazilian politics have always been organized on the basis of the rules, procedures, and (to some extent) normative principles that dominated the international system at any given time. However, neither specific political outcomes, nor the irrelevance of institutional design follow from the misplaced character of these norms, rules, and procedures of government. Instead, the effects of misplaced ideas and political institutions in Brazilian history may best be described by referring to Mario de Andrade who, along with other modern writers and artists in the 1920s, proclaimed the Brazilian capacity to digest

and restate the genres of European modernism to be *antropofagico* (cultural cannibalism).

The concept of cultural cannibalism may seem far-fetched, but it clearly suggests the need to surpass a type of structural dysfunction-alism [*sic*] that is found in studies of Brazilian party and electoral pol-itics. Brazilian parties and elections can be understood neither as de-viations from liberal ideals of representation,[19] nor as failed adaptations of ideological party systems.[20] The discovery that Brazilian parties do not conform to liberal ideals or formal models of European party systems requires reassessment of theory, not liberal lament, con-demnation, or recommendations for a broad redesign of Brazil's in-stitutions. In scientific terms, finding corruption, fleeting organiza-tions, and apparent ideological incoherence among Brazilian parties confirms the null hypothesis of traditional liberal models. Confirma-tion of the null hypothesis requires rejection of theory, not for calls by social scientists to remake reality in the image of a formal model. In sum, a better account is needed of how political parties mediated between the state and society in Brazilian history.

Misplaced monarchic, liberal, federalist, and democratic ideas adopted from abroad have generated unexpected institutional adap-tations and party systems in each period of Brazilian history since the nation's independence from Portugal in 1822. The following chapters describe these party systems in terms modeled on American history in the hope of both shifting the comparison from European to U.S. party development and clarifying the political context of Brazilian voters as their nation returned to democracy.

— Chapter 2 —

The First Party System

Political Clans, Provincial Accords, and Parliamentary Monarchy, 1822–1889

After 1836, the political history of the country is that of conflict between the two parties, Conservative and Liberal.
—*Barão do Rio Branco, 1857*

Although not in their image, the liberal and monarchic institutions introduced after Brazil gained its independence in 1822 generated a series of party-electoral and party-administrative practices of increasing autonomy and complexity that lasted a full sixty-seven years until 1889. This period of party predominance from 1836 until the end of the Brazilian Empire is defined as the first Brazilian party system. Unlike Hispanic Latin America, Brazil developed effective bureaucratic institutions, a prince and parliament, and a powerful military force during its empire. Explaining the uniqueness of Brazil in nineteenth-century Latin America requires a careful analysis of party and electoral politics, because they created the links between central imperial institutions and the variety of provincial and local institutions throughout the vast Brazilian territory. These links through party patronage machines were a consequence of the sequence of rules and procedures adopted from abroad over the course of the empire. Indeed, the consolidation of the first Brazilian party system is a com-

pelling example of how misplaced ideas from abroad can generate unexpected institutions and practices—a tendency that one might call (after Mario Andrade) political-institutional cannibalism.

A reconsideration of party-electoral politics during the Brazilian Empire is essential not only to explain the relative success of Brazilian polity building but also because existing perspectives underestimate both the importance of parties and the autonomy of politics in nineteenth-century Brazil. Earlier theoretical perspectives such as Marxist political economy and a concern with state building suffer from a type of republican evolutionism that sees the fall of the empire as a natural transition to liberal and republican rule. Recent studies by Richard Graham and José Carvalho do indeed emphasize the development of unique political links between central imperial institutions and county and provincial leaders. For Graham, under the empire local elites ceded power to central institutions to preserve the Brazilian ethos of order and progress and the class structure amid changing times.[1] Carvalho explains the relative absence of civil war and militarization in imperial Brazil by emphasizing common patterns of elite socialization.[2]

But the socialization of the ruling class and underlying class interests seem unable to fully account for polity building during the empire. Instead, this analysis returns to the classic works of Oliveira Vianna and Paula Beiguelman to emphasize the origins, development, and breakdown of specific party-electoral practices during the empire.[3] First, a few comments on the antecedents and institutional frameworks of imperial politics and the formation of the Liberal and Conservative parties are in order.

Antecedents and Institutional Frameworks: The First Empire, 1824–1831

Brazilian Independence surpassed even Machiavelli's expectations. Dom Pedro I (the prince who in 1821 remained in Brazil when the exiled king and court returned to Portugal after Napoleon's defeat) founded the Brazilian nation with a speech act, hired foreign mercenaries to impose political institutions on its society, and granted legitimacy to the incipient Brazilian state. Comparatively speaking, Brazil adopted few liberal institutions upon becoming independent in

1822.[4] All other Latin American nations were founded as independent republics, and most abolished slavery. However, in Brazil generalized demands for the nation's independence were heard only after attempts to liberalize Portugal's control failed, and few proponents of independence challenged the eminently nonliberal institution of slavery.

While historians still lack the documentation required to link political groups to patterns of economic and social change during the First Empire (1824–1831), there is relative consensus on the primary cause of political conflict during that era.[5] From Independence until the return of Emperor Dom Pedro I to Portugal in 1831, conflict arose because of differences between the centralized imperial administration and diverse national and nationalist groups in Parliament. This conflict lay behind the emperor's dissolution of the Constituent Assembly in 1823; the imposition of censorship and a centralizing monarchic constitution in 1824; revolts in São Paulo, Minas Gerais, and the northeast, and their suppression by German and Irish mercenaries in 1826. Finally, Dom Pedro I was forced to abdicate the throne in the shadow of further revolts in 1831.[6]

The most important institutional legacy of the First Empire was the 1824 constitution, which remained the legal framework for parliamentary monarchy until 1889—over sixty-five years. After dissolution of what has been called the "planters'" Constitutional Assembly in 1823, the constitution of 1824 established a unique four-power system inspired by Benjamin Constant's institutional formula for the French restoration.[7] This system was based on the principle of *poder moderador* (moderating power) and gave the emperor broad veto powers over Parliament.[8] As the *poder moderador* of a parliamentary monarchy, the emperor was empowered to appoint senators for life, dissolve the lower house, decree laws, name ministers, dissolve cabinets, and intervene in the provinces. The Parliament of the First Empire lacked the essential features of a parliamentary regime, such as powers of ministerial review or appointment. Not surprisingly, Parliament also proved inadequate as a site for resolving political conflicts between nativists and the imperial administration.[9]

Formation of the Liberal and Conservative Parties

Most scholars agree that the empire's two national parties—the Liberals and Conservatives—emerged from conflicts over decentraliza-

tion during the regency (1831–1841).[10] Upon the abdication of Dom Pedro I in 1831, the Liberal party program called for a federal republic, abolition of *poder moderador*, an elected, temporary Senate, and bicameral provincial congresses that could make appointments in the municipalities. Despite this far-reaching program of 1831, the party soon accepted the limited constitutional reforms of 1832–1834, a development no doubt related to the fact that the Liberals were called to form several cabinets during the regency. Whatever the explanation, by the 1830s the Liberal party had distanced itself from more radical movements calling for regional autonomy and institutional reform.

The Conservative party originated in the alliance between moderate Liberal politicians who were threatened by provincial revolts and court politicians who favored restoration of the monarchy. Both groups participated in the 1837 cabinet and shared an opposition to centrifugal, republican, and liberal tendencies. However, these groups coalesced into the Conservative party only after the death of Dom Pedro I (1837) suspended hopes for restoration. The ideology of the Conservative party centered on the need for centralized state authority. The party called for reconstitution of the State Council, reform of the decentralizing criminal code amendment, expanded citizenship requirements, extension of both *poder moderador* prerogatives in the imperial administration, and life terms for senators. The ascendancy of the Conservatives was confirmed during the 1840s when fifteen-year-old Dom Pedro II was declared heir-in-waiting, the justice system, the police, and the provincial presidencies came under central control, and the monetary threshold for elector status was raised.[11]

The *ideas* that defined the liberalism and conservatism during the empire focused on the great political issues of the nineteenth century. Paula Beiguelman observes that Brazilian liberalism arose in the "struggle against colonial power, in the struggle for liberty and equality, in the struggle against monopolies, privileges, and other restrictions that the metropole imposes on free production and circulation." But with the closing of the Constituent Assembly in 1823 by the emperor, it became clear that "the majority of representatives intended to limit the meaning of liberalism by distinguishing it from democratic revindications." Over the next three decades, liberal discourse centered on political decentralization within a federal form of government. After the 1860s, a new generation returned to the radical aspects of the first period and linked the political-institutional revin-

dications of state decentralization to greater questions of civil liberty, political participation, and social reform. This urban, reform-oriented, and cosmopolitan liberalism departed from earlier expressions and became the origin of the 1889 republic.[12]

The Conservative and Liberal parties, founded during the regency, were distinguished at that time by their divergent institutional formulas for the imperial state. However, as Weber reminds us, "All party struggles are struggles for the patronage of office as well as struggles for objective goals."[13] Because of the availability of a written record of Liberal and Conservative party *ideas* and *programs*, historians have paid less attention to the emergence and consolidation of party administration and patronage *practices* during the regency. In a notable exception, Sergio Buarque de Holanda identifies a quite different reason behind Vasconcelos's famous resignation from the Liberal party: the Liberal cabinet formed by Vasconcelos's rival Feijo in 1836 had taken control of the Rio de Janeiro customs office—the financial and organizational base of Vasconcelos's Liberal party faction.[14]

What then explains Liberal and Conservative control of parliamentary and administrative politics from 1832 to the end of the empire in 1889? The freezing of cleavages into durable parties and consolidated party systems is a characteristic of mass politics in the twentieth century.[15] But the "freezing" of the Liberal-Conservative division of the 1830s into a two-party parliamentary monarchy lasted through the 1880s. The central claim of this chapter is that the Liberal-Conservative cleavage of the 1830s remained central until the end of the empire because of the increasing importance of political parties in the imperial state administration. Contrary to prevailing views of imperial party and electoral politics, both Liberals and Conservatives expanded their control over administrative practices in state and society throughout the empire.

Why do so many accounts of the Brazilian empire underestimate the importance of parties and elections? First, an emphasis on liberal ideas has kept scholars from appreciating how party practices froze the Liberal-Conservative split of the 1830s into the imperial party system. Those in the liberal tradition tend to see party politics during the Brazilian empire as little more than a failure to fulfill idealized forms of political representation. Scholars in the Marxist tradition or those who work within more recent state-building approaches, stress the contrast between the dynamic evolution of liberal and republican ideas

against the devolution of liberal political institutions during the empire. Most tend to see the Conservative and Liberal parties as increasingly irrelevant because the classic idea of nineteenth-century Brazilian liberalism—decentralization—was no longer a goal of the Liberal party by the beginning of the Second Empire. However, this gap between founding ideas and subsequent practices is insufficient evidence of party weakness or party system devolution.

Classic analyses of imperial politics from a liberal perspective also tend to underestimate the importance of parties and elections because of an idealized conception of how parties should represent social and economic interests. For example, despite their fundamental differences, Raimundo Faoro and Nestor Duarte concur that parties and liberal political institutions were not representative because of corruption, fraud, and paternalism, especially in rural areas.[16] Faoro and Duarte draw critical attention to imperial interventions into liberal procedures such as centralizing the judicial system and other political structures during the 1840s and the abrupt dissolution of the Liberal cabinet in 1863. However, because they hold an idealized view of parties as mechanisms for articulating interests, they fail to fully appreciate the parties' role in wielding political power and building the Brazilian state.

Finally, while Marxist historians provided the first broad interpretations of imperial politics in Brazil, they also tend to underestimate the importance of parties and elections in that era. While relegating party politics to the role of imperial farce, they discuss Brazil's economic and social transformations of the second half of the nineteenth century.[17] For example, Caio Prado, Jr., interprets imperial politics as a consequence of the social and economic transformations following the abolition of the slave traffic in 1850. Once Brazil entered the changing world economy, free of Portuguese domination, capital was liberated from fixed investments in land and slaves. These patterns also generated new patterns of economic growth, new social groups, and new political issues in the late nineteenth century.[18] But Caio Prado's emphasis on the progressive nature of mobile and urban capital in the Second Empire to explain party conflicts and political outcomes risks both economic reductionism and republican evolutionism. He refers to the rigidity of imperial political institutions and the personality of the emperor as final causes in the fall of the empire, but fails to explain concrete political processes. The economic dynamism and progressive

character of new capitalists in the Second Empire did not make patronage party politics irrelevant or dysfunctional, nor do they explain specific political outcomes as the empire fell.[19]

The First Brazilian Party System

To avoid the assumptions of liberal evolutionism and the vices of economic reductionism, the analytic focus can be narrowed to pose the following questions. How were party and electoral practices organized in the state and in society under the empire? What practices by parties and the state bureaucracy were the result of rules and procedures based on liberal and monarchic ideas adopted from abroad? Vianna and Beiguelmen focus precisely on such questions: Vianna describes four stages in the emergence and transformation of party-electoral practices in Brazil and links them to the adoption of new liberal political rules and procedures during the empire;[20] Beiguelman describes the evolution of party practices at the state level.[21] Taken together, their work offers quite a different view of party empowerment and the place of party-electoral politics in the rise and fall of the Brazilian Empire.

Vianna begins with the legacy of colonial society. The spatial, geographic, cultural, and political isolation of the Brazilian *fazenda*—estate or plantation, became the fundamental context for electoral practices during the empire and, indeed, for subsequent Brazilian party systems. Vianna stresses, like others, the virtual absence of social and cultural interaction outside the *fazenda* in imperial Brazil.[22] Indeed, the autonomous *fazenda* generated what could be called, after Leonard Krieger, the paternalistic Brazilian idea of freedom.[23] This dramatic isolation of the *fazenda* confirms a core idea in dependent development theory: peripheral nations lack cultural, social, and economic integration because of their fragmented links to external markets.

The development of *political* institutions during the Brazilian Empire is another story. Instead of isolation, one finds integration; instead of dysfunction, adaptation. External influences and the adoption of liberal and monarchic rules after Independence were critical in the development of state-society relations in Brazil. Vianna discusses four phases in which the liberal rules and procedures introduced during

the empire produced unique party practices that organized political power and linked state and society. The first phase followed the adoption of universal free male suffrage with an extremely low income requirement after Independence in 1821.[24] The expansion of suffrage in the social context of isolated, quasi-feudal *fazendas* produced a novel paternalistic style of political organization. Vianna notes:

> The movement toward the party organization of the rural masses [caused by the democratic regime] had, as one can see, an origin outside of the municipalities. It came from outside, it was an exogenous suggestion, its only purpose was to attend a political-administrative necessity . . . the need to form, via elections, a provincial government and a national government. In short, the two new state structures which the 1822 Regency had instituted.[25]

Vianna describes this first moment in the organization of the Brazilian electorate as the transformation of *paternal* clan into *political* clan.

The second phase of party development in imperial Brazil, according to Vianna, was the expansion of politics beyond the borders of the *fazenda* to the more complicated terrain of the county, this time caused by the decentralizing Criminal Code of 1832.[26] This liberal legislative achievement had the effect of encouraging political clan leaders to enter into *county-level* accords. The first political practices to go beyond the borders of the *fazenda* and that could be called Brazilian were the result of the introduction of liberal political rules and procedures into Brazil. Vianna writes: "This solidarity, this understanding, this association, this syncretic impulse that occurred between *fazendeiros* was purely political—because it had exclusively electoral ends."[27] Liberal institutions were functional in nineteenth-century Brazil not because they embodied liberal norms, but because they determined the parameters for resolving party-electoral conflict and organizing state bureaucracies. Based on these municipal-level agreements, elites elected judges, police, municipal representatives, and National Guard officials—by force if necessary. During the regency, these municipal offices constituted a critical site for solving conflicts and nurturing patterns of association and state power based on party and electoral politics.

For Vianna, the third moment of party development during the empire came when the Conservative and Liberal parties were organ-

ized in response to the political centralization of the late 1830s. Centralization began with the Additional Act of 1836 and continued after the declaration of the Second Empire in 1841.[28] With the support of the Conservative party, the Brazilian monarch recentralized power by rescinding many prerogatives previously granted to provinces and counties. As a consequence, municipal-level political organizations forged political alliances, this time on the *provincial level*, both opposing and favoring centralization. Local, county, and provincial party-electoral practices thereby became the organizational and electoral bases for the Liberal and Conservative parties.

In sum, national political institutions during the empire relied on a dense set of party-electoral and administrative practices that lasted throughout the sixty-seven years of parliamentary monarchy. Vianna suggests that party-electoral practices evolved after the introduction of liberal and monarchic rules and procedures into Brazil. Because of the emphasis on liberal ideas and political economy in histories of the empire, the importance of party development in each moment is by and large ignored. Elections, parties, and liberal legislation mattered in imperial Brazil—not because they set a standard or realized a progressive ideal, but because they established the institutional and legal parameters for party development. From this perspective, nineteenth-century Brazilian politics reveals practical innovation and institutional adaptation, not party dysfunction or increasing irrelevance.

Parties in imperial Brazil also had an important place in government. Beiguelman describes the Brazilian Empire as a "constitutional four-power monarchy with life-long Senate and two asymmetric patronage parties."[29] The place of parties and the relations between these institutions can be summarized as follows:

Poder moderador. The *poder moderador* forms the executive cabinet with one of the two parties, which then constitutes Parliament through elections.

Parliament. Party members nominated to the executive cabinet "create" a parliamentary majority via elections and nominate, administer, and govern on the basis of the parliamentarians elected.

Senate. Lifetime nominations to the Senate guarantee the two-party system by assuring that even politicians who are out of power have material and political support.

Patronage parties. After 1836, the persistence and practices of the two national parties is not due to ideological differences over centralization versus decentralization but to their insertion into state administration processes.

Asymmetric parties. The Conservative party, which retained a majority in the Senate, was called more frequently to form cabinets than the Liberals. The Liberal party remained a source of political innovation, true to the dictum, "The Liberal party proposes, the Conservative party executes."[30]

While this succinct description of party practices in the imperial state summarizes institutional and procedural innovations of the era, it is a somewhat inaccurate portrayal of the period of Conservative supremacy from 1836 to 1848 and the period of republican dynamism after 1864.

Several factors impeded the full realization of liberal parliamentary monarchy in Brazil: the absence of parliamentary review of ministers; the conservatism of the Senate and State Council; the primacy of Conservative cabinets; and electoral fraud. However, these characteristics do not explain the decadence and eventual fall of the empire. Regarding general trends, parliamentary debates on electoral legislation and the electoral strength of the Liberals in 1860, after electoral reform, suggest that change was perhaps possible within the framework of the imperial monarchy.[31] Furthermore, the fall of the empire may reflect not the dysfunctionality and irrelevance of party politics, but the militarization of the state after the war with Paraguay in 1865–1870.[32]

Political parties became increasingly autonomous, complex, and coherent as the empire evolved. Both the classic works of Vianna and Beiguelman and data collected by Carvalho on the social and career origins of imperial political leaders support this claim.[33] The increasing complexity and autonomy of political career paths among imperial ministers, senators, and federal deputies suggest that political parties became increasingly important for organizing the Brazilian state and society (see table 2.1). From 1822 to 1889, the percentage of imperial ministers with prior experience in the Senate and State Council remained stable. But the significant increase in the percentage of ministers who had passed through the lower party-administrative posts of general deputy, provincial president, and provincial deputy reveal the

Table 2.1   Previous Political Offices Held by Imperial Ministers,
1822–1889 (percent)

	First Empire/Regency 1822–1840	Second Empire 1840–1889
Senator	54.2	58.7
Counselor	30.5	35.6
General deputy	37.2	67.5
Provincial president	13.5	21.8
Provincial deputy	3.3	31.2
(N)	(59)	(160)

Source: José M. Carvalho, *A Construção da Ordem,* p. 98.

growing complexity and routinization in party and political careers. The increasing importance of regional political offices in ministerial nominations suggests that parliamentary and party politics became more complex, autonomous, coherent, and adaptable.[34]

The data also suggest that there is an excessive emphasis on the domination of Parliament and parties by leaders of the state bureaucracy throughout the empire.[35] The increasing importance of party careers in ministerial nominations can be contrasted to the *decreasing* percentage of those with experience in the state bureaucracy among nominated senators and elected federal deputies (see tables 2.2 and 2.3). The percentage of nominated senators whose careers have been primarily in the state bureaucracy falls steadily from an average of 69.9 percent in the 1820s to 29.6 percent in the 1870s and 1880s. The percentage of elected federal deputies who rose primarily through the state bureaucracy falls from 39.0 percent in the 1822 chamber to 8.0 percent in 1886. The domination of society by the state bureaucracy did not occur because state personnel took direct control of imperial political institutions; instead, party professionals seemed to come primarily from the liberal professions.

Conclusion

While wars and aborted attempts to consolidate their national governments wracked other Latin American nations during much of the

Table 2.2 Occupational Origins of Imperial Senators, 1822–1889 (percent)

	1822–1831	1831–1840	1850–1853	1853–1871	1871–1889
State bureaucracy	69.9	66.6	62.2	45.8	29.7
Liberal professions	8.4	11.2	16.2	31.2	51.8
Business or agriculture	11.7	5.3	18.9	20.8	16.7
Church	10.0	16.6	2.7	2.2	1.8
Total	100.0	100.0	100.0	100.0	100.0
(N)	(60)	(36)	(37)	(48)	(54)

Source: Carvalho, *A Construção da Ordem*, p. 81.
Note: Figures are percentages of the total number of senators for each period.

Table 2.3 Occupational Origins of Federal Deputies, 1822–1886 (percent)

	1822	1834	1838	1845	1850	1857	1867	1869	1878	1886
State bureaucracy	39.0	37.5	47.5	46.6	47.7	37.6	17.2	28.7	11.5	8.0
Liberal professions	6.0	13.4	11.9	15.5	15.3	26.6	40.5	23.7	52.4	35.2
Business or agriculture	10.0	5.7	5.9	5.8	7.2	14.5	7.7	11.4	8.2	7.2
Church	23.0	23.0	11.9	7.7	7.2	5.1	1.7	2.4	0.0	3.2
Other	22.0	20.4	22.8	24.4	22.6	16.2	32.9	35.8	27.9	46.6
Total	100.0	100.0	100.0	100.0	100.0	100.0	100.0	100.0	100.0	100.0
(N)	(100)	(104)	(101)	(103)	(111)	(117)	(122)	(122)	(122)	(125)

Source; Adapted from Carvalho, *A Construção da Ordem*, p. 83.

nineteenth century, elections and party organizations linked the Brazilian state and society through a sequence of political developments eloquently described by Vianna and Beiguelman. The record suggests that party-electoral politics were critical for building political institutions and mediating state-society relations in imperial Brazil. Indeed, its "cannibalism" of other nations' political institutions stands in bold contrast to the prevailing economic fragmentation and social isolation of the time. Adopted liberal and monarchic ideas produced adaptation and political integration in Brazil. What first appeared as institutional adaptations to the juridical innovations of the empire eventually became enduring elements of electoral and party politics in Brazil.

After Independence in 1822, a grant of free male suffrage with low income requirements by Dom Pedro I transformed the paternal clans that ruled the large *fazendas* and vast rural areas of Brazil into political clans. Once electoral resources were thereby established, the decentralizing Criminal Code of 1832 encouraged *fazendeiros*-cum-political-clan leaders to resolve conflicts with their counterparts and build institutions on the county level. The final phase of party development during the empire occurred in response to the recentralization of power, beginning with the Additional Act of 1836 and culminating in the 1841 regency. Alliances for and against centralization on the national level between county and provincial party-electoral machines evolved into the Liberal and Conservative parties that dominated imperial politics until 1889.

Unfortunately, the role of party politics in the political crises of the 1880s and the fall of the empire in 1889 remains difficult to establish. Emilia Costa notes that interpretations of the late empire and the declaration of a republic have changed dramatically.[36] Recent work stresses the dissatisfaction of military officers during the final decades of the empire.[37] Perhaps Frank Colson, who calls for more research on the period, makes the most convincing case.[38] This cursory review of imperial politics suggests that more attention should be given to the role of the Liberal and Conservative parties—specifically to their programs for the new era in the wake of abolition, their economic and political differences, and the factionalism that led to the formation of republican parties and eventually to the military coup and declaration of a republic in 1891.

— Chapter 3 —

Devolution in the Second Party System

Oligarchs, Single-State Parties, and Gubernatorial Federalism in the Old Republic, 1889–1930

In imperial Brazil, monarchist, liberal, and republican ideas dominated debate, informed institutional design, and set the context for party-electoral politics. The most influential idea during the Old Republic (1889–1930) was federalism. Inspired by the U.S. federal and presidential system, the authors of the 1891 constitution sought to reverse the centralization of state power during the empire by establishing states' rights to contract foreign loans, levy export taxes, write constitutional, criminal, and electoral law, and perhaps most important, to form autonomous military organizations.[1] Once again, the adoption of federalist ideas from abroad by Brazilian political elites generated unexpected outcomes. The combination of broad states' rights and direct presidential elections during the Old Republic generated two new elements that comprised the second Brazilian party system: the predominance of governors in national politics and the hegemony of single parties within states.

Important work has been done since Thomas Skidmore remarked in 1967 that "the historiography on the Old Republic (1889–1930)

is relatively meager."[2] Several U.S. historians have done regional and comparative studies of the major Brazilian states during the Old Republic. The cooperative research of Joseph Love, Robert Levine, and John Wirth enables us to ask more precise questions about the formation of single parties in the states, unity and discord among political leaders, and the impact at the state level of crisis in the 1920s and dictatorship in the 1930s.[3] However, by focusing on the states, they leave unanswered important questions about national politics.

Brazilian historians and social scientists tend to examine politics in the Old Republic within a broader interpretive framework.[4] Early views of the Old Republic stressed the congruence between its agrarian and export-based economy, its oligarchic society, and its clientelistic politics.[5] For these scholars, the Brazilian Old Republic is seen as the oligarchic calm before the storm of mass politics. The problems of modern Brazil, such as organizing mass inclusion, modernizing government administration, and fostering industrialization through state-led import substitution policies, are all associated with the post-1930 period.

This picture of oligarchic stability and unproblematic hegemony of the big states a century ago collapses on closer investigation.[6] Instead, scholars now emphasize specific problems in the emergence, consolidation, and breakdown of oligarchic federalism from 1889 to 1930. Indeed, the current description of Old Republic politics as *politica dos governadores* (governors' politics) focuses on the rise of specific electoral and party practices that linked local and regional political machines with national politics.[7] Although debate continues, historians and political scientists today have a far better understanding of asymmetric federalism on the national level and party-machine politics on the state and local levels in the Old Republic. The following sections briefly consider three aspects of the second Brazilian party system: the establishment of gubernatorial prerogatives in federal politics; the organization of single parties in the states; and the role of party-electoral politics in the breakdown of the Old Republic in 1930.

Governors' Politics and Asymmetric Federalism

The colloquial description of Old Republic politics as *cafe com leite* (coffee and milk) agreements between governors of the major states

(coffee-producing São Paulo and dairy-producing Minas Gerais) implies a gentlemanly rotation of the presidency that conceals both the difficulty of reaching national consensus among states and the assertion of hegemony within states. The powerful states with the largest electorates could choose the federal president in alliance with several smaller states, form majorities in the national congress, and control the federal bureaucracy. But while three successive presidents from São Paulo State dominated the federal government from 1889 through 1906, *Paulistas* failed to elect a president between 1907 and 1926—hardly the kind of rotation implied by *cafe com leite*.[8] Love argues that despite the absence of presidents from São Paulo, the *Paulista* elite still retained control over the critical federal ministries and policies of foreign exchange, domestic monetary levels, and commodity (coffee) price support programs.[9] However, Mauricio Font questions the extent of compatibility between federal fiscal and monetary policies and the coffee interests of São Paulo State, especially during the 1920s.[10] Given the complexity of this debate, the concept of governors' politics—instead of assuming the gentlemanly character of oligarchic politics, a compatibility of rural and urban interests, and the unchanging local domination by paternalistic landowners—focuses on the specific mechanisms that built single-state parties and national party alliances.

The central mechanism of governors' politics on the federal level was to create viable majorities in congressional and presidential elections.[11] Elections were adopted because other institutional procedures failed to resolve conflicts. From the military coup that deposed the emperor in 1889, through selection of President Campos Salles in late 1891, military leader Deodoro Fonseca simply nominated governors—a practice that exacerbated friction in most states and caused a civil war in Rio Grande do Sul.[12] The 1891 constitution only deepened regional differences, and Fonseca responded by dissolving the first congress of the Old Republic and imposing a state of siege. This attempt to centralize power failed, Fonseca resigned, and his successor Floriano Peixoto attempted to reconstruct the federal government by dissolving the state assemblies. This also provoked armed revolts and full-scale war in Rio Grande do Sul in 1892–1895.

By 1892, national leaders feared additional violence and recognized that factionalism within the states threatened the very existence of the central government. The solution engineered by President Cam-

pos Salles was to hold elections but to seat only those federal deputies supported by state governors. Governors retained this unusual legal prerogative to seat their congressional delegations throughout the Old Republic. The ability of governors to present lists of legitimate federal deputies established their predominance, not only within their states, but also as key actors in negotiating electoral alliances and legislative coalitions among the single-state republican parties on the federal level. In the United States, parties developed during the nineteenth century through senators who served as the primary links between local patronage machines and the federal government. Although Brazilian governors lost the prerogative to seat congressional delegations in 1930 and never regained it, their influence in electoral and party politics on the state and federal levels remains critical until today.

The Organization of Single-State Republican Parties

The *coroneis*, oligarchs, and municipal political machines left over from the empire were forced to adapt to this unorthodox power of governors to seat federal congressional delegations. The classic account of *coronelismo* by Victor Leal emphasizes that, despite the relative modernization of politics and bureaucracies during the Old Republic on the state and federal levels, the power of *coroneis* remained unchallenged on the local level and continues into the twentieth century.[13] Leal's argument remains a classic, but Oliveira Vianna and Mauricio Font differ with him on one important account, asserting that the power of *coroneis* was not timeless and unchanging. Several institutional and political developments occurred during the forty-one years of the Old Republic that altered both the context and content of local electoral machines. Vianna suggests that the Old Republic, instead of reinforcing the private patrimonial control of *coroneis*, actually produced a "vertiginous absorption of municipal power by the state."[14]

Font also emphasizes the changes in the states once governors dominated federal politics and the federal and state bureaucracies of the Old Republic began to modernize: "A new group of *coroneis* emerged. Usually holders of law degrees, the "doctors" were often key figures in the state bureaucracy or the party who acted as political bosses."[15] Furthermore, once new political bosses appeared on the scene, the content of local electoral and party politics also changed:

"New *coroneis* did not start out, as the traditional ones did, by claiming generalized dependency status from their supporters and followers. They had to attain a following by political entrepreneurship."[16] In sum, observers now emphasize not the timeless patrimonial power of rural *coroneis* as reinforcing the predominance of traditional oligarchic society, which in turn reinforced the distortions of an agricultural export economy, but achievements in state building, economic modernization, and other processes of change.[17]

This new emphasis on change during the Old Republic helps us to understand the third Brazilian party system in a new way. Perhaps the most important consequence of social, economic, and state-administrative modernization is that, at least in some states, a new professional class of politicians emerged during the Old Republic. Traditional oligarchs may have replaced military elites and dominated parties and states at the beginning of the Old Republic. In the case of São Paulo, Font remarks, "At the beginning of the republican regime the PRP was a mixture of patrician oligarchy and clientelistic networking projecting subregional interests directly onto the state apparatus." Traditional oligarchs also seem to have retained this power in some states.[18] But during the forty-one years of the Old Republic, politicians and state personnel who ran single-state republican parties became increasingly specialized, centralized, and autonomous from oligarchs, *coroneis*, and traditional elites.[19] A pattern that James Malloy emphasizes after 1930 describes this process well: those who establish organizations often lose control to professionals who have risen through the ranks.[20]

Although it is a matter of debate, Font argues that several developments in the state of São Paulo let a new generation of professional politicians wrest control of the day-to-day operations of the PRP from traditional oligarchs. The modernization of agriculture, industry, and commerce generated new classes that broke traditional bonds with local oligarchs. Immigrants, laborers, urban capitalists, and state administrators became voters and party activists. Font suggests that new professional politicians asserted control over the PRP and state agencies, not by extending oligarchic power, but by turning to new groups in the city of São Paulo and the newer coffee farms of western São Paulo State. Indeed, old planter families from the Paraiba Valley were forced into opposition, first within the party, later by forming the Partido Democratico (Democratic party, PD).[21]

In sum, electoral-party politics emerged as an increasingly autonomous sphere during the Old Republic, to such an extent that both
traditional oligarchs and new claimants from the middle classes were
excluded from power. Further analysis is required to fully understand
the rise and fall of the third Brazilian party system and the variations
among states in the relative power of traditional oligarchs and emerging professional politicians. But whatever the variation, two central
characteristics of the third Brazilian party system provide new perspectives on the course of politics during the Old Republic: the establishment of gubernatorial prerogatives to seat federal deputies and
the predominance of single-state republican parties.

Parties and the Breakdown of the Old Republic: From Marxist to Tocquevillian Theories of Revolution

New perspectives on the Old Republic also pose new questions about
the 1930 revolution. Since Fausto's paradigm-shifting book of 1970,
scholars have rejected interpretations of the 1930 breakdown of the
Old Republic as a revolution in the Marxist sense, as caused by an
ascendent bourgeoisie.[22] But, ironically, recent accounts of the events
leading up to 1930 bear a striking resemblance to the accounts of
major revolutions by Theda Skocpol (and Tocqueville) that focus on
the decline of traditional landed oligarchs in the face of new state
bureaucracies and parties.[23] Although further research is needed on
how the causal sequence differed in other Brazilian states, the experience of São Paulo suggests that Skocpol's and Tocqueville's theories
may reveal much about party-electoral politics and the 1930 revolution in Brazil.

The predominance of professional politicians and state bureaucrats in the PRP by 1920 has been noted. The first indications that
single-state party structures in São Paulo began to exclude members
of the traditional coffee elite appeared in the 1919 municipal elections,
when widespread violence erupted against state party leaders.[24] From
1919 until open calls for revolution in 1930, opposition to the PRP
in São Paulo was centered in traditional rural leaders in São Paulo
State and took several forms. Local disputes escalated to a *munici-
palismo* movement, while contested elections split coffee producers
and other agrarian interest groups. After a dissident movement of

traditional planters within the PRP failed, opposition increasingly took place outside the party. Font argues that 1920 newspaper campaigns, formation of the Liga Nacionalista, and "rising malcontent among the established coffee elite" culminated in the rebellion of 1924, during which military leaders, backed by traditional oligarchs, took over the state government for three weeks.[25] The censorship, repression, and state of emergency required to restore order after the 1924 rebellion marked the end of political tranquility in São Paulo.

This escalating tension between traditional oligarchs and newer groups may be clearer in São Paulo because revolution was articulated through party politics: the leading opposition force in the state after 1926 was the PD.[26] While the PD first attempted to "organize and articulate big coffee capital with financial, commercial, professional, and interest groups to which it felt closely related," the party subsequently pursued alliances with popular sectors in São Paulo and coalitions with parties and groups from other states opposed to the PRP.[27] But, as Font notes: "Instead of being the revolution's immediate victims (they were indeed long-term casualties), planters actually played a significant part in articulating a national movement against the PRP."[28]

Traditional arguments about how deep social and economic divisions produced political conflict in the 1920s are convincing only if the analysis is extended to the political level.[29] Indeed, scholars now agree that the striking characteristic of economic development and social change in the Brazilian Old Republic is the unusual unity of interests between old and new groups. Given this unity, the division of capitalists into agrarian, commercial, industrial, and state fractions does not hold. Neither does the distinction between oligarchy and middle class. In fact, these types of businesses were owned by, if not the same people, often by the same family. Indeed, the Brazilian oligarchy controlled both state and commercial enterprises in the empire, and continued to participate in newer stages of capital during the Old Republic.[30] Brazilian commercial, agrarian, and industrial interests also coincided during the Old Republic because the federal government adopted complementary policies such as currency devaluations, import taxation, and price subsidies in the coffee sector that favored all three sectors. This compatibility of interests had an important impact on the organization of parties: the Brazilian Old Republic is conspicuously lacking in opposition parties promoting industrialization.[31]

Other Latin American countries differed in this regard. For example, in Argentina the *frigoríficos* (packinghouses) were originally dominated by foreign business, while the Sociedad Rural Argentina represented the interests of ranchers. Economic differences between agrarian and commercial sectors were grafted onto the explosive cleavage between national and foreign interests, defining much of Argentine politics until the *frigoríficos* were nationalized.[32]

If a greater compatibility of interests characterized the Brazilian Old Republic, the 1930 revolution must be understood in political terms as a contest for power—not the outcome of underlying economic or social transformation. Interpreting the 1930 revolution as a type of bourgeois rebellion, as a transition from oligarchic liberalism to the industrialism of the Estado Novo, or as the military expression of an emerging middle class have all been criticized because social cleavages in Brazil simply were not that deep. The causes of popular exclusion, dissent, and rebellion in the 1920s must now be sought on the political level, in the mechanisms of the *politica dos governadores* system and the rigidity of single-state republican party machines.[33]

— *Chapter 4* —

Mass Inclusion in the Third Party System

Populism and Patronage in Party Development and Passive Democratization, 1945–1964

The mechanisms of party development that Max Weber described as *passive democratization* in nineteenth-century America emerged together for the first time in Brazilian history after World War II. Direct presidential, gubernatorial, and mayoral elections were held throughout the 1945–1964 period. Elected officials freely appointed party politicians to administrative posts. Governors and regional party politicians thereby linked local patronage machines to their party-electoral organizations, which, in turn, were linked to presidential campaigns through electoral alliances, legislative coalitions, and promises of administrative nominations typical of spoils systems.[1] In addition, local, state, and national party organizations were also built out of—and from opposition to—the new corporatist institutions and the symbolic legacies of national populism established by Getulio Vargas.

Understanding the rise and fall of the third Brazilian party system between 1945 and 1964 again requires a shift away from models taken from Europe to the U.S. experience with presidential and federal institutions. Scholars often describe Brazilian political parties in 1945–

1964 using terms and models derived not only from European party organizations, but also from the European experiences of polarized pluralism and democratic breakdown.[2] But comparisons with ideological party systems and disciplined, effective parliamentary elites misrepresents the role of party and electoral politics in causing the crises leading up to the events of 1964. Instead, by comparing the third Brazilian party system in 1945–1964 to the U.S. experience, one can better describe how popular pressures, machine politics, presidential elections, and the constraints on change in capitalist society precipitated political crisis and the military intervention of 1964.

In 1978 Juan Linz and Alfred Stepan first suggested that the structure of party competition must be considered a central intervening variable in the sequence of polarization and political crisis that produces democratic breakdown.[3] In the same edited volume, J. Samuel Valenzuela explained the fall of the Allende government and military intervention in Chile by emphasizing how polarized pluralism caused political radicalization.[4] But both Stepan and Sartori argue against emphasizing the autonomous causal weight of centrifugal party competition in pre-1964 Brazil. For Stepan, because populist leaders overloaded the state's capacity to execute policy and tended to circumvent the party system, their leadership is a better explanation of the crisis and breakdown of the regime.[5] For Sartori, party-system analysis also seems inappropriate for Brazil before 1964, because its parties never achieved the structural consolidation found in competitive mass party systems.[6]

Bolivar Lamounier and Rachel Meneguello have classified four other perspectives on the relation between party politics and democratic breakdown in 1964:

1. Theories of social modernization and political development that emphasize the traditionalism and backwardness of Brazilian parties.
2. Political economy explanations that emphasize constraints on populist policies due to the end of the easy phase of import substitution industrialization.
3. Analyses that emphasize the lack of party control over state resources and decision making, thereby reducing their legitimacy and increasing populist demagoguery.
4. Explanations of party politics and political crisis in the 1960s as a case of polarized pluralism.[7]

Scholars of the first category correctly stress Brazil's growing class divisions and other social conflicts in the early 1960s, but misconstrue the origin of social paralysis.[8] Political exclusion did not simply arise from weak political institutions or the unwillingness of political leaders to incorporate mass claimants.[9] Instead, it is more accurate and precise to say that the plebiscitarian bias of populist leaders encountered structural constraints to change typical of dependent capitalist development. Both international and domestic business reduced investments and mobilized against President João Goulart once the Kennedy administration canceled loans to Brazil and the IMF rejected San-Tiago Dantas's anti-inflationary plans.[10]

The second perspective, political economy, identifies precisely such concrete historical constraints on populist state policies and popular inclusion.[11] These explanations supplement political development approaches to the pre-1964 crisis by clarifying the underlying causes of economic stagnation, the class character of social mobilization, and the place of international actors—political and financial—in the breakdown. However, most political economists interpret events as caused by social mobilization, political conflicts, and the constraints of capitalism. The political and institutional characteristics of the Brazilian party system are relegated to a peripheral role.

Scholars in the fourth category such as Wanderly G. Dos Santos and Lucia Hippolito make the bolder assertion that the causes of polarization, crisis, and democratic breakdown in 1964 can be found in the institutional features of Brazilian party and electoral politics.[12] Santos presents a two-pronged polemic,[13] first against Sartori by arguing that theories of polarized pluralism are indeed appropriate in Brazil, despite the premass character of its party system. But Santos also confronts widespread assumptions about how economic crisis, social conflict, and military intervention in 1964 are sequentially linked.[14] Contrary to these assumptions, Santos argues that the centrifugal tendencies of party elites *in Congress* had already created negative politics and legislative impasse by 1962, well before the exacerbation of social conflicts or deepening economic crisis. Because this process within political institutions preceded heightened social and class mobilization, Dos Santos's argument is not only provocative; it is also plausible.

The third category refers primarily to the ground-breaking work of Maria C. C. Souza entitled *Estado e Partidos Politicos no Brasil,*

1930–1945 (1976). Souza provides a new explanation for electoral trends, party politics, and democratic breakdown in 1964 in part because it avoids problematic comparisons to European party systems. Souza focuses both on structural problems of pre-1964 party competition and the prospects for overcoming those problems through the mechanisms that drive Brazilian parties: the links between direct executive elections and patronage machines. Far from focusing on the weakness or dysfunctionality of Brazilian parties, Souza fundamentally claims that the pre-1964 party system produced military intervention because it had generated the political outcomes associated with the democratization and consolidation of mass politics: "Our central hypothesis . . . is that the critical character of the (pre-1964) conjuncture derives from the simultaneous strengthening of the state and the party system, presenting in an immediate way the following dilemma: state without parties or party government."[15]

The third Brazilian party system produced political crisis and caused military intervention in 1964 not because of its backwardness or inability to express and represent popular interests. The plebiscitarian appeals of Brazilian party-electoral politics had raised popular expectations for political change to such a point that the system challenged the political and economic constraints of Brazil's dependent capitalist society. In sum, Souza offers both a compelling theory of how the third Brazilian party system generated political crisis and a broader account of how direct plebiscitarian appeals worked toward the democratization of Brazilian society.[16]

Souza recognizes that for much of the postwar period party politicians had failed to influence state policies that confronted core questions of redistribution.[17] Because the Estado Novo established centralized ministries and secretaries responsible only to federal and state executives, parties and legislators dealt only with less critical policies of regulation and distribution. Souza insightfully suggests that because core questions about redistribution were isolated in centralized ministries controlled by the executive, party leaders gained little experience in core policy areas.[18] Instead, they developed irresponsible populist discourses and patronage practices, thereby reinforcing corporatism, clientelism, and patronage in Brazilian party politics.

But another consequence of concentrating redistribution questions and policies in the executive has not been fully recognized: in the pre-1964 system, plebiscitarian appeals to social justice could be

brought directly into state policies. Here is the critical and unappreciated link between Brazilian party-electoral politics and the political crises that wracked the nation before 1964. Directly elected presidents increasingly relied on plebiscitarian appeals and sought to impose redistributive policies, while failing to recognize their impact on party-electoral alliances, the consequences of widespread social mobilization, and the political and economic constraints of capitalism. The following sections review the role of the third Brazilian party system in the crises that precipitated military intervention in 1964.

Origins of the Third Party System:
The Estado Novo and Transition to Democracy, 1945

Getulio Vargas's declaration of a provisional government in 1930 is widely recognized as the major turning point in modern Brazilian history; the institutional and symbolic legacies of the Estado Novo dominated Brazilian politics from the return to competitive party-electoral politics in 1945 until the breakdown of democracy in 1964. From 1930 to 1938, Brazil experienced, in rapid succession: proclamation of a provisional government in 1930; a revolt against the new government based in São Paulo in 1932; election of a constitutional congress in 1933, followed by a new constitution in 1934; emergence of a broad popular front on the left during 1935 that challenged Vargas's increasingly authoritarian government; an attempted coup by the Communist party in the same year; and the emergence of an *integralist* (fascist) movement that was subdued only after an aborted coup attempt in 1938.

The events of revolution were rapid and puzzling because imported ideas of liberalism, corporatism, fascism, and Marxism informed various attempts to organize mass politics after 1930. None prevailed. Despite the institutional innovations of the provisional government such as functional representation and a national "nonpolitical" party, alongside continued reliance on traditional liberal kinds of geographical representation, Brazilian revolutionaries failed to build legitimate state institutions. Indeed, the constitution of July 16, 1934 remained sovereign only until national security legislation was enacted in April 1935. Thereafter, the government of Getulio Vargas, while elected by the constitutional congress in 1934, increasingly relied on intervention, decree, and repression to maintain power.

Instead, the 1930 revolution produced an unexpected combination of paternalistic, inclusionary corporatism and national populism. By 1937 Getulio Vargas had reconstituted the political center, built centralized modern state institutions, and created clientelist, corporatist, and populist political links to Brazil's emerging mass society. Beyond the complexity and diversity of politics following the 1930 revolution, the manipulation of events by Getulio Vargas is perhaps the most notable phenomenon. Vargas was declared head of the provisional government in 1930, was elected president by the constitutional congress in 1934, and led the military coup that overruled the selection of his successor in 1937.

The organization of the Estado Novo once again confirms the utility of analyzing the unexpected articulation of foreign ideas into political power in Brazil as the "cannibalization" of foreign political institutions. Although the Vargas–anti-Vargas cleavage failed to overwhelm Brazilian politics to the extent that occurred in Argentina between supporters and opponents of Perón, it would be difficult to overestimate the implications of Getulio Vargas's reconstitution of the political center and organization of mass political linkages (under authoritarian rule) for the future.[19] Indeed, Brazil's experience of Tocquevillian tragedy, wherein democratic equality threatens liberty, begins here. The first national measures of mass inclusion and redistribution, such as a minimum wage and social security programs, were introduced under the authoritarian national populism of Vargas's Estado Novo. The new corporatist institutions and patronage machines constructed by Vargas and his nominated governors were transformed into the two parties that dominated national elections from 1945 to 1960, the PSD and PTB. Liberal groups who opposed Vargas and organized the UDN failed to win the Brazilian presidency until 1960, and then only by fielding Janio Quadros, the unstable governor of São Paulo, as their candidate.

Two Transitions: 1945 and 1985

The inclusionary corporatism of Getulio Vargas's national populism (1937–1945) and the exclusionary corporatism of bureaucratic authoritarianism (1964–1985) were dramatically different contexts for party organization and electoral politics during the two transition pe-

riods that followed.[20] The fall of Getulio Vargas in 1945 was due more to the democratic climate of the postwar world than to the organizational weakness or unpopularity of the Estado Novo among Brazilians.[21] The Estado Novo also gave authoritarian state leaders the political experience, patronage resources, and popular support necessary to win competitive elections. The combination, inherited by the PDS and PTB, of diffuse plebiscitarian support for Getulio Vargas and the favor of local-level machine politicians is still a formula for winning elections in Brazil. In sum, the Estado Novo was a comparatively well-organized political regime, with solid support among both new national leaders and the public at large.

By comparison, the fall of the military government in 1985 was caused more by internal weaknesses than the international climate or internal social opposition.[22] And the recent period of bureaucratic-authoritarian rule left military and state elites without legitimizing symbols, material resources, or reliable local-level contacts for winning national elections. The prolonged transition period, 1974 to 1985, permitted authoritarian state leaders to manipulate elections, temporarily prevail in party politics, and pursue various public relations strategies designed to increase public support for the military government. But these efforts could not compensate for the exclusionary and bureaucratic character of the regime, the absence of compelling populist images or personalities, and the lack of solid local-level support from party-electoral machines.[23]

The new institutions that centralized state power in the Vargas regime also produced a new generation of political leaders. Newly nominated governors, new federal and state Departments of Public Service (DASP), new ministries of labor, industry, and commerce, social security, and newly modernized armed forces—all produced new regional leaders with solid local backing. Estado Novo state leaders also retained control of bureaucratic and administrative resources (as well as their political contacts) long after the fall of the authoritarian regime. Two of the major parties of the 1945–1964 period (the PSD and the PTB) were organized by Getulio Vargas and this new generation of Estado Novo politicians.

During the recent authoritarian period, the scope of administrative reform and bureaucratic innovation was considerably smaller. Instead, most scholars accept Fernando Henrique Cardoso's characterization of politics in the military regime as loosely organized by

informal rings of interest articulation.[24] Because the mechanisms of political centralization during bureaucratic authoritarianism were so ad-hoc, few durable political resources were left to state leaders competing in open elections. In fact, the organization of parties in the recent transition was controlled by party politicians with comparatively minor positions in the authoritarian state. National leaders under the military government fared poorly in elections during the transition period.

Electoral Laws and Their Intended Consequences

Unlike the 1985 transition (which most scholars agree actually began in 1974), the electoral timetable of the 1945 transition was clear and rapid. In two strokes of Machiavellian anticipation, on February 28, 1945, Getulio Vargas decreed Constitutional Law 9 (Lei Agammenon) and on May 28, 1945, a supplementary Electoral Code.[25] These decrees outflanked growing liberal opposition by setting the procedures and regulations for party and voter registration, as well as the electoral timetable. The Lei Agammenon determined that the electoral calendar would be set within ninety days. Subsequently, the Electoral Code scheduled direct presidential elections for December 2, 1945, and elections on May 6, 1946, for governors, the constitutional congress, and state and municipal chambers.[26]

The 1945 electoral code was arranged to benefit the candidates supported by Getulio Vargas (there were no parties in spring 1945, only prospective candidates).[27] For example, the 1945 electoral code permitted the registration of individual candidates in several races. Getulio Vargas's simultaneous victories in the Senate and Chamber of Deputies in 1945 (over 100,000 votes in several states) made clear the purpose of the law. This clause violated the original intent of Assis Brasil's representation system that was to remove the plebiscitarian tendencies of majoritarian elections from legislative races. Under the system of statewide PR lists, the coattails of Getulio Vargas were a principal explanation for the PTB's success in the 1945 elections. The representation formula was skewed further toward plebiscitarianism and *getulista* candidates by a law requiring that votes which remained unassigned according to the PR formula should be given to the party that had received a plurality.[28]

Perhaps the most innovative manipulation of the 1945 code was the organization of ex-officio voter registration. Voters were registered at their workplace from employers' lists. All offices of public administration registered their employees, and all government-recognized labor unions registered their members. This ingeniously transferred the corporatist principle of functional representation within the democratic procedures of geographical representation. Although the practice was abolished in 1950, ex-officio registration accounted for 23 percent of Brazilian voters in 1945.[29] Ex-officio registration and multiple candidacies granted significant political advantages to *getulista* candidates in 1945. But the blatantly manipulative intent of the decrees also united the civilian and military opposition. In fact, they were a key factor in ensuring support for the military coup against Getulio Vargas that guaranteed the transition to democracy.

In comparison, the reregistration of voters conducted in early 1986 was not only universal and mandatory, but also impartial—its fairness facilitated by computerization and the autonomy of the Tribunal Superior Eleitoral (TSE). Computer programs were developed to identify the classic types of fraud, such as multiple registrations and the use of false identification card numbers. Fraudulent voters were deleted from lists across Brazil.[30]

The Organization of Parties

Getulio Vargas and the governors he nominated between 1937 and 1945 built the Partido Democratico Social (Social Democratic party, PDS) on the political machines and corporatist ties developed during the years of authoritarian rule. The Partido Trabalhista Brasileiro (Brazilian Labor party, PTB) was also organized on the basis of the new corporatist labor institutions forged in eight years of authoritarian rule. Both parties benefited from the immense personal popularity of Getulio Vargas.[31] Indeed, a central reason for the continuity between the Estado Novo and the period after 1945 was that opposition to and support for Getulio Vargas remained the primary political cleavage. Electoral legislation introduced after Vargas left power ruled out the possibility of Estado Novo interventors (nominated governors) running for governorships in 1946. But eight years of experience in

public administration and political organization still gave the PSD a considerable advantage over opposition candidates and parties.

The classic anecdote about how Estado Novo political machines were transformed into the PSD describes how former interventor Benedito Valladares called for a reunion of Minas Gerais politicians in the Belo Horizonte sports stadium and asked for their affiliation. In São Paulo, the path from nominated governor to elected governor was less direct. Adhemar de Barros was dismissed from the *interventoria* of São Paulo by Getulio Vargas in 1941 and joined the opposition party, the UDN, in 1945. However, he retained enough popular and professional political support to defeat the *getulista* candidate in the 1945 gubernatorial campaign. With the governorship in hand, Adhemar de Barros organized the Partido Social Progressista (PSP, Progressive Social party), which remained an important minor party throughout the pre-1964 period and polled 16 percent in the 1960 presidential election. Adhemar de Barros skillfully cultivated local patronage systems and introduced populist politics to the people of São Paulo over the radio—speaking each evening at seven o'clock during his tenure as nominated governor.[32] In Rio de Janeiro, the inheritance of the Estado Novo was not only political, but also familial. Amaral Peixoto, a central figure in Brazilian politics until his death in 1985, was Getulio Vargas's son-in-law, was nominated governor in Rio de Janeiro, was elected national president of the PSD, and won the 1950 gubernatorial elections.[33]

Opposition to authoritarianism during the 1940s was organized primarily by oligarchic groups damaged by the 1930 revolution, regional liberal leaders, other malcontents after 1937, and the organized left.[34] These groups coalesced around General Eduardo Gomes's candidacy for president and formed the UDN only afterward, in 1945. Storybook accounts of liberal opposition to the Vargas regime cite the Manifesto of Minas Gerais as the spark that brought down authoritarian rule. But liberal opposition to Vargas failed to receive significant mass support. Nor could the UDN win majoritarian elections after the end of the Estado Novo. In 1945, General Eduardo Gomes polled only 35 percent of the vote and lost to the PSD/PTB candidate, General Eurico Dutra, with a solid majority of 55 percent. In the first legislative elections of the democratic period, the UDN fared worse, receiving 29 percent nationally. Indeed, the UDN represents another compelling example of the disjuncture between liberal ideals and de-

mocratization in Brazil. Even the symbol of moral renovation chosen for the 1945 presidential campaign—a white handkerchief—revealed the antipopular and elite meaning of liberalism and the UDN.

Queremos Getulio: Mass Support for National Populism

Another critical difference between the 1945 and 1985 transitions was the character of mass mobilization. During both transitions there was an unprecedented, and relatively spontaneous, rise in popular interest in politics. However, in 1945, the *queremismo* movement was an expression of popular *support* that sought to legalize the candidacy of Getulio Vargas for president. The *queremista* movement was the first indication that the peculiar populist and paternalistic image of the authoritarian leader would define Brazilian political discourse throughout the postwar democratic period.[35] In comparison, the 1984 campaign for *diretas ja* (direct presidential elections now) expressed popular *opposition* to military government, not support. But unlike 1945, popular expectations failed to find durable political images in 1984. Instead, a carefully organized public relations campaign portrayed President-elect Tancredo Neves as offering a cordial, gentlemanly solution to a threatened confrontation between the military and the radical opposition.

The mobilization of labor also differed during the two transitions. Because of the inclusionary corporatism of the Estado Novo, authoritarian state leaders had enough institutional and symbolic resources in 1945 to simultaneously organize the PTB and forge an effective political alliance with the Partido Communista Brasileira (Brazilian Communist party, PCB). By comparison, the exclusionary corporatism of the recent military government left state leaders with few resources for mobilizing labor during the transition period. Instead, independent new labor unions, and even leaders of state-controlled corporatist unions, became major opponents of the military regime.

The Third Party System and the Breakdown of Democracy in 1964

In their analysis of political parties before 1964, Lamounier and Meneguello summarize what scholars have learned about electoral and

party politics from 1945 to 1964. The following assertions have been made:

1. After the mid-1950s, the two principal parties—the PSD and the UDN—declined in the face of more urban-based parties. This did not mean (except in the case of the PTB) a realignment in favor of parties with governing capability, but instead fragmentation into minor and personality-based parties.
2. None of the thirteen legal parties developed a complex and continuous organizational structure during the period: they were clearly parties of notables or associations run by populist chiefs.
3. The mass public felt little subjective identification with these parties, while more educated voters saw little ideological differentiation among them.
4. The three principal parties—the PSD, the UDN, and the PTB—were internally fragmented into widely known ideological, regional, and personalistic factions.
5. The parties were extremely heterogeneous and conflictual because of rapid urbanization and divisions in the federal state structure.
6. Permissive laws regarding alliances and coalitions led to a splintering of parties and complex party alliances during electoral campaigns—alliances that often differed radically from one state to another.[36]

This summary helps to explain how Brazil's third party system differed from the consolidated party systems of advanced democracies. But once again the focus is on deviations from idealized models derived from the European experience. Indeed, this list could be taken for a series of liberal laments rather than empirical descriptions of pre-1964 party politics in Brazil.

For example, to say that before 1964 Brazilian parties were mere parties of notables or associations run by populist chiefs reminds us that Brazilian parties of that era did not meet the formal criteria—having a permanent organization and a well-defined national hierarchy—typical of European mass parties. But this observation fails to recognize important dynamics and political consequences of party development during Brazil's third party system. Far from notables, lead-

ers of state and local patronage machines were political professionals. They were not populist chiefs; winning direct mayoral, gubernatorial, and presidential elections and forming complex alliances through the spoils system were complex political tasks that produced regional and national leaders of considerable talent.

The third description stresses the lack of party affinity among Brazilian voters in general, and in particular the failure of educated Brazilians to find much ideological difference among the parties. While survey data before 1964 is sparse, the evidence from subsequent social and electoral surveys conducted during the period of military rule and democratic transition strongly indicate that ideological party images are simply not relevant to Brazilian voters; nor do they function in Brazil's party-electoral politics. From this perspective, "low levels" of party identification and ideological images among voters before 1964 are not surprising. Lamounier and Meneguello cite party factionalism and the laxity of laws regulating party alliances as defining features of the period. But they fail to place these characteristics within their broader institutional, political, and social context.

This lack of synthesis is all the more surprising because when Lamounier and Meneguello discuss specific matters such as clientelism, corporatism, and the lack of party discipline, they identify clear, concrete causes for these phenomena. For example, weak party discipline is seen as the logical outcome of a system that requires vertical and horizontal flexibility among politicians seeking state resources for their districts. The overrepresentation, political strength, and conservatism of federal deputies from the traditional regions of Brazil is explained, among other institutional factors, by the greater experience and professionalism of rural politicians. Conservative federal deputies from rural regions were influential because their districts were less competitive, and their experience and seniority greater. Finally, one can explain corporatism among business leaders before 1964 not as a cultural trait, but because the clientelist practices and distributive decisions that characterize party politicians were irrelevant to the types of government policy that concerned business people. Instead, business groups tended to deal directly with state agencies under the executive. In sum, Lamounier and Meneguello stress the functionality and adaptation of specific party practices, but they characterize these practices as dysfunctional for the party system as a whole because they

compare them to ideal European models and liberal theories of representation.

If the comparison is shifted to the United States, these same empirical trends can be interpreted very differently. Instead of seeing electoral decline among major parties, electoral fragmentation, polarized pluralism, and other indications of party deterioration, this analysis suggests that competitive party-electoral politics produced crisis and democratic breakdown in 1964 because, in Souza's words, they threatened to "simultaneously strengthen the state and party system."[37]

The sequence of events is critical: although Janio Quadros's resignation in August 1961 precipitated a series of political crises, no one could have predicted the subsequent course of events and military intervention. Vice-President Goulart assumed a weakened presidency on September 7, 1961, proposed moderate reforms, negotiated with both foreign and domestic interests during 1962, regained full presidential powers through direct popular referenda by January 1963, and continued to pursue viable policies of economic adjustment and structural reform through May 1963. Nonetheless, the prospects for moderation evaporated when during the first part of 1963 the confidence of foreign and domestic business eroded and the United States refused to exercise financial leadership among Brazil's foreign creditors. President Goulart's subsequent proposals for agrarian reform and regulating the flow of capital galvanized opposition by the upper classes, while conservative provocateurs quickly generated reaction among conservative parties, national and international business, and the armed forces.

Before discussing the place of party competition in this sequence of events, a brief review of what scholars have asserted about the decline of major parties and party polarization up to 1964 is appropriate. First, the results of congressional elections between 1945 and 1962 do indeed give the impression that the major parties—the PSD, the UDN, and the PTB—declined at the polls (see table 4.1). The total vote for the PSD declined steadily from 42.6 percent in 1945 to 15 percent in 1962. The vote for the UDN went from 26.5 percent in 1945 to 10.8 percent in 1962. After the PTB peaked at 18.6 percent of the vote in the 1950 election (when Getulio Vargas won the presidency), the party declined to 11.6 percent in the 1962 elections.

Table 4.1 Official Results for Federal Chamber Elections, 1945–1962 (percent)

	1945	1950	1954	1958	1962
PSD	42.6	30.5	21.6	18.1	15.0
UDN	26.5	19.2	13.3	12.9	10.8
PTB	10.1	18.6	14.6	14.4	11.6
Party alliances	—	22.9	25.2	32.6	39.7
Other parties	17.2	21.7	18.5	12.6	4.9
Blank/null[a]	3.3	0.8	6.6	9.1	17.7
Total	100.0	100.0	100.0	100.0	100.0
(N)	(5,934,332)	(6,763,273)	(9,889,827)	(12,687,997)	(14,747,221)

Source: Estatísticas Históricas do Brasil (Rio de Janeiro: IBGE, 1990).
a. Nullified because of mistake.

But several caveats are in order. First, votes lost by the major parties did not necessarily go to minor parties. The number of votes obtained by minor parties running isolated candidates fell from 17.2 percent in 1945 to 4.9 percent in 1962.[38] Instead, voters shifted their preferences to *party alliances*, which increased their share of the total congressional vote from 22.9 percent in 1950 to a full 39.7 percent. Hence, trends during the third party system that appear to be fractionalization and polarization are in fact the result of increasingly complex party alliances. In an abstract model of ideological parties and disciplined parliamentary politics based on European conventions, a growing number of electoral alliances would indicate the decline of a governing majority, an increase in negative politics, and other problems. But if one sees electoral alliances as critical mechanisms that link legislators to executives through the spoils system, alliances can be interpreted as facilitating realignment among congressional, state, and local party leaders in response to broader electoral realignments on the national level. Further evidence about presidential elections and federal deputies is required to resolve these different interpretations of electoral alliances.

If one examines the representation of parties in the Chamber of Deputies from 1945 to 1964, one cannot continue to claim that the major parties declined and suffered fragmentation or that electoral alliances caused significant problems of governability before the growing political crisis of 1963. While candidates for federal deputy entered into increasingly complex party alliances at election time, few affiliated with minor parties after taking office (see table 4.2). In 1945, federal deputies representing the three major parties (the PSD, the UDN, and the PTB) made up 89.5 percent of the chamber. In 1962, the three parties controlled 83.5 percent. A decrease of 6 percent over seventeen years hardly indicates major party decline, electoral fragmentation, or polarized pluralism during the 1945–1964 period.

Furthermore, not all the major parties lost seats in the Federal Chamber. The PTB, the major populist party of the period, more than quadrupled its representation of deputies in the Federal Chamber from 22 in 1945, to 116 in 1962. The representation of the PSD and UDN did fall from 52.8 to 30.3 percent, and from 29.0 to 23.4 percent, respectively. But this realignment of federal deputies from the state-centered PSD and conservative UDN to the populist PTB cannot be considered an indication of major party decline, fraction-

Table 4.2 Party Representation in the Federal Chamber,
1945–1962 (percent)

	1945	1950	1954	1958	1962
PSD	52.8	37.0	35.0	35.3	30.3
UDN	29.0	24.4	22.7	21.5	23.4
PTB	7.7	16.8	17.2	20.2	29.8
PCB	0.9	7.9	9.8	7.7	5.4
Minor parties	4.9	—	—	—	—
Total	5.6	13.9	15.4	15.3	16.2
(N)	100.0	100.0	100.0	100.0	100.0
	(286)	(303)	(326)	(326)	(389)

Source: Maria Campello de Souza, *Estado e Partidos Políticos no Brasil, 1930–1964* (São Paulo: Alfa Omega, 1976), p. 144.

Note: Four of the UDN federal deputies elected in 1945 were elected in alliance with the minor party, PR. In 1962, the Partido Democrático Cristão, PDC the largest minor party, elected twenty deputies.

alization, or polarized pluralism. Instead, the evidence suggests a significant realignment of party leaders toward "a party with governing capacity."[39]

The evidence from presidential elections also fails to show weakened major parties, electoral fractionalization, or polarized pluralism. The total direct popular vote for the PSD/PTB alliance, which elected three successive presidents, did indeed fall from 54.1 percent in 1945 to 28.5 percent in 1960 (see table 4.3). But the UDN, which polled roughly 30 percent of the popular vote in the first three presidential elections, won the presidency with Janio Quadros as their candidate with 41.7 percent of the vote in 1960. Perhaps more important, minor parties fared poorly in the 1960 election, falling from a peak of 32.2 percent in 1955 to 16.3 percent. Finally, the three major parties of the pre-1964 system together polled 75.0 percent in the 1950 presidential elections. By 1960, their hold in the presidential contest remained strong—70.2 percent. A decrease of less than 5 percent in the total electoral vote for the PSD, PTB, and UDN in presidential elections is insufficient proof of major party decline, fragmentation, or polarized pluralism.

Table 4.3 Official Results of Presidential Elections, 1945–1962
           (percent)

	1945	1950	1955	1960
PSD-PTB alliance	54.1	46.6	33.8	28.5
UDN	33.9	28.4	28.6	41.7
Other parties	9.6	20.6	32.2	16.3
Blank/null[a]	2.2	4.3	5.2	6.7
Total	100.0	100.0	100.0	100.0
(N)	(6,003,209)	(8,254,979)	(9,097,014)	(12,586,354)

Source: Estatísticas Históricas do Brasil, 1990.
a. Nullified because of mistake.

Indeed, presidential election returns before 1964 suggest that success at the polls required candidates and parties to carefully mediate populist appeals, negotiate with state and local political machines, and build presidential campaigns through complex alliances with party fractions. For example, a candidate for president before 1964 could not rely exclusively on broad plebiscitarian appeals to urban voters. Instead, even a candidate with charismatic and populist appeal had to form alliances with regional and local machine politicians. Souza writes:

> A competitive presidential candidate required these two components of electoral support: on the one hand, generalized support that went beyond specific social and demographic groups, starting with the virtual unification of their own state; and, on the other hand, considerable control in several minor states through agreements with local leaders.[40]

This is an example of a functional interrelation between the local, state, and national levels of the pre-1964 party system. Souza's examination of 1960 electoral results suggests that the two major presidential contenders still received the majority of their votes from rural areas. Both candidates mounted national campaigns by systematically forming alliances with regional and local party machines.[41]

In sum, the evidence from presidential and legislative elections, as well as party representation in the Chamber of Deputies from 1945 to 1964, simply does not support the argument that Brazil's party system declined because of political crisis along the lines of European experiences with electoral fragmentation and polarized pluralism. If major parties declined, how can we explain the surge of the UDN in the presidential election of 1960 and the role of party alliances in shaping electoral realignment? Moreover, the share of major parties in presidential elections and the Federal Chamber remained largely unchanged during the 1945–1964 period.

If one shifts the comparison to the United States, it is possible to view party-electoral politics before 1964 as articulating popular pressures through direct elections for executives as well as reconciling these demands with both patronage systems and the realities of governance in dependent capitalist society. If one recognizes the plebiscitarian character of Brazilian presidential elections, Goulart's rapid reassertion of presidential authority through a direct referendum in 1962 can be seen as a master stroke for achieving political change modeled on de Gaulle's inauguration of the French Fifth Republic in 1958. Given the tendency of state and local party leaders to form electoral alliances and legislative coalitions through the spoils system, the increasing number of party alliances during the early 1960s shows that electoral realignment was possible. Finally, if one considers the rapid deterioration of relations between the Goulart administration and both foreign and domestic business interests after May 1963, one can usefully describe military intervention in 1964 as an example of an averted realignment. Military intervention prevented populist-led political change.

This argument does not seek to discredit other explanations for political crisis and democratic breakdown in 1964 but to clarify the character of critical political moments. Economists have shown how both structural problems such as intensified import substitution and short-term trends of inflation, currency reserves, foreign exchange policy, and a negative balance of payments severely limited the prospects for the inward-oriented populist and nationalist policies that were stubbornly proposed late in the Goulart administration.[42] Sociologists have dramatized the disjuncture between the national-populist policy tradition and the new social classes and business associations that had been generated by Brazil's phenomenal economic

growth and unprecedented levels of foreign investment since 1945.[43] Studies of military politics have also eloquently described both the roots of military intervention and how it occurred on March 31, 1964. Indeed, only historians may be capable of narrating objectively the emotionally charged events that produced military intervention in Brazil.[44]

But, led by Juan Linz's landmark work, political scientists seem especially suited to clarify how structures of party competition, political leadership, and other intervening factors explain the human element in the breakdown of Brazil's democracy. The task of political science is to make such events—in retrospect—avoidable, rather than predetermined by deep structural causes. This review of electoral and party politics from 1945 to 1964 suggests that structures of party competition and mistakes of political leadership were indeed critical in the deepening political crisis after May 1963. But this escalation of party-electoral polarization occurred much later than one might expect from an abstract model of polarized pluralism, major party decline, or electoral fragmentation. Until May 1963, the direct election of presidents and the complex negotiations between executives and legislators that cut across party lines had guaranteed as much state authority and party autonomy as could be expected from institutional arrangements at that time.

The political achievements and possibilities for sustaining democracy in Brazil before military intervention in 1964 should not be minimized. After Janio Quadros and the UDN mobilized the necessary popular support to win the presidency in 1960 and defeat the PSD/PTB alliance for the first time since 1945, he resigned twenty months later while attempting to expand both presidential legislative prerogatives and emergency powers. During the crisis of succession that followed Janio Quadros's renunciation of the presidency on August 24, 1961 (the anniversary of Getulio Vargas's suicide), full military rule was averted by grafting a parliamentary system onto the third Brazilian party system. Only after Tancredo Neves was named prime minister and the powers of the presidency were significantly reduced in late 1962, did Vice-President João Goulart, a PTB leader and Getulio Vargas's protégé, succeed in assuming the weakened presidency.

By January 1963 President Goulart had used referenda to reassert full power as president, had begun to implement economic adjustment policies to reduce inflation, and had presented an agenda of

moderate, viable, and concessionary populist-nationalist reforms. While events moved swiftly thereafter, their sequence indicates the power of presidential initiative and the reality of conservative reaction and other constraints to change in pre-1964 Brazil. Many actors and institutions, both foreign and domestic, played critical roles in producing the breakdown of democracy in Brazil. Goulart failed to recognize the new realities of Brazil's international economy and overestimated both the strength of his traditional populist coalition and his capacity to galvanize support through direct appeals.[45] The Kennedy administration failed to overcome its distrust of Goulart and lost an opportunity to support a moderate leader in Brazil. Under the Johnson administration, U.S. diplomats openly encouraged military coup-makers.[46] In Brazil, conservative opposition groups accepted foreign assistance, flagrantly exacerbated polarization, and provoked military intervention.[47] The rational investment decisions made by foreign and domestic businesses produced outcomes that eventually made it impossible to sustain not only the Goulart administration, but democratic government itself.

Conclusion

Brazil's third party system emerged from an authoritarian era of centralized state power and developed in a context dominated by clientelist machines, corporatist organizations, and gaping social inequalities. Despite these birth defects and structural shortcomings, the mechanisms of passive democratization produced significant political change in Brazil between 1945 and 1964. Few analyses of pre-1964 politics recognize that the development of political crisis and military intervention was due to the *clarity* of populist party politics. Populist politicians were not blocked by voters unable to perceive their own interests, but by the political-economic constraints on social change in dependent capitalist society. Indeed, given the sequence of events after imposition of parliamentary rule in 1962, the institutional parallels with Charles de Gaulle's organization of the Fifth French Republic could hardly be closer. While center-right Brazilian politicians attempted to appease the military by reducing the popular pressures articulated through presidential elections, João Goulart used direct appeals and popular referenda to reassert presidential authority and

avert the alliance between conservative parties and military interventionists.

This reassessment of events in Brazil leading up to 1964 suggests that arguments about major party electoral decline, polarized pluralism, and electoral fragmentation derived from European models must be rejected. Comparing Brazilian and American trajectories of party development provide a better understanding of how party-electoral politics produced political conflict and democratic breakdown. This comparative perspective also suggests that debates about institutional reform may be amiss. Unlike recent arguments favoring broad institutional reorganization and the adoption of parliamentary institutions, Weber and other observers of U.S. politics argued that the bureaucratic complexity of existing party organizations and the routinization of party careers is sufficient to weed out demagogues and avert problems of governance.[48] This level of analysis may be more appropriate than generalizing about party systems, presidential institutions, and parliamentary forms of government.

— *Chapter 5* —

Toward the Fourth Party System

Plebiscitarian Appeals, Patronage Machines,
and Mass Party Politics, 1974–1989

In the beginning there were new kinds of party apparatuses emerging. First, there were amateur apparatuses. They are especially often represented by students of various universities, who tell a man to whom they ascribe leadership qualities: we want to do the necessary work for you; carry it out. Secondly, there are the apparatuses of businessmen. But both apparatuses were fast-emerging bubbles which swiftly vanished again.

—*Max Weber, "Politics as a Vocation"*

This chapter reviews the place of plebiscitarian appeals, administrative appointments, and patronage machines in party and electoral politics in Brazil from 1974 through 1990.[1] Because military rule and competitive elections were mixed during the transition to period from 1974 to 1985, this chapter examines both the attempts at political engineering by leaders of the military government and the unexpected consequences of increasingly competitive national elections. After introducing how military elites sought plebiscitarian acclaim between 1967 and 1973, the discussion covers the liberalization project adopted by President Geisel in 1974, the national elections of that year, the constitutional amendments by executive decree of 1976 and

1977, the 1978 national elections, the Party Reform Act of 1979, the 1982 national elections, the movement in 1984–1985 for direct presidential elections, the selection of Tancredo Neves by a restricted electoral college and the transition to civilian rule in 1985, and the 1985, 1986, 1989, and 1990 elections.

Although this period requires further research, comparison of electoral and party politics from 1974 through 1990 suggests that the mechanisms of party development and passive democratization described in preceding chapters still prevail in Brazil. To understand the emerging characteristics of what may become Brazil's fourth party system, this analysis once again emphasizes the impact of direct executive elections, the power of executives to appoint politicians to administrative posts, and the autonomy of local and regional patronage machines during the post-1974 transition period in Brazil.

Brazilian Voters Under Military Rule, 1964–1973

Upon taking power in 1964, military leaders considered favorable public opinion essential to their success. They believed that engineering public opinion would ensure the stability of sociocultural affairs and permit the military government to implement the economic and political policies necessary to achieve national security and development. Indeed, the Medici administration (1969–1974) initiated plans, elaborated since the 1950s, for monitoring and controlling public opinion. This centralized technical approach to managing popular attitudes under military rule is typical of the bureaucratic character of Brazilian authoritarianism.[2]

Mass propaganda, monitoring of public opinion, and public relations campaigns first emerged in the curriculum and as conference themes at the Escola Superior de Guerra (Superior War College, ESG) in 1955.[3] Since 1955, the War College has held seminars with chief executives from the best marketing and public relations firms in Brazil and has taught methods of managing public opinion, marketing, and propaganda in core courses.[4] In 1959, five years before the military took power, the Servico de Pesquisa e Planejamento da Opinião Publica (Service of Planning and Research on Public Opinion, SPPOP) was created by General Golbery within the National Security Council. After military intervention in 1964, personnel from both the SPPOP

and public opinion groups of the political action organizations IPES/ IBAD formed the core staff of the Grupo de Trabalho de Relacões Públicas (Working Group on Public Relations, GTRP) created by President Costa e Silva in 1968.[5] Finally, a cabinet-level Assesor Especial de Relacões Públicas (Special Assessor of Public Relations, AERP), which reported directly to President Medici, was formed in 1969.

In a conference at the Superior War College in 1970, AERP director Col. Otavio Costa outlined the public opinion campaigns of the Medici administration and their place in both the war against subversion and general strategies to secure national development.[6] The AERP organized several public relations offensives, including an advertising campaign to celebrate the "Brazilian Economic Miracle," which targeted foreign banking centers; a campaign to celebrate *Brasil Grande* at home, and finally the incorporation of the 1970 World Cup victory into government publicity programs. Public relations campaigns targeted both internal and external publics to create the psychosocial conditions necessary to defeat subversion and encourage economic development. Judging by the amount of private foreign bank loans made to Brazil, the military government apparently succeeded in influencing international financiers. Did military public relations campaigns also generate support at home?

Youssef Cohen and Bolivar Lamounier offer convincing explanations for why the public temporarily supported the military regime by stressing how far public perceptions of government had been depoliticized in authoritarian Brazil. Using evidence from social surveys conducted during 1972–1973, Cohen argues that the heritage of corporatist inclusion still kept many popular sectors apolitical.[7] Given this historical legacy, Cohen suggests that public support for the Medici administration was based on popular perceptions that military government was effective (without mention of substantive issues), that— in any event—subversive threats to the nation's security were real, and that there was no viable opposition. In analyzing a separate social survey of Salvador Bahia in 1971, Lamounier also found that respondents made extremely few references to political matters and figures, that when such expressions were made, they seemed to be less than logical and lacked substantive content, and that few were aware of opposing ideas.[8]

The results of the 1970 elections also suggest that the military government during its most repressive era had unexpectedly strong support. The government party, ARENA, polled 49.8 percent in Chamber of Deputies races, and 43.7 percent in the Senate, securing a plurality in each house (see table 5.1). Part of ARENA's success was certainly due to a climate of fear and apathy. The government retained a virtual monopoly over political resources and information, had banned or exiled opposition leaders, and continued to severely restrict electoral contestation. Repression does seem to have produced apathy and fear: the percentage of blank and null voting rose in Senate races from 21.0 percent in 1966 to 30.5 percent by 1970. But to explain the degree of public support for ARENA and the government, one must consider factors beyond repression, apathy, and fear, and rec-

Table 5.1   Official Results of the 1970 National Elections (percent)

	ARENA	MDB	Blank/ Null	Total (N)
Total				
Federal Chamber	49.8	19.5	30.5	(21,013,388)
Senate	43.6	28.6	27.7	
Southeast				
Federal Chamber	47.3	17.0	35.7	(9,858,069)
Senate	37.7	32.3	29.8	
Northeast				
Federal Chamber	54.8	17.2	27.9	(5,092,464)
Senate	52.2	20.1	27.7	
South				
Federal Chamber	50.4	26.8	22.6	(4,597,489)
Senate	39.5	21.6	19.3	
Center-west				
Federal Chamber	49.9	22.3	27.7	(913,841)
Senate	47.0	33.4	19.5	
North				
Federal Chamber	45.4	21.9	32.6	(551,525)
Senate	45.3	25.0	29.6	

Source: Dados Estatísticos. Tribunal Superior Eleitoral, Vol. 8, Brasilia, D.F.
Note: For the composition of each region, see Appendix 1.

ognize the short-term legitimacy the government received from strong economic growth (GNP increased by an average of 11 percent per year from 1969 to 1973), the effectiveness of government publicity programs, and the use of local and regional political machines to support ARENA candidates.

Unfortunately, because most social science accounts of Brazilian voters under hard-line rule share the same general assumptions about voters' cognitive constraints, they fail to examine the possibility that military rule itself, through stiff restrictions on information, contestation, and participation, constrained Brazilian public opinion. Empirical democratic theory once held that the vast majority of voters in mass society tend to be poorly informed, uninterested in politics, and satisfied with the government in power. The primary causes of these unflattering characteristics were also thought to be long-term factors such as socialization, lack of education, and limited knowledge, thereby hampering the possibility of change. Few who have studied public opinion in authoritarian Brazil have considered an alternative explanation: that because of state control over information, participation, and challenges by opponents, voters only appear to be uninformed, uninterested, unpoliticized, and relatively satisfied.

The period of hard-line military rule in Brazil from 1968 to 1973 presents an extreme example of state control over the dissemination of information and electoral contests. In this context, Brazilians' ignorance of politics in 1972–1973 has two explanations: cognitive and educational limits, as proposed by empirical theorists, and limited political options and information, as stressed here. But the evidence shifts after 1972. A significant increase in political knowledge among Brazilian survey respondents during the liberalization period suggests that the apparent lack of sophistication among Brazilian voters in 1972–1973 was not due to ignorance, apathy, or lack of education, but to military restrictions on information and political challenge. The number of survey respondents correctly identifying the State Literacy Program (MOBRAL) in open-ended questions increased from 30.4 percent in 1972 to 83.1 percent in 1978. Correct responses describing the Unemployment Compensation Fund (FGTS) increased from 32.5 percent to 44.5 percent. The number of respondents able to describe Institutional Act V (authoritarian legislation decreed on December 13, 1968) rose from 19.4 percent in 1972 to 24.6 percent by 1978, despite an agreement by opposition party (MDB) leaders not to men-

tion the act during the 1978 campaign. Finally, even the number of respondents correctly naming the current president rose from 60.9 percent in 1972 to 70.9 percent in 1978.

What then explains these patterns of opposition and support during the period of hard-line rule? In a landmark essay, Linz argues that public support for authoritarian regimes depends primarily on creating durable institutional links between the state and society.[9] If one focuses on how the authoritarian regime was organized circa 1970—with only fleeting legitimizing symbols, loosely organized political parties, unstructured voting patterns, and the absence of an institutional formula for military rule—the Brazilian regime appears to have been rather weakly constructed. Authoritarian leaders censored information, blocked opposition, and prohibited political participation. Despite public relations efforts to the contrary, military rule hobbled public opinion and impeded the development of mass political institutions.

In sum, military rule before the onset of liberalization in 1974 indicates that the plebiscitarian appeals of direct executive elections, the distribution of administrative appointments to party professionals, and the formation of complex party alliances with patronage machines are critical to the success of mass politics in Brazil. Until 1973, Brazil's military rulers attempted to shift public opinion in their favor. The Medici administration formed new cabinet-level agencies to monitor and control public sentiment as part of the government's broader mission to guarantee national security and foster economic development. But this experiment suggests that it takes more than good marketing to organize the vote in Brazil. Instead of solidifying support, military leaders only temporarily reduced opposition through repression, depoliticized support by relying on economic performance and public relations campaigns for acclaim, and created a void between the state and society.[10] By 1973, the Geisel-Golbery faction convinced military leaders that the Medici administration's Orwellian techniques must be abandoned in favor of a new strategy.

Adoption of the Strategic Liberalization Project, 1973

The question of democratic normalization centered on the ability of the government to develop a project of institutional engineering

which could establish a dynamic of decompression sufficiently powerful to be irreversible. Yet, at the same time, this process required objectives of sufficient clarity so that this project would capture the imagination of the majority of the military—effectively altering the internal military coalition of the system.

— *Wanderley Guilherme Dos Santos*

Why and under what military, political, economic, and social pressures did the Geisel government inaugurate and the Figueiredo administration continue the "strategic conservative" plan of liberalization? Political scientists have yet to adequately explain and historians to completely reconstruct why Brazil's authoritarian leaders turned to liberalization strategies in 1973.[11] There are various explanations. Some emphasize the instability of the Brazilian authoritarian regime,[12] others the usefulness of liberalization strategies,[13] and still others internal pressure within the military state.[14] It seems likely that the lack of institutional rules and procedures to regulate military power, the loss of traditional feedback and control mechanisms due to the centralization of authority, and fear of internal military opposition all played a role in producing change.

Although the causes of liberalization are unclear, most agree that "Brazil's slow road to democratization" began with General Geisel's victory over hard-line military groups in the presidential succession of 1973 and his strategic adoption of more liberal policies during 1974.[15] The new administration's attitude toward more open elections can be traced both to Brazil's tradition of instrumental authoritarianism and the military doctrine of national security and development. President Geisel retained a typically military perspective on elections, political parties, and democracy. Indeed, the authoritarian state policy of decompression was formulated explicitly within the concepts and methods of Brazilian military theory.[16] Liberalization was conceived of as a series of strategies and tactics designed to achieve the government's objectives of national security and development. The new administration's expectations were typically instrumental authoritarian because it viewed Brazilian society as not quite ready for competitive elections and full democracy.[17]

Brazil represents the most protracted and controlled case on record of the liberalization of an authoritarian regime from above. Speeches by President Geisel in 1974 and 1975 first confirmed the

government's intent to liberalize.[18] However, the speech made by General Golbery (Geisel's minister of civil affairs and architect of liberalization) to the Superior War College (ESG) in 1980 is more instructive because it outlines the "strategic conservative" policies of liberalization and the place of parties and elections in their plans.[19] In Golbery's words:

> The objective is to maintain and enlarge a central operating area. This is necessary for the tranquil and secure promotion of our national objectives [national security and development].[20] Meanwhile, successive and irregular tricks [*golpes*] could be used unexpectedly against the opposition to divide the various opposition groups already discordant among themselves. Again, limits to adversaries actions should be set early in the process . . . it is a sort of Skinnerian pedagogic situation; reinforcing what is productive, and opposing counterproductive or suicidal attitudes.[21]

Minister Golbery then outlined the strategic goals that follow from this primary objective of maintaining and enlarging a central operating arena:

▲ to prevent the erosion of centralized power in the executive and "superministries,"
▲ to preempt the threat of a coup d'état or bid for power from the extreme right, and
▲ to coopt or forestall pressures outside the centralized state apparatus by opening channels between society and the state while retaining control and power of veto over the process.

Finally, Golbery enumerated the tactics and policy alternatives available to the Geisel administration:

▲ to divide and conquer opposition groups through a party reform law,
▲ to liberalize censorship selectively and under state control, and
▲ to coopt the emerging opposition social and labor movements into institutionalized arenas of political conflict.

The executive decrees and constitutional amendments of the authoritarian government after 1973 emerge from this military conception of liberalization. The policies of the Geisel administration were derived from the government's objectives of national security and development and sought a controlled decompression, which would institutionalize the centralized power of military elites.

The 1974 National Election: The First Test of "Strategic Conservatism"

The results of the 1974 elections stunned the "strategic conservatives," dismayed military leaders, and indeed remain a puzzle for political scientists to this day.[22] The opposition party, the MDB, won sixteen of twenty-two contested seats in direct elections for the Senate, raising its delegation from 18 to 30 percent.[23] The MDB also increased its representation in the Federal Chamber from 22 to 44 percent of the house and won a majority in all five of the most important southeast state legislatures (See table 5.2). The gains by the opposition MDB (from 28.6 to 50.1 percent in Senate races, from 19.5 to 36.6 percent in Chamber of Deputies races) were considerable, given the political atrophy that prevailed during hard-line rule. The 1970 elections were held under extremely controlled conditions, with Congress in forced recess, opposition politicians banned, intimidated, or unable to campaign, and the government conducting military operations against guerrilla movements. Indeed, with few patronage resources and little chance to win elections, leaders of the opposition party actually proposed disbanding the MDB in 1972.

The success of the MDB in the 1974 elections undermined support for liberalization among military leaders because it cast doubt on the government's ability to control the electoral process. The perception of defeat was aggravated by charges made by ARENA politicians, who characterized the MDB as antirevolutionary.[24] The reaction of hard-line military groups went beyond talk. New antisubversive campaigns were mounted in several regional military commands during 1975. As popular expectations were raised for a return to democracy and some exiles returned following the 1974 elections, Brazil witnessed an unexpected resurgence of political detainment and torture. President Geisel reasserted control over hard-line military groups in

Table 5.2 Official Results of the 1974 National Elections (percent)

	ARENA	MDB	Blank/ Null	Total (N)
Total				
Federal Chamber	42.0	36.6	21.3	(27,252,464)
Senate	34.7	50.1	15.1	
Southeast				
Federal Chamber	34.5	42.0	23.4	(12,709,680)
Senate	27.8	56.6	15.4	
Northeast				
Federal Chamber	59.2	20.4	20.3	(6,370,642)
Senate	47.6	36.6	15.7	
South				
Federal Chamber	38.7	43.4	17.8	(5,861,066)
Senate	35.2	51.5	13.3	
Center-west				
Federal Chamber	50.3	27.9	21.7	(1,284,454)
Senate	39.6	45.5	14.8	
North				
Federal Chamber	36.5	44.2	19.3	(1,026,622)
Senate	47.7	34.6	17.6	

Source: Dados Estatísticos. Tribunal Superior Eleitoral, Vol. 10 (Brasilia, D.F.)

regional commands and intelligence services only after the violence culminated in the deaths of Vladimir Herzog (director of São Paulo Public Television) in October 1975 and Manuel Filho (a labor union leader) in January 1976, while both were in custody at the Second Regional Army Headquarters in the city of São Paulo.

Ironically, the 1974 elections also generated concern for the electoral viability of ARENA. After all, conditions were liberalized, in part, to avoid the self-dissolution of the MDB. Before 1974, few opposition politicians were able to win elections and build careers. The MDB was crippled by the forced reorganization of the pre-1965 party system, the banning and exile of party leaders, the restriction and suspension of Congress, and the monopoly of state resources by the government party, ARENA. Nonetheless, in the liberalized atmosphere after 1974,

there was concern over the electoral viability of ARENA. This rapid reversal of party fortunes suggests that political change was driven by the plebiscitarian character of elections early in the liberalization process.

The Strategic Conservatives Strike Back: The Amendments of 1976 and 1977

Once military hegemony was restored and far-right terror reduced by 1976, the Geisel administration focused on winning the 1976 and 1978 elections. Shortly before the 1976 municipal elections, decree no. 6,639 of July 1, 1976 (named the Lei Falcao after Geisel's minister of the interior) prohibited television campaigning beyond broadcasting still photos captioned by the candidate's name, party affiliation, and a brief curriculum vitae. Similar restrictions were imposed on radio advertising. The Geisel administration also convinced the Supreme Electoral Court (STE) to ban all campaign advertising before the 1976 municipal elections. While these measures gutted the MDB's informational campaign, ARENA made full use of state resources and patronage machines in local-level electioneering. The combination of state and party clientelism on the municipal level, as well as the restriction and intimidation of MDB candidates, produced ARENA victories in most rural areas and small towns and cities in the municipal elections.[25] The plebiscitarian appeal of the MDB as the party of opposition to military rule worked only in the large cities in 1976, with the MDB winning a majority in the assemblies of São Paulo, Rio de Janeiro, Belo Horizonte, Porto Alegre, Salvador, Campinas, and Santos.

Authoritarian leaders altered the rules and procedures once again in April 1977, hoping to retain a majority in the 1978 national elections. When legislation to reform the judiciary proposed by President Geisel failed to receive the necessary two-thirds vote of the Congress required for a constitutional amendment, General Geisel simply closed the National Congress in accord with Institutional Act V. Legislative powers thus in hand, President Geisel decreed Constitutional Amendments VII and VIII, known thereafter as the Pacote de Abril (April Package). The Pacote de Abril

▲ added municipal council members to the gubernatorial electoral colleges (made up of state assembly members),

▲ increased the number of senators from each state from two to three, (the additional Senate seat henceforth to be selected by the above-mentioned state electoral colleges),

▲ reduced the electoral college for selecting the president by excluding representatives from state assemblies,

▲ restricted campaign media advertising by extending the jurisdiction of the Lei Falcao from municipal elections to state and national elections as well,

▲ altered the proportional representation formula for the Chamber of Deputies; once calculated as a percentage of the electorate, now to be calculated as a percentage of the total population (thus further overrepresenting the rural and less developed areas where illiterates—i.e., nonvoters—make up a larger percentage of the population), and

▲ weakened the power of the legislature by reducing to a simple majority the requirement for amending the constitution.

After the rules and procedures for elections were altered once again by these executive decrees, Congress was reconvened on April 15, 1977, while political interests shifted focus to the 1978 elections.

Stalemate: The 1978 Elections

The Pacote de Abril legislation succeeded in reducing the government party's losses in the 1978 elections. While the MDB received 17.5 million votes in Senate races to ARENA's 13.2 million, the MDB won only nine of forty-five contested Senate seats (See table 5.3). ARENA won twenty-one Senate seats in the newly created electoral congresses (subsequently dubbed bionic senators) and fifteen Senate seats in direct elections. In the Chamber of Deputies, the MDB's 49.5 percent of the national vote produced only 189 seats, while ARENA's 50.4 percent of the vote translated into 231 seats. Furthermore, the proportional representation formula favored ARENA in state assemblies. The 15.4 million votes for ARENA nationwide meant the control of 492 seats, whereas the MDB's 14.8 million votes translated into only 353 seats.

Table 5.3 Official Results of the 1978 National Elections (percent)

	ARENA	MDB	Blank/ Null	Total (N)
Total				
Federal Chamber	39.9	39.4	21.0	(37,666,000)
Senate	35.1	46.3	18.5	
Southeast				
Federal Chamber	29.7	47.8	19.5	(18,648,000)
Senate	23.0	53.3	22.7	
Northeast				
Federal Chamber	57.8	21.9	20.1	(8,671,000)
Senate	52.6	20.1	14.4	
South				
Federal Chamber	42.9	41.6	8.9	(7,194,000)
Senate	33.6	49.0	12.3	
Center-west				
Federal Chamber	46.3	34.1	19.5	(2,089,000)
Senate	45.6	37.0	17.2	
North				
Federal Chamber	43.5	29.2	26.9	(1,144,000)
Senate	41.8	35.7	22.5	

Source: Tribunal Superior Eleitoral, *Dados Estatísticos,* Vol. 11 (Brasilia, D.F., 1989).

The 1978 election results suggest that the military government maintained control of liberalization only after severely restricting campaign activity and blatantly manipulating electoral rules in favor of the government party. Indeed, liberalization in Brazil failed to produce a linear evolution toward competitive politics. The 1978 elections were held under even greater intimidation and overt repression of opposition candidates than in 1974. In 1978, a complementary act prohibited media coverage of MDB politicians, revoked the mandates of three MDB federal deputies, and indicted the president of the MDB, Federal Deputy Ulysses Guimarães.

Hard-line military opposition to the policies of the Geisel administration also increased military factionalism during the negotiations for choosing his successor. By challenging President Geisel's informal

prerogative to select his successor, General Frota brought conflict among military leaders to the surface and endangered the core principal of military hierarchy.[26] Furthermore, another recurrence of far-right terror destabilized the liberalization process. Despite breaches of military discipline and attempts to politicize the military during 1978, President Geisel secured the nomination of his chosen candidate in the restricted electoral college, General João Batista Figueiredo, an insider of the strategic conservative group and head of Geisel's National Information Service (SNI). After reasserting control, President Geisel reinforced liberalization with several important institutional reforms during the final months of 1978: Institutional Act V was allowed to expire, habeas corpus was formally reinstated, and the banishment of over 120 exiles was lifted.

Divide and Rule Over the Opposition: The 1979 Party Reform

Despite an economic downturn and an increasingly confrontational labor movement, President Figueiredo reaffirmed the government's commitment to liberalization and introduced several institutional changes early in his administration.[27] The centerpiece of authoritarian state strategy early in the Figueiredo presidency was the Party Reform Act of 1979. Because the two-party situation tended to unite the opposition and threatened the ability of state leaders to control the liberalization process, dividing the opposition became a major policy priority. In the 1980 address to the Superior War College, referred to above, Minister of Civil Affairs Golbery argued that the government must "proceed with a liberalization policy for achieving the disarticulation of the opposition and the birth of different and multiple fronts; . . . the heterogeneity inherent in the opposition should facilitate such an objective. In political terms this is a prescription for a policy encouraging a plurality of parties."[28]

By enacting the Party Reform Bill, the Figueiredo administration attempted to split the opposition into several smaller parties, to prevent any successor party from using the MDB's image as the party of opposition to military rule, and to revive the pre-1964 Brazilian Labor party (PTB) under the government's control. Hence, the Party Reform Act of 1979 disbanded the two parties created by the regime in

1965, required the use of *Partido* in all campaign logos, and set a series of organizational criteria to be met within a calendar year from the bill's enactment.

The immediate consequence of the Party Reform Act was to channel the political resources of opposition groups away from direct political action and confrontation toward the day-to-day tasks of party organization. Two major parties emerged after a year of local directory meetings and municipal conventions. First, the MDB cleverly circumvented the logo requirement by creating the Partido do Movimento Brasilero Democratico (PMDB, Party of the Brazilian Democratic Movement). Furthermore, the *P* appeared in PMDB campaign literature in light colors against a larger and darker *MDB*. The second major party to emerge from the 1979 party reform was the Partido Democratico Social (Social Democratic party, PDS), composed almost exclusively of politicians from the pre-1979 government party, ARENA.

Four new parties also met registration requirements. First, the Partido Popular (Popular party, PP) was organized by conservative regional politicians (primarily from Minas Gerais) and is best known for its dissolution soon thereafter. When the Supreme Electoral Court (STE) upheld the *sublegenda*[29] law for the 1982 elections (decreeing mandatory voting by party list), politicians exited en masse from the party and returned to the safer electoral coattails and proportional representation lists of the PDS or PMDB. The PP led an exceedingly short existence as a centrist alternative.

The second minor party to meet the registration requirements in 1980 was the Partido Trabalhista Brasileira (Brazilian Workers party, PTB), which retained little of its pre-1964 heritage because of military manipulations. The Supreme Electoral Tribunal (STE) denied Leonel Brizola (heir to Getulio Vargas's regional and populist political tradition) use of the logo of the pre-1965 PTB upon his return from exile. Instead, the PTB was given to Ivette Vargas, a niece of Getulio Vargas and confidante of General Golbery from São Paulo. Despite this blow to Brizola, his populist appeals and financial support from the Socialist International enabled the organization of a new party within the final six months of the registration period.

The last of the four smaller parties to meet the organizational threshold (having directories in 20 percent of the municipalities in five states) was the new Partido dos Trabalhadores (Workers party, PT).

Core support came primarily from the new labor and social movements of São Paulo and its industrial suburbs. The PT was able to meet the organizational criteria because of its strong ties with Catholic base communities, neighborhood organizations, and the dedication of its young activists. However, the registration of the PT was controversial because, in fact, it appeared to fall short of requirements. The military government's determination to divide the opposition (and avoid a confrontation with the PT) led to waiving minor details of the registration requirements and recognizing the PT in 1980.

The 1982 Elections: Elected Governors and Military Government

In November 1982, Brazilians elected twenty-two governors and a third of the Senate in direct majoritarian elections, as well as the entire Chamber of Deputies and all state and municipal assemblies in statewide proportional representation lists. Direct elections for governor were held for the first time since 1965 because, among other reasons, the government had lost secure majorities in the restricted electoral colleges of states designed by authoritarian legislation. Furthermore, because the presidential decree powers of Institutional Act V (AI 5) had expired, changes of electoral and party regulations would now have to pass through Congress. This deterioration of executive power led President Figueiredo to lament, "If I only had AI 5."[30] The agreement between the government and opposition groups to postpone the 1980 municipal elections until 1982 produced a slate of candidates considerably larger than is usual in Brazil.[31] The only offices excluded from the ballot (except the presidency) were the Senate seats decided in 1978. And because half the Senate seats chosen in 1978 were nominated (under Pacote de Abril legislation), this seemed to assure a PDS majority in both the Senate and the Electoral College, which would select the next president in 1985. Nonetheless, to be on the safe side, the military government changed the rules twice before the 1982 elections.

The electoral reform of 1981 was designed to use the resources of state patronage to benefit the PDS in this wide range of contested offices. The reform required a straight party vote across offices (the *voto vinculado*),[32] prohibited party alliances, and reintroduced the Lei

Falcao, which limited campaign coverage in the mass media. The *voto vinculado* intended to build on the electoral strengths of the PDS by linking votes for federal and state offices—where PDS strength was weakest—to the municipal level, where PDS and state patronage was strongest. Subsequent legislation altered the ballot itself shortly before the 1982 election. Departing from the practice of printed lists of candidates by party, voters were to write in the name of their chosen candidate, a task open to coercion and fraud.

Contrary to expectations, the *voto vinculado* created large coattails for the PMDB and PDT legislative candidates in states with popular opposition candidates for governor and senator. The PMDB won governorships in the southeast states of São Paulo, Minas Gerais, Parana, and Espirito Santo, as well as Amazonas, Acre, and Para in the north, and Mato Grosso and Grosso do Sul states in the center-west (see table 5.4). The PMDB won a majority in all of the above state assemblies, except the two states in the center-west. Without legislation requiring a straight ballot vote, these successes in legislative races would not have been possible.

Nonetheless, a second authoritarian strategy achieved its intent. Unable to form electoral alliances, the opposition was weakened in several key states—if not in gubernatorial races, certainly in legislative elections. For example, in the state of Rio Grande do Sul, the PDT fielded a strong candidate and the PDS won the governorship. The inability to form opposition alliances also favored Moreira Franco and the PDS in Rio de Janeiro. However, the populist discourse of Leonel Brizola mobilized support, primarily in the northern suburbs of Rio de Janeiro, at an unimaginable rate and increased his ranking in the polls by 20 percent during the last month of the campaign.

Results of the 1982 Gubernatorial Elections

The election of opposition governors in 1982 while the federal executive remained under military control created a situation of dual power, which Juan Linz describes as diarchy, that posed serious problems for new party organizations.[33] The first problem was symbolic. Newly elected opposition governors were unable to meet the inflationary democratic expectations of Brazilians because, despite the fanfare surrounding their election, they did not control the government

Table 5.4 Official Results of the 1982 Elections for Governor, by Party, State, and Region

	PDS	PDT	PT
North			
Acre	33,879	—	4,637
Amazonas	164,190	—	5,352
Para	461,969	—	11,010
Northeast			
Alagoas	257,898	—	—
Bahia	1,623,422	—	25,113
Ceara	1,149,468	—	9,961
Maranhão	673,916	12,738	8,643
Paraiba	509,855	—	3,198
Pernambuco	913,774	—	4,027
Piaui	398,818	—	5,814
Rio Grande do Norte	389,677	—	3,207
Sergipe	256,385	1,133	1,354
Center-west			
Goias	470,184	845	9,818
Mato Grosso	203,605	899	887
Mato Grosso do Sul	237,144	5,414	4,541
Southeast			
Espirito Santo	282,728	1,236	10,588
Minas Gerais	2,424,197	11,160	113,950
Rio de Janeiro	1,530,706	1,709,180	152,614
São Paulo	2,728,732	94,395	1,144,328
South			
Parana	1,127,175	6,679	12,047
Rio Grande do Sul	1,294,962	775,546	50,713
Santa Catarina	838,150	4,572	6,803
Total	17,965,834	2,623,797	1,589,645

Source: Tribunal Superior Eleitoral, *Dados Estatísticos*, Vol. 13 (Brasilia, D.F., 1989).

PTB	PMDB	Blank/ Null	Total
3,152	36,369	8,519	86,556
4,203	201,182	26,198	401,125
7,214	501,605	92,333	964,252
—	206,856	99,307	401,125
—	1,030,111	468,589	3,147,235
—	478,853	318,465	1,956,747
632	180,287	180,896	1,057,112
—	358,146	92,333	964,252
7,872	816,085	211,458	1,953,216
—	271,274	107,517	778,423
411	283,366	72,163	748,854
—	77,965	46,687	383,524
—	964,179	115,394	1,560,420
—	188,878	36,041	430,310
—	258,192	48,179	553,470
—	448,074	83,308	825,934
—	2,667,595	606,639	5,823,541
536,383	1,073,446	438,337	5,440,666
1,447,328	5,209,952	972,930	11,597,985
30,202	1,708,785	312,055	3,196,943
—	1,272,319	405,473	3,799,013
2,281	825,500	154,505	1,831,811
2,039,708	19,059,019	4,910,953	48,188,955

bureaucracy. For example, soon after the new PMDB administration was inaugurated in São Paulo, antiausterity demonstrators tore down the gates of the governor's palace. This blot on the democratic credentials of the PMDB was organized by minor opposition parties eager to step into the symbolic void. In sum, the PMDB lost support, like any government party, without actually governing.

The 1982 elections also generated protracted conflict between newly elected governors and the federal government over fiscal, bureaucratic, and political resources. While opposition politicians had gained formal control of nine governorships, the alliances and political relationships of conservative politicians inside federal, state, and local agencies built during eighteen years of military rule remained. Attempts to implement new policies produced party skirmishes, and the more experienced bureaucrats and politicians of the PDS often prevailed. Economic adjustment policies after 1982 exacerbated confrontations between federal and state governments. For example, President Figueiredo undercut the new PDT administration of Leonel Brizola by withdrawing the deposits of federal companies and agencies in BANERJ, the Rio de Janeiro state bank. Brizola avoided insolvency only after receiving considerable deposits from leaders of gambling rings from the Rio de Janeiro suburbs.[34]

The 1982 elections also produced new conflicts among party leaders, both within and between parties. Permissive membership rules forced candidates to calculate their electoral chances according to both their ranking on party lists and the total allocation of offices to parties expected under the proportional representation formula. Being a minor party candidate often improved prospects of election by relying on the coattails of a strong candidate for governor. For example, the gubernatorial candidacies of Luis Inacio da Silva and Janio Quadros in São Paulo, despite defeat, increased their party representation in municipal, state, and the federal chamber. In comparison, the crowded lists of the major parties often made it more difficult to be elected to legislative office. Even where opposition parties were assured of winning the governorship, competition between partisan colleagues on the PR lists was often more heated than the campaign against other parties.

The 1982 election also inaugurated a new phase of multiparty bargaining in Congress. While the government lost a majority in the Chamber of Deputies, only four votes from opposition deputies were

needed to form a majority. The proto-opposition party PTB (with thirteen federal deputies) received many overtures, but deputies from other parties were also convinced to support legislation proposed by the military government. Creating legislative majorities with the administrative resources of the executive is a classic pattern of Brazilian competitive party politics. To the extent that this practice returned after 1982, the multiparty situation opened up bargaining arenas between the authoritarian executive and the legislature and facilitated the reemergence of professional party politics.

Presidential Succession: Direct Elections or Electoral College?

Unlike his predecessors, President Figueiredo failed to secure a consensus among military, party, and political leaders for selecting his successor. Instead, a majority of military leaders favored neutrality during the presidential succession, despite the widespread conviction that political radicalization would follow from the victory of a PMDB candidate. Without presidential leadership, a procedural void emerged wherein government candidates were either vetoed by the military, blocked by President Figueiredo, or defeated on the PDS convention floor. First came Vice-President Aureliano Chaves. Chaves seemed a strong candidate during 1983, and, despite support from ex-President Geisel and several influential military leaders, Chaves suffered a persistent veto by President Figueiredo and military leaders from the information services.[35] When the possibility of a compromise Chaves candidacy emerged once again in late 1984, it was craftily blocked by President Figueiredo's crossing the border into Paraguay for the Itaipu Dam opening ceremony. Vice-President Chaves was momentarily promoted to president and thereby prohibited from seeking a second term.

Without military consensus, politics centered on the government party (PDS) because it appeared to retain a secure majority in the restricted electoral college that would select the president. Former governors Paulo Maluf and Antonio Carlos Magalhães, both PDS members, quickly dominated the selection of delegates for the PDS national convention in August 1984. Despite the opposition of military leaders, Paulo Maluf presented himself as a candidate who prom-

ised continuity. He remained confident that President Figueiredo, military leaders, and PDS governors and politicians would, as in previous presidential successions, respect the convention's nomination, support his candidacy, and veto PMDB contenders.[36] But neither President Figueiredo, nor the military, nor many PDS politicians wholeheartedly supported Maluf's candidacy.

Instead, public opposition to Maluf and his lack of tact in negotiating with political leaders produced what had appeared impossible only months before: a PMDB victory in the restricted electoral college. After the PDS National Directorate refused to liberalize the convention rules, party president José Sarney resigned. Soon thereafter, other PDS leaders resigned to form the new Partido da Frente Liberal (Liberal Front party, PFL). Remaining PDS leaders also negotiated support for Tancredo Neves. The leader of the PDS in Congress assured Tancredo Neves of seventy votes from PDS delegates in favor of a PMDB candidate as early as March 1984.[37] Former Governor Magalhaes and Vice-President Chaves also lived up to oral agreements with Tancredo Neves to ally themselves with the PMDB if Maluf succeeded in winning the PDS nomination.

While military leaders failed to agree on presidential succession, popular demands for direct presidential elections challenged the very legitimacy of military rule. The first demonstrations for direct elections in late 1983 were based on an unusual degree of cooperation between opposition parties and social movements, but they received little public support.[38] However, by early 1984 rally attendance consistently surpassed predictions, often by a factor of ten. Unexpectedly, rallies for direct elections soon became the largest political demonstrations in Brazil to occur since the death of President Getulio Vargas in 1954. Opinion polls suggested that up to 80 percent of Brazilians favored holding direct elections for president; even 75 percent of PDS supporters were in favor.[39] The public's spontaneous endorsement of an apparently procedural issue puzzled organizers and observers alike. But the endorsement of direct elections by Brazilians in 1984 was due neither to their commitment to liberal government, nor support for the agenda of political change promoted by rally organizers. Instead, the direct elections movement focused on the political symbol most apparent and most important to Brazilians—the presidency—precisely when neither military leaders nor party politicians could resolve the problem of succession.

For opposition leaders, the direct election campaign served as a powerful bargaining chip in electoral college negotiations. While Paulo Maluf cajoled electoral college delegates with the bluff of threatened military resistance to the PMDB, PMDB leaders bluffed by raising the specter of popular mobilization. Throughout the electoral college campaign and until the end of 1984, military groups in the information services mounted undercover operations to discredit the candidacy of Tancredo Neves. But the time for a bid from the right had passed. Anti-coup sentiment had prevailed in most military groups since the 1981 Rio Centro bomb incident[40] and the Military High Command refused to endorse further anticommunist and antisubversive efforts in September 1984. Threats of a military veto lost credibility thereafter, despite secret operations, red-baiting, and grandstanding by General Newton Cruz, commander of the troops stationed in the nation's capital.

A confrontation between popular demands for direct presidential elections and military disapproval of radicalization loomed during 1984. But instead of seeking to expand the scope of politics, party notables proceeded to negotiate within the restricted electoral college designed by military rulers. The Aliança Democrática (Democratic Alliance) that secured the 1985 presidential succession and Brazil's transition to civilian rule was built on agreements to distribute an estimated 130,000 administrative appointments in the federal government. And because negotiations occurred in the electoral college, state power would be shared according to those who guaranteed the victory of Tancredo Neves—PDS dissidents.[41]

The 1985 Mayoral Election

After Tancredo Neves was hospitalized hours before the inauguration ceremony, his sickness and death created a depoliticized interregnum that lasted from January through April 1985.[42] Vice-President Sarney was sworn in as president but was unable to reconstruct the complex commitments made by Neves to political leaders. Instead, President Sarney relied on military leaders, public relations consultants, traditional political leaders, and the Catholic church. Furthermore, instead of responding to popular demands for direct presidential elections, the new civilian government called municipal elections to replace the

nominated mayors in capitals and other cities declared to be national security zones by military governments.

The 1985 elections were once again unusual. Since 1932, Brazil's electoral system balanced the plebiscitarian character of majoritarian elections for executive offices by including on the same ballot proportional representation elections for legislatures. The 1985 elections were not municipal elections, but mayoral elections in selected cities without accompanying slates for municipal chambers. The new civilian government made a poor decision by calling elections that favored populist appeals and opposition voting. The fact that the parties of the democratic alliance supporting the Sarney government enjoyed organizational breadth and state patronage mattered little in the 1985 mayoral elections.

The electoral debut of the New Republic—a name since abandoned—also suffered from liberalized, but not necessarily democratic, rules and procedures. The central problem was that the law permitted many parties but called for only one ballot. Congress voted to open debate, to ease candidate affiliation, and to grant media exposure to all registered parties; but the motion for runoff elections was defeated. Single-ballot elections with many candidates in executive elections are notorious for their failure to produce a majority. This unfortunate combination allowed the resurgence of provocative right-wing attacks and the proliferation of personalist candidates. Dozens of minor parties and fringe candidacies were financed by PDS politicians and former leaders of the authoritarian regime. These puppet parties proceeded with the dirty work of political libel and assured a drop of 3–5 percent in the vote for PMDB candidates—tactics well known to pre-1964 professional politicians and indeed to democratic politicians the world over.

The 1985 elections suggested that winning elections in contemporary Brazil still requires both mastery of populist discourse and the support of patronage machines. Older politicians such as ex-President Janio Quadros and veteran Carioca politician Saturnino Braga won not because the public recognized their personalities but because these candidates knew campaign tactics, alliance strategies, and other *practices* of Brazilian electoral politics. Names were not enough. On declaring his candidacy for the São Paulo mayorship, Adhemar de Barros Filho, a federal deputy and son of the São Paulo populist leader Adhemar de Barros, achieved a 13 percent preference in public opin-

ion polls within one week. However, three weeks later, his ratings fell to around 2 percent, where they remained until election day. Brazilian voters recognize the substantive political meaning of traditional political leaders.

Brazilian voters also responded to the patronage practices of politicians on the local level. Recent scholarship has demonstrated the importance of local brokerage for federal deputies in the opposition party, the MDB, during both the authoritarian and transition periods.[43] At election time, vote-getting entrepreneurs on the local level called *cabos eleitorais* (literally, electoral infantry) require not only campaign funds, but also resources above and beyond their steady income from political appointments to state jobs. Most *cabos eleitorais* will vote according to the alliances and advice of the state or federal deputy whom they support and depend on. However, a more direct technique for organizing support in a region controlled by a state or federal deputy, municipal representative, or some other *cabo eleitoral* is simply to write a check. Votes delivered by local machine politicians matter even in the city of São Paulo—a center of opposition voting. The half-hearted support of many PMDB machine politicians significantly weakened Cardoso's candidacy in the 1985 mayoral campaign. For many state and federal deputies and their professional associates, the possibility of a Cardoso victory threatened their control of the regional party's executive committee.

Television and radio coverage was critical in the 1985 election. Unlike previous elections held under military rule, censors acted only in cases of gross slander or character assassination. A full two hours per day were reserved for campaign programming, distributed according to the percentage of party representation in the Federal Chamber and state assemblies. The audience for campaign programs rivaled even those for popular commercial television and radio productions, while media journalists made and unmade political careers. Some candidates scrambled to secure the good will of media executives, while others became media executives themselves. The Ministry of Communications is one of the most politicized ministries in Brazil because it controls the concession of broadcasting rights. Professional politicians often own radio and TV stations, media personalities often become politicians, and de facto electoral districts can often be mapped by the circumference of a broadcast signal.

The 1985 campaign produced a bonanza for marketing, public relations, and campaign consulting firms. Standard research techniques and marketing strategies were adopted. However, because of the distance between the assumptions of marketing and the immediate and personalistic terms of Brazilian political debate, consultants erred at crucial points in the 1985 campaign. For example, private firms supplied opinion polls to Fernando Henrique Cardoso during the São Paulo mayoral campaign that consistently underestimated the vote for Janio Quadros by 5 percent. The problem was not sampling error. Instead, pollsters later realized that supporters of Janio Quadros (and conservative candidates in general), whether owing to timidity, fear, willful deceit, or shame, tend not to identify themselves as such.[44] It took the loss of a crucial election to improve campaign techniques.

Meanwhile, Janio Quadros, in defiance of conventional marketing practices and the advice of consultants, refused to grant interviews or appear on news programs, physically assaulted reporters before the camera, and spoke at length without props or prepared text during his allotted time on television and radio. The Quadros campaign also financed a series of minor right-wing parties to handle mudslinging, and, during the last week of the campaign when rebuttals could no longer be mounted, Janio Quadros launched a series of unexpected personal attacks, denouncing Cardoso as an atheist, a marijuana smoker, and a communist who had taught Marxism in foreign universities. These attacks cut support for Cardoso in the lower socioeconomic classes by an estimated 3–5 percent—enough for him to lose the election.[45]

The 1986 National Elections

The PMDB won twenty-two of twenty-three contested governorships, majorities in the Constitutional Congress, and virtually all state assemblies in the 1986 elections. This landslide, which proved to be short-lived, was caused not by a surge of opposition, but by a rapid transfer of allegiance by regional and local politicians from conservative parties to the PMDB. The pattern of electoral realignment in the United States suggests that such electoral shifts, from presidential elections down through state and local politics, can take decades.[46] But in Brazil during 1985 and 1986, local and regional politicians

rapidly transferred to the PMDB: first in expectation of the roughly 130,000 federal administrative nominations to be made after President Sarney's inauguration on January 15, 1985; later in expectation of perhaps five times that number of state-level administrative jobs to be distributed by governors after the 1986 elections.[47]

Mayors and municipal representatives from towns across Brazil distributed state patronage and delivered votes for ARENA/PDS parties and the military government. However, by the end of 1985 many of these local-level politicians had negotiated their affiliation with the PMDB. These links between the opposition image of the PMDB in national elections and local-level patronage machines were perhaps clearest in Minas Gerais State. In late 1985, Helio Garcia, governor of Minas Gerais, boasted that he would no longer accept individual "cattle" (mayors) into the PMDB, but only complete "herds" (mayors with secure majorities in municipal chambers). The realignment of local politicians to the PMDB also occurred in other states. Eleven of the twenty PDS mayors from the Rio de Janeiro suburbs had affiliated with Leonel Brizola's opposition PDT by the end of 1985. In Rio Grande do Sul State, the other core area of Brizola support, over 1,000 mayors from the provinces had signed on with the PDT. During the 1986 campaign, Senator Fernando Henrique Cardoso expressed assurance of his reelection and a sweeping PMDB victory in São Paulo State because of support from local politicians in small towns and rural areas.

Populist appeals also worked during the 1986 elections. Despite the eccentricity of many campaigns, gubernatorial candidates often cut to core issues of substantive social and economic equality. For example, the turning point of Orestes Quercia's campaign to become governor of São Paulo was his insistence on federal intervention into the cattle markets. What do fattened cattle have to do with democratization? The question, "Where's the beef?"—a campaign slogan in the 1984 U.S. presidential election—clarified a deepening conflict between the new civilian government and business that centered on withholding fattened cattle from slaughterhouses. The low price of meat during the first months of the anti-inflationary Plano Cruzado (an unintended consequence of the plan's wage and price freeze catching meat prices before they were raised against inflation) put beef on the table of lower-income Brazilians. Despite opposition from foreign creditors, the Plano Cruzado caused a surge in domestic consumption

and production. GNP grew at an annual rate of 10 percent for eight months, while real wages increased by 30 percent.

Competitive electoral politics clarified what was at stake. Prices for consumer goods remained frozen, and long lines at retail stores both resolved the disjuncture between supply and demand and became an important means of political socialization in 1986. The spectacle of shoppers waiting in long lines is commonly associated with economic failure by economists and those with disposable income. However, populist politicians transformed these lines into a political asset by blaming shortages on producer slowdowns. State intervention into the cattle markets became a campaign issue during 1986 because it represented the redistributive impact of the Plano Cruzado and, by extension, raised core questions of distributive justice. Instead of a burden, long lines at the stores were perceived by poor Brazilians as an acceptable pricing mechanism because populist discourse transformed the issue to suit their purposes. In sum, direct popular appeals, realignments by party leaders, and forging campaign alliances by distributing administrative jobs to professional politicians—these describe Brazil's electoral politics through 1986. But these mechanisms, occurring in the states, failed to affect national politics after the transition to civilian rule because direct elections for president were not held until 1989.

The 1989 Presidential Elections

Presidential elections are always critical events in Brazilian politics. However, the 1989 election brought mass participation and modern media techniques to the contest after a thirty-year hiatus. Suffrage expanded more than fivefold, from 18 million in the last presidential election before military rule in 1960, to over 82 million in 1989. Furthermore, over 85 percent of registered voters viewed four live television debates and two hours of party campaign programming that were broadcast every day on prime-time television and radio for two months before November 15, and two weeks prior to the December 15 runoff election. Television became the principal forum during the 1989 presidential campaign and intensified its plebiscitarian character because the 1989 election failed to combine legislative elections based on proportional representation with majoritarian races for executive

posts. Because elections for governor, as well as federal, state, and municipal legislatures were scheduled for November 1990, party alliances and machine politics mattered little in 1989. Politicians' careers were not directly at stake in the presidential election.

A young, conservative governor of the small northeastern state of Alagoas named Fernando Collor de Mello unexpectedly emerged in this volatile context. Collor increased his popular support from 17 percent in the first polls, taken in April, to 46 percent in early September by negotiating appearances on television, purchasing publicity, and popularizing his denunciations of bureaucratic abuse. Collor's lead began to erode in September once the media programs of other parties appeared during the two hours of preelection campaign programming, distributed according to party representation in Congress rather than money or informal support from media groups. After falling to 26.6 percent in the polls, Collor's fortunes were reversed when Silvio Santos, the conservative media star and owner of SBT television, unexpectedly entered the race. While the Supreme Electoral Court disallowed Santos's bid for the presidency on the ninth of November, Santos thereupon endorsed Collor, effectively ensuring a plurality for Collor in first-round voting.

Collor received over 28 percent of the first-round vote, well ahead of the 16 percent received by Inacio da Silva (Lula), the candidate for the Partido dos Trabalhadores (Workers party, PT) who edged out Leonel Brizola, ex-governor of Rio de Janeiro and candidate for the Partido Democrático Trabalhista (Democratic Workers party, PDT) by half a percentage point to challenge Collor in the runoff elections (see table 5.5). By dominating the first television debate of the second round, Lula surged in the polls to tie Collor only ten days before the December 15 vote. However, Lula failed to dominate the second debate as he did the first, unable to counter the damaging effects of personal attacks and negative advertising in the final days of the campaign. Collor mounted a series of devastating personal and political attacks seven days before the election, convincing voters that a victory of Luiz Inacio da Silva and the PT would destabilize society and turn Brazil away from a liberalizing world. On December 15, Collor received 35,089,998 votes (42.7 percent), defeating Lula, who received 31,076,364 votes (37.8 percent).

The election of a conservative president after three decades of military rule and a transition largely controlled by political leaders

Table 5.5 Official Results of the 1989 Presidential Election
(percent)

	First Round				Second Round		
	PRN	PT	PDT	PSDB	PRN	PT	Total (N)
North	25.5	19.4	4.6	5.4	48.5	20.3	(4,424,718)
Northeast	29.2	18.3	11.6	6.7	41.2	32.8	(21,529,617)
Center-west	44.6	18.8	5.9	9.0	48.8	28.3	(5,087,499)
Southeast	24.0	16.9	13.3	15.4	42.8	42.0	(37,538,389)
South	45.5	7.7	36.3	6.0	39.0	39.9	(13,476,003)
Total	28.5	16.0	15.4	10.7	42.7	37.8	(82,074,718)

Source: Tribunal Superior Eleitoral, 1989.
Note: Blank/null votes excluded.

suggests that the new opposition groups and parties that emerged under military rule failed to master the techniques of mass party and electoral politics. Leonel Brizola won over 50 percent of Rio de Janeiro State and pluralities in the southern states of Rio Grande do Sul and Santa Catarina. However, he polled only 1.4 percent in São Paulo State, whose 18 million voters composed 22 percent of the national electorate in 1989. Five favorite-son candidates occupied the ideological spectrum and shut Brizola out of the São Paulo electorate, from former Governor Paulo Maluf and Federal Deputy Afif Domingos on the right, Ulysses Guimaraes and Mario Covas in the center, and Lula on the right. Brizola's masterful oratory and embodiment of the Brazilian national-populist tradition failed to convince voters in the intense competition of São Paulo politics. Brizola also failed to receive support from the center-west and northeast regions where his exposure was limited and support from party leaders weak.

The candidate for the Brazilian Social Democracy party (PSDB), São Paulo Senator Mario Covas, remained at 7 percent in the polls until October, then surged after he hired the director of the highest-rated commercial television news program to produce his daily thirteen-minute media slot. Nonetheless, Covas placed fourth in the 15 November runoff election, receiving 7,790,392 votes, 4.3 percentage points below Lula. The Covas campaign was weakened by a lack of support from machine politicians after he split from the PMDB to

found the PSDB in May 1988. Furthermore, because Collor received widespread support from media and business, Covas's expectation of becoming the most viable centrist candidate against either Lula or Brizola never materialized. Finally, Covas's strategy to broaden support beyond São Paulo and the southeast was blocked when his choice for vice-president (Roberto Magalhaes, governor of the northeast state of Pernambuco) was vetoed in the PSDB national convention of July 1989.

After winning twenty-two of twenty-three contested governorships in 1986, the PMDB polled below 5 percent in the 1989 presidential race. The candidate and elder statesman of the party, Federal Deputy Ulysses Guimarães, could not reverse the erosion of public support for his party associated with the Sarney government nor overcome the electoral defeats on the left and right in the 1988 municipal elections. Despite hiring a brilliant media team for the largest time allowance on television and radio (22 minutes per day), Guimaraes never rose above 5 percent in the polls. While a formal split between right, center, and left factions occurred during the July 1989 party convention, Guimaraes failed to secure the support of powerful governors early in the campaign. Governors Orestes Quercia of São Paulo, Alvaro Dias of Parana, and Miguel Arraes of Pernambuco declared their unwillingness to be associated with a Guimaraes candidacy as early as March 1989.

The remaining nine official candidates received unexpectedly low support. Despite winning mayoral offices in the capital cities of Pernambuco and Ceara in 1988, the conservative PFL candidate former Vice-President Aureliano Chaves polled less than 3 percent in first-round voting. Disputes between PFL factions led by Senator Marco Marciel and ex-governor Antonio Carlos Magalhães weakened the campaign, despite a full sixteen minutes per day allotted to the party on television and radio. The conservative candidate of the Partido Liberal (Liberal party, PL), São Paulo Federal Deputy Affif Domingos, surged to third place in the polls during early October, only to become the target of sustained negative advertising from rivals eager to protect their bases of support in São Paulo.

The exception to this pattern of opposition party decline is the new Workers party (PT). During the 1980s, the PT grew from a minor left opposition party to a major presidential contender with enthusiastic militants and professional staff in all corners of Brazil. Start-

ing from its core supporters among new union movements in the industrial suburbs of São Paulo, the PT won support among young urban voters in the southeast capitals during the early 1980s. After sending representatives to local, state, and federal legislatures, the PT won important mayoral contests across Brazil in the 1985 and 1988 municipal elections. Furthermore, while PT administrations elected in 1985 faced both protracted opposition from conservative municipal bureaucracies and provocation from far-left factions within the party, the administrations elected in 1988 avoided direct confrontation and reduced party factionalism.

The 1989 presidential race confirmed earlier evidence that the meteoric rise of the PT is not a result of radicalization among voters. Victories by the PT in three state capitals and several smaller cities in the November 1988 mayoral elections do not indicate a general drift to the left. Voters were simply disgusted with brazen corruption, rising inflation, and the lack of leadership from the Sarney administration. Likewise, Lula's success in the 1989 presidential contest appears to have more to do with his youth, honesty, and convincing popular discourse than with the political ideology of the PT. The success of the PT in the 1989 election must not be underestimated: Lula defeated nine national leaders from the major parties to enter the runoff election and emerged from the 1989 race poised for the 1990s.

As President Collor took office in March 1990, hyperinflation loomed, the federal deficit surged and Brazil ended its first decade of negative per-capita growth since 1945. Nine months later, few could doubt the ability of directly elected presidents to initiate and implement policy in Brazil. President Collor reasserted executive authority after years of policy drift under the Sarney administration and shocked both foreign and local business on 16 March 1990, the day after his inauguration, with a comprehensive plan to reduce inflation, lower the federal deficit, and liberalize the economy. The political consequences of the Collor Plan were to dramatically reinforce the power of the executive and the government's capacity to make economic policy. The confiscation of government securities and private savings transformed the government from Brazil's largest debtor to its largest creditor—a position used to restart the economy and consolidate political support. The Collor Plan also restored the government's ability to set monetary and credit policies through the central bank, instead

of manipulating interest rates on the volatile overnight market for government securities.

Throughout 1990, the new administration received strong support from the media and public, faced virtually no congressional and little social opposition, and overrode governors who were more concerned with consolidating the support of state and local machines for the 1990 elections than organizing national opposition at the end of their term. Although his party controlled only 5 percent of the Chamber of Deputies upon inauguration, President Collor confiscated roughly 80 percent of the nation's liquid financial assets, implemented a dramatic package of economic reforms, and maintained the policy initiative. His perception of a plebiscitarian mandate, use of patronage resources, and recourse to the provisional decree powers of the Brazilian presidency permitted Collor to quickly build legislative majorities in Congress, retain popular acclaim, and dominate the political agenda.

The 1990 National Elections

The 1990 elections reproduced the mechanisms of party development and passive democratization on the state level. Direct gubernatorial elections endowed twenty-seven governors with both popularity and the prerogative to nominate professional politicians to thousands of administrative posts. Gubernatorial elections were won by combining broad popular appeals and alliances with local patronage machines. Indeed, because the 1990 elections were driven primarily by state and local politics rather than national matters, traditional politicians reasserted control over local machines and either left or rebuilt the national parties that had artificially controlled patronage on the federal level during military rule and the Sarney administration.

A review of Brazil's major parties and party leaders in the wake of the 1990 elections confirms the importance of both popular appeals in executive elections and alliances with patronage machines. Within the PMDB, center-right machine politicians, commonly called *fisiológicos* (political insiders) led by Orestes Quercia gained control of the party, defeating the center-left wing of those who openly opposed military government, *históricos*, led by São Paulo Federal Deputy Ulysses Guimarães.[48] After securing the election of his successor to the São

Paulo governorship, former Secretary of Security Luiz Antonio Fleury, Orestes Quercia (former governor of São Paulo) moved to control the PMDB national organization and plan his 1994 presidential bid. Quercia was elected president of the party in March 1991, nominated close political allies to both the presidency of the Congress and PMDB leaders in the Federal Chamber, retaining control of a party with 108 of 503 federal deputies, over 200 state deputies, and more than 1,600 mayors throughout Brazil.

The conservative PFL also lost representation in Congress. Despite the humiliation of receiving less than 1 percent in the first-round 1989 presidential elections, the PFL reinforced its position as the second-largest party in Congress, with eighty-seven federal deputies and nine governorships, and won more governorships than any other party. The unexpectedly strong performance of the PFL is further evidence of the importance of local and state-level patronage in the 1990 elections. The PFL was built by conservative ministers from the period of authoritarian rule, such as Antonion Carlos Magalhaes and Marco Maciel, and continues to dominate politics in many states of the less developed northeast region.

After a strong showing in the 1989 presidential race, the PT failed to win a governorship and controls only one Senate seat in the new Congress. Nonetheless, the PT increased its representation in the Federal Chamber from seventeen to thirty, significantly expanded its number of state deputies across Brazil, and until 1992 retained control of several mayorships, including the city of São Paulo. The PT continued to expand and consolidate as a political party but, after loosing the second-round presidential elections to Collor in 1989, the presence of the PT decreased during 1990 due to the decisive action, economic successes, and protection of real wage levels during the first semester by the Collor administration.

Several minor parties remain on the scene after the 1990 elections. The Brazilian Social Democracy party, PSDB, founded in 1988, lost twenty seats in the Federal Chamber and now joins three other minor parties with forty to fifty federal deputies. The PDT, led by populist firebrand Leonel Brizola who won the governorship of Rio de Janeiro in 1990, increased its congressional representation by four to forty-six. President Collor's PRN increased its representation from thirty-one to forty in the 1990 elections. The conservative PDS also in-

creased its representation in 1990 from thirty-two to forty, also winning four Senate seats.

In a new development of considerable concern, the 1990 election also appears to have generated significant apathy toward legislative elections. In the state of São Paulo, a full 65 percent of votes for federal deputy were blank or null, considerably greater than the norm of 15–25 percent. Indeed, under the statewide proportional representation system that traditionally generates large thresholds for elected office, candidates won seats in the Federal Chamber from São Paulo State (which contains 25 percent of Brazil's over 82 million voters) with a mere 20,000–30,000 votes.[49]

Conclusion

Chapters 2 through 5 suggest that understanding the political context of voter choice in Brazil requires making theoretical and conceptual shifts away from paradigms based on European history to new comparative perspectives grounded in the U.S. trajectory of party development in a presidential and federal system. American political history provides fundamentally new perspectives on presidential institutions and party development both in Brazilian history and during the recent events of democratic transition by drawing attention to the importance of popular appeals in direct executive elections, emphasizing the realities of machine politics, and suggesting that Brazilian executives build and maintain legislative alliances because of their ability to appoint professional politicians directly to administrative posts.

The preceding chapters compare party development in Brazil and the United States by conceptualizing Brazilian political history as a succession of party systems. Chapters 2 and 3 suggest that monarchic centralism and oligarchic federalism dominated the first and second party systems during the Brazilian Empire (1822–1889) and Old Republic (1889–1930). But chapter 4 argues that the third Brazilian party system (1945–1964) fully embodied the mechanisms of party development and passive democratization first described by Max Weber. After 1945, the popular appeals of direct executive elections and the ability of presidents, governors, and mayors to directly appoint party politicians to administrative posts rapidly reorganized the corporatist and patronage machines of Getulio Vargas's Estado Novo

(and opposing groups) into the political parties (PSD, PTB, UDN) that dominated politics until military intervention in 1964. Chapter 5 argues that, despite the absence of presidential elections until 1989 and despite the context of military rule, the executive-centered presidential and federal system of authoritarian Brazil allowed the direct nomination of professional politicians to administrative posts during liberalization, thereby producing a rapid and sweeping organization of parties based on alliances with local patronage machines.

These characteristics of mass politics in the era of democratic transition not only call for shifting comparisons from Europe to the United States, but also counter scholars who advocate parliamentary government, cast doubt on those who view Brazilian political institutions as underdeveloped, and pose new, difficult normative and theoretical questions about party development and passive democratization. Theories that focus on civil society empowerment or the desirability of parliamentary institutions fail to capture the rapid organization of mass politics through direct popular appeals, patronage systems, and the ability of executives to appoint party professionals to administrative offices. Indeed, this analysis suggests that local problems were linked to the national issues of the day during the democratic transition not by opposition groups, but by the patronage practices of professional party politicians.[50]

Although it is difficult to interpret recent events, the impeachment of President Collor in December 1992 suggests that he failed to transform the direct popular appeals of presidential elections into durable legislative coalitions.[51] Far from offering grounds for condemning presidential institutions, the conflicts that produced his downfall appears to have been caused by both his extreme centralization of authority and stubborn unwillingness to develop legislative and political coalitions with leaders from the developed southeast region. Furthermore, the impeachment proceedings also suggest that presidential systems may be less rigid than proponents of parliamentary institutions recognize. While the ability to remove executives through a vote of the legislature in parliamentary systems is considered unique, congressional impeachment of President Collor achieved precisely that.

Finally, it should also be noted that Brazilians voted overwhelmingly to retain presidential institutions in a national referendum on April 21, 1993. Originally scheduled by the 1988 constitution, voters were asked to either retain the traditional presidential system or

change to either parliamentary government or a monarchy (the latter presumably parliamentary as well). Many scholars of Brazilian politics strongly endorsed the campaign for parliamentary government.[52] But the evidence presented herein about presidential institutions and party development in Brazil suggests that many opportunities for democratic reforms exist short of wholesale abandonment of existing institutional arrangements.

Given that inflammatory populist appeals can be ameliorated by scheduling legislative elections alongside direct executive elections; given that budgetary reforms may reduce corruption and that civil service reform could further that goal; given that popular identification with government occurs more through presidential elections than durable partisan affinities or European ideologies, and given the exclusive character of previous periods of parliamentary rule in Brazil (1822–1889, 1962–1963), this analysis suggests that abandoning direct presidential elections would risk disenfranchising large portions of Brazilian society. Without direct presidential elections, the representation of popular sectors so critical in Latin American politics, which Guillermo O'Donnell describes as "lo popular," would decrease.[53] The incentives for politicians to articulate alliances between popular appeals and patronage machines would also decrease, and the latter would most likely prevail in the corridors of a legislature already skewed toward traditional rural areas, reducing not only popular input but effective government as well.

PART III

Brazilian Voters in Democratic Transition

Introduction to Part III

Chapters 1–5 argue that the mechanisms of party development and passive democratization first described by Max Weber—the rapid reorganization of patronage machines into mass parties by directly elected executives through the distribution of administrative appointments to professional politicians—provide a powerful new theoretical perspective on how party-electoral politics work in Brazil. Unlike studies derived from models of European party development, which conclude that Brazilian parties are weak and dysfunctional, this book suggests that shifting the comparison to the United States offers substantial evidence that the sequence of party systems in Brazilian history has been critical for building state-society relations since independence in 1822.

The next four chapters build on this historical review by examining how these mechanisms of party development and passive democratization affected Brazilian voters in the era of democratic transition: their partisan loyalties, positions on issues, judgments about government performance and accountability, participation in campaigns, and attitudes toward democratic institutions during 1974–1985.

Analysis of sequential data from electoral surveys conducted before the 1974, 1978, and 1982 national elections reveals a rapid organization of mass belief among Brazilians during the transition to democracy. Rapid change can be seen away from both the unstructured patterns of voting under hard-line rule, *and* pre-1964 political and partisan cleavages. However, because the concept of *realignment* in a democratic system suggests that one ideological divide or social cleavage is superimposed on another, it fails to highlight the kind of change that occurred in Brazil during 1974–1982. Fundamentally new, nationally based patterns emerged in Brazilian public opinion and voter alignment after 1974. Hence, not realignment, but *alignment* more adequately describes these changes among Brazilian voters.

The multiple regression analysis reported in chapter 1 introduced the similarities and differences between Brazilian voters and advanced democratic electorates by suggesting that respondents' self-placement on a left-right scale, their perceptions of executive performance, and their positions on national issues provide a robust explanation of their intended vote in the 1982 election. Chapters 6 through 10 take a closer look at Brazilian public opinion and voter alignment by carefully examining the causal logic and political context of these factors and others that scholars consider critical in democratic electorates:

Party identification: voting that reflects enduring partisan attachments based on political socialization, largely in the family;

Issue voting: voting that reflects one's stand on national issues;

Accountability voting: voting based on judgments about government policy and performance, primarily on economic issues;

Participation: voting influenced by membership in social organizations and participation in political campaigns;

Attitudes toward democratic institutions: the extent to which voters value liberal and democratic political institutions.

The following chapters examine each of these dimensions by reviewing their origins in the liberal tradition, their place in patterns of public opinion and voter alignment in advanced democracies, and the extent to which the accurately describe Brazilian voters in democratic transition.

Focusing on these political and conceptual dimensions of Brazilian voter choice is possible because sociologists have systematically explored diverse demographic determinants such as class, region, gender, race, and the urban-rural cleavage in Brazil.[1] This knowledge of electoral sociology permits us to shift away from demographic characteristics and aggregate data to directly examine individuals, their political conceptions, the causal factors behind their choices, and the impact of institutions and other contexts. These matters often appear in the demographic characteristics of survey respondents and official electoral data as simple rigidities.[2]

Indeed, clear national demographic patterns often fail to appear among Brazilian voters because plebiscitarian appeals, patronage, and

complex links between local, state, and national politics in Brazil tend to cut across class and other demographic divisions and thereby weaken their explanatory power. The following analysis of the political conceptions of individual voters and aggregate patterns in electoral survey data seeks to provide new perspectives on Brazilian voter choice and its context.

— Chapter 6 —

Plebiscitarian Appeals and Patronage Machines

The Development of Party Images and Partisanship

The MDB's role was less that of representing the interests of any particular group or class, and more of symbolizing a protest.
—*Fernando Henrique Cardoso, on the 1974 national elections*[1]

In São Paulo, and generally throughout the large urban centers, the broadest and possibly most stable party identifications were formed of our entire electoral history.
—*Bolivar Lamounier, on the 1978 national elections*[2]

These comments by Cardoso and Lamounier contain the central paradox about party images and popular responses among Brazilian voters after 1974. The rapid shift toward the MDB in the first elections held under liberalized military rule in 1974 was, at best, an amorphous manifestation of opposition by a depoliticized and inexperienced electorate. How could such a vote in 1974 lead to broad and stable party identifications by 1978? If voters identified with parties by 1978, why did the 1979 Party Reform Law split MDB voters into four opposition parties that competed among themselves in the

1982 election? If opposition voters were split in 1982, how did the PMDB secure such landslide victories in the 1986 election? Full explanation of rapid changes in partisanship during 1974, fractionalization of the opposition after 1979, and the fleeting success of the PMDB in 1986 requires an analysis of how the plebiscitarian appeals of elections and patronage organized party images and party loyalty. This chapter begins to integrate the historical analysis of part 1 into study of the causal factors behind voters' choices during the democratic transition era by clarifying the meaning and measuring party identification; by reviewing expectations about civilian society empowerment; and by arguing that contrary to theories of party identification, Brazilian party-electoral politics rapidly created short-term partisan affinities during 1974–1985.

Did direct plebiscitarian appeals and patronage organize party images and popular partisan affinities during the Brazilian transition? Most social scientists see Brazilian parties as undisciplined, clientelistic, and underdeveloped political organizations that keep Brazilian voters politically ignorant and passive.[3] By comparing Brazil to Europe and other Latin American countries, such as Chile, Argentina, and Uruguay, with their well-organized parties and ideological voters, analysts emphasize the short-lived and inchoate nature of Brazilian party images. It is also common to suggest that because Brazil's party leaders build complex, often hermetic, back-room electoral and legislative alliances on the national, state, and local levels, Brazilian parties lack internal discipline and ideological clarity. And because voters lack information about the programmatic content of parties, they consequently fail to develop durable identifications with parties. But formal models of party identification tells us little about public opinion and voting in Brazil, where voter alignment is largely driven by populist appeals and personality-based links between individual politicians and voters.[4]

Contrary to these widely accepted views, the partisan affinity of Brazilian survey respondents two weeks before the 1982 election correlates strongly with their intended choice for governor (see table 6.1). The odds as expressed in partial correlation coefficients (R) from logistic regression are quite high, ranging between .44 and .58.[5] The causal logic and political context of party loyalty in Brazil certainly differs from patterns found in advanced democratic electorates. But the weight of partisan affinity in Brazilian public opinion and voter

Table 6.1 The Effect of Party Affinity on Voter Choice, by Party, 1982 (logistic regression)

	PT	PDT	PDMB	PTB	PDS
Southeast	.44	.44	.56	.58	.53
(N)	(129)	(272)	(491)	(107)	(282)
Northeast	—	—	.54	—	.56
(N)			(490)		(294)
Rural area #1	—	—	.52	—	.52
(N)			(62)		(115)
Rural area #2	—	—	.54	—	.48
(N)			(32)		(106)

Source: 1982 electoral survey.

Note: Reported Partial Correlations (R) are maximum likelihood estimates for the odds of a respondents intent to vote for governor by party, given their expressed partisan affinity.

alignment, at least upon first examination, cannot be described as weak.

Three theoretical perspectives offer competing explanations about the cognitive content and political context of emergent partisan affinities among Brazilian voters during democratic transition. The conventional wisdom is that *long-term* factors such as political and family socialization are necessary before individuals can form a durable identification with a political party.[6] But recent studies on the empowerment of civil society under military rule and during transitions to democracy suggest that new social, political, and party alignments can rapidly emerge in times of political change. Finally, this analysis argues that explaining how party images and partisan affinities develop during democratic transition requires closer examination of direct plebiscitarian appeals and patronage in party-electoral politics.

Empirical theorists hold that stable democracy requires stable partisan attachments.[7] Enduring party allegiances are important because they organize voting patterns and representation (for the system as a whole), while they simplify the dissemination of information on the individual level. This perspective suggests that solid party identification among voters tempers electoral change, provides leaders the free-

dom they need to implement policy, and guards against demagogic politicians and flash parties. These ideas about party identification have been central to the analysis of public opinion and voter alignment for three decades, and scholars have achieved an impressive understanding of party images and partisan affinity in most of the advanced democracies.[8]

However, several core assumptions about party identification are both at odds with liberal democratic theory and fail to describe the relation between party images, public opinion, and voter alignment in Brazil during 1974–1985. The most problematic assumptions are the following:

1. Voters possess rather simple and unconstrained belief systems in which party attachment plays an important role.
2. Constraints on electoral change lie primarily in the intellectual and educational endowments of individuals, not levels of political information available to them.
3. Political socialization and party loyalty are basically shaped by long-term influences, chiefly within the family.

These assumptions are problematic because they differ considerably from liberal democratic theory and do not apply to Brazilian public opinion. An emphasis on the simplicity of voters and cognitive, temporal, political, and social constraints on change seems quite distant from liberal ideas and democratic theories about political development and change. Furthermore, these assumptions fail to account for the rapid shifts in partisan affinity among Brazilians in recent decades. If stable democracy requires voters with durable party identifications, consolidated over three generations, then this theory is simply inappropriate for Brazil and other countries in transition from authoritarian rule. Building and deepening new democracies urgently requires viable theories about how partisan affinity can develop in the short term.

Recent studies about the empowerment of civil society do indeed emphasize the prospects for change during the dramatic events of democratic transition. Nonetheless, this perspective still fails to accurately describe how party-electoral politics organize partisan affinity in Brazil. The empowerment of civil society emerges not only from organized social opposition to authoritarianism, which can produce

regime change. There is also the possibility that the realities of life under authoritarianism may have created new conditions for the emergence of democratic politics in these countries.[9] The resurrection of civil society as a political force during the transition to democracy in Brazil and other Latin American countries has generated new terms of discourse, endowed new actors, and created new cleavages. However, both survey data and the preceding historical review suggests that the consolidation of these new cleavages and politics occurs in the day-to-day context of competitive mass party and electoral politics.

The central argument of this chapter is that both theories of party identification and civil-society empowerment fail to explain the content, context, and prospects for partisan affinities among Brazilian voters in democratic transition. Instead, the mechanisms of party development and passive democratization provide a much more compelling explanation: party images first emerged during the Brazilian transition because of the plebiscitarian character of the 1974 election. Opposition to the military government predominated in the southeast urban regions, while support of the military government prevailed in the less developed rural areas and northeast region. However, during the following eleven years of gradual, state-controlled, elite-centered transition in Brazil, the presidency and other executive offices remained above electoral review. Military control of the federal government meant that, instead of a directly elected president building electoral alliances and legislative coalitions through the spoils system, conservative politicians thrived on state patronage and predominated in semicompetitive elections. The preceding historical chapters suggest that Brazilian party images and partisan affinity must be constantly reproduced through intra- and interparty alliances for legislative and executive races across the national, state, and local levels of Brazilian politics. Without direct elections for governor (until 1982), for mayor of capital cities and others declared security zones (until 1985), and for president (until 1989), these patterns failed to fully materialize for much of the transition period.

Indeed, elite-centered politics culminated in selection of a civilian president in 1985 within the restricted electoral college designed by military rulers. Direct presidential elections were postponed until 1989, then held—unusual for Brazil—in isolation from legislative, state, and local elections. Executive and legislative elections have been held concomitantly in Brazil since 1932, based on Assis Brasil's pro-

posals for electoral legislation designed to reduce the populist and plebiscitarian character of majoritarian elections for executive office by holding contests for legislatures at the same time.[10] Under military rule, public relations campaigns mounted by nonelected executives were linked to patronage politicians through distribution of administrative appointments and state patronage. After the transition to civilian rule, the machine politicians who controlled local and state electoral politics under military rule rapidly aligned themselves with the national leaders of the opposition PMDB preceding the 1986 elections.[11] This is not just a lament: of interest here is understanding how party and electoral politics set the context for party images and partisan affinities during the Brazilian transition.

In sum, three perspectives offer three competing explanations for how party images and partisan affinity developed among Brazilian voters in democratic transition. The success of the opposition party (P)MDB after 1974 suggests, at first glance, that the empowerment of civil society during the transition period rapidly produced national mass party images and affinities. The growing number of survey respondents who identify themselves with a political party between 1972 and 1982 reveals the meteoric expansion of the (P)MDB's popularity among Brazilians and the steady decline of those who identified themselves with the government parties, ARENA and PDS (see table 6.2).

These rapid changes of partisan loyalty among Brazilians in democratic transition present a puzzle for theories of party identification. Scholars working in the Schumpeterian tradition of elite democratic theory are profoundly skeptical about the possibility of rapid changes in party identification—except in times of dramatic political experiences such as revolution, violent regime change, or civil war.[12] Recent analysis of Spain during and after the transition to democracy also suggests that "growth in party identification has lagged behind the acquisition of left-right placement and opinions of leaders."[13] Nonetheless, the evidence suggests that Brazilian partisan affinities changed rapidly during the transition period, despite the gradual, elite-centered, and nonviolent character of politics.

But the development of partisanship during the Brazilian transition also presents a puzzle for theorists of civil-society empowerment. Instead of a consolidation of Brazilian voters who identify with opposition parties, the 1982 data suggests the fragmentation and differ-

Table 6.2   Partisanship Among Voters in São Paulo and Porto
Alegre, 1972–1982 (percent)

Partisan Affinity	1972	1974	1978	1982
Government party				
ARENA or PDS	35.5	21.3	17.1	16.3
Opposition party				
MDB or PDMB	10.4	45.8	8.7	23.1
PT	—	—	—	7.9
PDT	—	—	—	9.0
Party formed after 1979				
PTB	—	—	—	4.6
Other or no response	54.1	31.8	32.2	39.7
Total	100.0	100.0	100.0	100.0
(N)	(1,314)	(1,287)	(1,271)	(1,247)

Source: 1972 social survey; 1974, 1978, 1982 electoral surveys.

Note: Percentages are from surveys of São Paulo and Porto Alegre because they were the samples with comparable questions about partisan affinity across the period of hard-line rule and transition.

entiation of opposition affinities after the 1979 Party Reform Law.[14] The effectiveness of the government's "divide and rule" tactic can be seen by the extent to which the PMDB lost support in 1982, while the number of those identifying with the PDS remained about the same as those supporting ARENA in 1978. Furthermore, when the opposition party, the PMDB, finally achieved success in the 1986 elections (winning twenty-two out of twenty-three governorships, and majorities in the Constitutional Congress and many state assemblies), the primary strength of the PMDB was no longer its image as an opposition party.

By 1986, the PMDB's electoral success was caused not by spreading popular opposition among Brazilian voters but by the popularity of the Plano Cruzado and electoral alliances forged between national PMDB leaders and patronage systems on the local and state levels. The historical review in part 1 shows that Brazilian party images and partisan affinity are usually recreated in each election through a combination of direct popular appeals in majoritarian races for executive

offices and patronage politics in local and state legislative campaigns. The PMDB broadened its support in 1986 only after the military left power and the new civilian government of Jose Sarney (and the party alliance that supported him) gained the prerogative to nominate politicians to administrative posts, thereby enabling it to make electoral alliances with regional and local politicians throughout Brazil.

The following sections describe, first, how direct popular appeals and patronage machines generate *immediate* and *personalistic* ties between parties and voters in Brazil. The next section takes a closer look at the emergence of new party images on the national level after 1974. The final section argues that the extended coexistence of authoritarian and democratic power from 1982 to 1985 weakened Brazilian party politics because the plebiscitarian appeals that emerged after 1974 could not be linked to government policies or patronage systems as long as the military retained control of the federal executive.

Party Images and Partisanship in Brazil

National party images and broad popular affinities first appeared in modern Brazil through the practices of populism and patronage. In Brazil, citizenship did not develop along the lines suggested by classic liberal theory or European experiences, but through populist and machine politics. The predominance of populism and patronage in Brazil has produced radically different types of partisan affinities among Brazilian voters, first during the period of inclusionary corporatism of Getulio Vargas's populist-nationalist government and then in periods of competitive politics thereafter.[15]

The rationales given by Brazilians for their choice of political party tend to be grounded in direct judgments of parties or admiration for a particular political leader. The vast majority of Brazilian voters who declared a party loyalty in the 1982 survey tended to conceive of politics in these terms (see table 6.3). With the exception of PT adherents in the southeast region and PDS identifiers in rural areas, the proportion of party identifiers who think about politics in terms of ideology or group interest rarely surpasses 10 percent. In comparison, the proportion of those who think about politics in terms in specific political personalities ranges from 39.2 to 80.8 percent. The proportion of party identifiers who in general evaluate politics directly (although

Table 6.3 Conceptualizations of Politics by Partisans, Compared to Voters in General, 1982 (percent)

	PT	PDT	PMDB	PTB	PDS	Voters in General
Southeastern cities						
Ideological	36.6	12.0	9.8	7.7	6.6	6.4
Personality-based	43.4	76.0	63.5	80.8	63.9	34.1
Immediate	20.0	10.8	23.1	7.7	26.3	12.6
None or no response	0.0	1.2	3.6	3.8	3.3	46.7
Total	100.0	100.0	100.0	100.0	100.0	100.0
(N)	(145)	(167)	(386)	(78)	(274)	(2,463)
Northeastern cities						
Ideological	7.1	—	9.5	—	11.5	4.7
Personality-based	64.3	—	56.8	—	39.2	32.2
Immediate	28.6	—	24.9	—	36.9	13.9
None or no response	0.0	—	8.9	—	12.3	49.2
Total	100.0		100.0		100.0	100.0
(N)	(14)		(169)		(130)	(1,297)
Rural areas						
Ideological	—	—	13.8	—	26.5	10.8
Personality-based	—	—	60.0	—	49.7	7.5
Immediate	—	—	13.3	—	13.5	26.5
None or no response	—	—	12.3	—	10.3	55.2
Total			100.0		100.0	100.0
(N)			(65)		(155)	(481)

Source: 1982 electoral survey.
Note: On types of conceptualizations, see Appendix 2.

lower among smaller parties and rural areas) varies between 23.1 and 36.9 percent among the major parties in the southeast and northeast region.

The different conceptual bases of Brazilian partisan affinity also extends to respondents who stated that they strongly identified with parties. In absolute numbers, few respondents with a strong affinity for a particular party considered politics in terms of ideology or group interest. And the proportion of respondents with immediate or personalistic conceptions of politics who declared themselves strong partisan identifiers, while fewer than those who classified themselves as ideologues, remained considerably above the number in the control category of not applicable/no response. Of the 131 party identifiers with *ideological* conceptions of politics in the southeast urban sample, 64.1 percent strongly identified themselves with a political party. In comparison, 47.3 percent of the 662 with *personalistic* conceptions, and 48.1 percent of the 210 with *immediate* conceptions of politics also stated they were *strongly* identified with their party (well above the 32.0 percent in the control category). Indeed, in the survey of São Paulo City, personalistic and immediate conceptions not only predominated numerically but also seem to have produced stronger partisan affinities: 51.4 percent of party identifiers with *personalistic* conceptions of politics and 48.1 percent of respondents with *immediate* conceptions of politics, responded that they were *very* closely identified with their party. In comparison, only 26.9 percent of party identifiers in São Paulo who think about politics in *ideological* terms declared themselves to be *very* much identified with their party.

In sum, the complex alliances that link local patronage systems to the broad popular appeals and candidacies for executive office appear to be central mechanisms that reproduce Brazilian conceptions of politics in terms of political personalities and immediate or direct judgments of parties. If one recognizes that Brazilian voters traditionally choose on the basis of direct judgments of plebiscitarian appeals by parties in national politics, the rapid shift to the MDB after 1974 no longer seems puzzling. The first political party in Brazilian history that approached the ideal of acquiring a broad, nationally based image among voters, did so because electoral campaigns after 1973 placed the choice between military government and the opposition MDB squarely before the Brazilian voter. Unencumbered by the ideological rigidities of a highly structured mass belief system, and with infor-

mation, organization, and contestation no longer constrained by military rule, Brazilians quickly identified with and voted for the (P)MDB, especially in the more advanced urban areas of the southeast.

Because access to state resources and the distributive practices of patronage machines are necessary for the local organization of parties throughout Brazil, the fractionalization of Brazilian parties after the 1979 party reform law also becomes understandable. The military's unwillingness to relinquish political power during the transition (producing what Linz called a situation of diarchy) allowed authoritarian state leaders to retain control of money and the power to distribute administrative nominations—both necessary to form alliances with professional politicians on the regional and local levels. Consequently, the (P)MDB leaders remained isolated, without patronage support on the local and regional levels, and vulnerable to an erosion of its image as an opposition party.

Plebiscitarian Appeals and Party Images on the National Level

Did the plebiscitarian character of Brazilian elections create broad, meaningful, and durable party images and popular affinities during the transition period? Scholars have debated whether opposition voting in the 1974 election was an informed expression of opinions, or merely a negative vote.[16] In a fine polemic, Santos defines the normal Brazilian vote as a negative vote—meaning that most voters do not value or remember party, issue, class, or group interest when they vote.[17] Instead, Brazilians tend to vote against whatever government is in power. Santos reviews electoral trends in the pre-1964 system to support the idea that a certain level of "instinctive" opposition voting is a constant in Brazilian electoral politics. By questioning the extent to which opposition voting is based on substantive political judgments, Santos placed the burden of proof on the other side. Lamounier's claim that opposition voting during the transition period produced the broadest and most durable patterns of party images and affiliations among Brazilian voters in history must be supported with empirical evidence about the type of mass belief structure behind such changes.

Does the survey data provide such evidence? Did new patterns of partisanship emerge in response to the plebiscitarian appeals of elections under military rule? The first indication that Brazilian voters considered primarily the present rather than the past when voting is that—among survey respondents—there is little correspondence between their party identification before 1964 and partisan affinity after 1974. While stronger correlations between pre-1964 identifications and support for ARENA/MDB appear in survey data from 1972 to 1974 in the politicized southern city of Porto Alegre, this relationship weakened thereafter.[18] Indeed, researchers preparing survey questionnaires after 1978 omitted questions tapping the partisanship of respondents before 1964 because it failed to explain party loyalty after that time. Such a rapid weakening of preauthoritarian political cleavages would be unthinkable in the highly politicized publics of Argentina, Chile, or Uruguay, whether during or after military rule.[19]

Another indication that the direct appeals of parties had an impact on Brazilian public opinion during the transition period is the clarity of public perceptions about the parties' positions on new political issues. In the 1978 survey, both ARENA and the MDB were perceived by respondents on the basis of their positions on the critical issues of the day. The responses in table 6.4 suggest that Brazilians perceived the MDB as the opposition party on the basis of new, post-1965 political issues. In the four southeast cities covered by the 1978 survey, the MDB was seen as the opposition on all national political issues. While public perceptions of ARENA are more ambiguously distributed in questions about its position on income distribution, greater government control of foreign business, and the enfranchisement of illiterates, most were unequivocally convinced that ARENA was the government party when questioned about the post-1964 issues of holding direct elections and whether the military should leave power. The degree to which survey respondents can identify the parties' positions on a series of issues indicate the range of individual beliefs and is a central measure of mass belief structure and ideological sophistication in public opinion.[20]

To summarize, public perceptions of the MDB and ARENA were based on new national issues that arose under military rule. The images of Brazilian parties emerged on the basis of issues, symbols, and political identities that referred not to values or principles formed in the past, but to the immediate question of whether parties supported

Table 6.4   Perceptions of Party Positions on National Issues in Four
Southeastern Capitals, 1978 (percent)

National Issue	Position	MDB	ARENA
Does the party favor or oppose the salaries of those with low income?	Favor	53.5	23.8
	Oppose	6.8	29.7
Does the party favor or oppose direct elections?	Favor	56.3	14.1
	Oppose	6.1	50.7
Does the party favor or oppose the military leaving power?	Favor	43.1	6.7
	Oppose	14.5	50.7
Does the party favor or oppose greater control of foreign firms?	Favor	41.9	21.2
	Oppose	6.8	26.0
Does the party favor or oppose granting the vote to illiterates?	Favor	39.0	22.3
	Oppose	13.5	28.3
(N)		(2,669)	(2,669)

Source: 1978 electoral surveys.

Note: Reported frequencies are average responses from the four capital cities in the 1978 survey: São Paulo, Porto Alegre, Belo Horizonte, and Rio de Janeiro. "Other" and "no response" figures are omitted for readability. Including these two categories, responses would sum to 100 percent.

or opposed the military government. The decreasing importance of pre-1964 party identification as a referent for politics after 1974 once again suggests that Brazilian party images are not based on long-term socialization but, instead, must be constantly reproduced through competitive electoral politics. While Brazilian partisan affinities are quite distant from ideals of durable identifications with ideological parties, the flexibility of the Brazilian public seems to have actually facilitated the organization of new patterns in opposition to or support of the military government. Indeed, in historical perspective, the emergence of party images across Brazil during the transition period is an extremely important development. Party images and identification in the pre-1964 system were based primarily on regional leaders

and local political machines. Before 1964, electoral politics was driven primarily by state and local concerns in an electorate of 18 million voters. With 48 million Brazilians voting by 1982, the plebiscitarian politics of the transition period appear to have produced, perhaps for the first time in Brazilian history, a *nationalization* of party and electoral politics.

Diarchy and the Differentiation of Opposition Party Images

Linz has called the extended irresolution of political power during the Brazilian transition a situation of diarchy.[21] While direct elections were held for governorships in 1982, military leaders retained control of the federal government until 1985. An important consequence of this blurring of distinctions between democratic and authoritarian power was that the MDB could not transform its popular appeals and promises into government policies. Control of executive offices and agencies—or alliance with those who control state resources—is required not only to implement policies, but also to win elections in Brazil. Because no direct elections were held for important executive offices before 1982, and then only for governor (and selected mayorships in 1985), the MDB gained only limited access to state resources. Thus diarchic ambiguity, authoritarian state elite manipulation of elections, and the inability of opposition parties to control state bureaucracies impeded the transformation of plebiscitarian appeals and opposition voting after 1974 into a principle of political action and party organization.

Given the importance of executive offices for pork-barrel politics and patronage on the local level, the extent of party contact with survey respondents during the 1982 campaign is revealing (see table 6.5). The reach of the PDS into the far corners of the Brazilian territory is reflected in the large number of personal contacts in the 1982 campaign. Because they retained control over the vast financial and administrative resources of the centralized Brazilian state, authoritarian leaders secured the support of important regional and local politicians across Brazil. Historical analyses of the post-1979 conservative parties, the PDS and PFL, are not yet available.[22] However, the 1985 and 1986 elections suggest that these parties were organized on the basis of alliances between authoritarian state leaders and regional and

Table 6.5   Voters Personally Contacted by Political Parties During
the 1982 Electoral Campaign (percent)

Party That Contacted Voter	Southeast	Northeast	Rural Areas
Government party			
PDS	15.7	17.8	47.3
Opposition party			
PMDB	18.8	8.2	34.6
PDT	7.1	—	—
PT	2.1	—	—
Semi-opposition party			
PTB	5.4	—	—
Not contacted or no response	50.9	74.0	18.1
Total	100.0	100.0	100.0
(N)	(2,463)	(1,860)	(481)

Source: 1982 electoral survey.
Note: The follow-up question read as follows: "Have you been contacted by
a candidate or someone associated with a political party to ask for your vote? If
so, which party did this person or candidate represent?"

local-level professional politicians. Local *cabos eleitorais* worked in favor of authoritarian state leaders as long as they controlled, in Barry
Ames's blunt words, pork.

The preceding historical chapter argues that the 1979 party reform law split the Brazilian opposition because the choice between
MDB and ARENA before 1979 concealed the many differences
among Brazilian voters. But the differentiation of opposition voting
after 1979 does not imply its weakening. On the contrary, the founding of new opposition parties helped to define the real differences and
similarities between both leaders and voters previously concealed in
the catch-all opposition party, MDB. In the effort to meet party registration requirements, energy and organization were directed toward
membership drives and publicity campaigns at a rate almost unequaled
in Brazilian history. This sharpened party images and partisan affinities. Furthermore, given that Brazilian parties and party images function on the national, regional, and local levels, the organization of
party images on these levels also indicates a consolidation of party

identification, not its fragmentation or weakening.[23] Indeed, this increasing complexity and diversity among Brazilian voters is consistent with recent scholarly emphasis on flux, multidimensionality, and historicity in the electorates of advanced democracies.[24]

In sum, the plebiscitarian character of national elections after 1974 created fundamentally new party images and patterns of partisanship on the national level. While the nationalization of party images differed in important respects from the primarily regional nature of pre-1964 politics in Brazil, the consolidation of party images and partisan affinity was blocked by the extended diarchy of the Brazilian transition. Because direct presidential elections were not held until 1989, opposition parties could not transform their electoral appeals into political realities. Instead, military leaders and the conservative parties retained control of patronage resources in the federal executive, nominated professional politicians to administrative posts, and retained political alliances with local and regional politicians.

Conclusion

Which theory best explains the organization of party images and partisan affinity during the Brazilian transition? Conventional wisdom about party identification falls short on three counts. First, because theories insist that long-term improvements in education and political socialization through the family are required for the creation of durable partisan affinities, this perspective fails to consider alternative mechanisms for building popular identifications with parties during the rapidly changing events of the democratic transition. We still lack the perspective and adequate survey evidence that only time can provide to analyze today's many new republics and democracies. Theorists who study party identification may be right: voters did indeed embrace fascist parties and caused a breakdown of democracy throughout Europe in the 1920s and 1930s. But this is a time of unprecedented transitions from authoritarianism to democracy. We need plausible theories about how party affinities are built and democracy is strengthened in the short term. The insistence on long-term causes and constraints on party identification fails to recognize the sudden impact of plebiscitarian appeals and patronage politics on

Brazilian voters and contradicts core elements of liberal democratic theory that portray voters as rational and government as responsive.[25]

Second, ideas about party identification that are grounded in assumptions about ideological parties and group interest politics poorly describe the links between voters and parties in Brazil. Very few Brazilians think about politics or embrace parties in terms of ideology or group interest. Instead, their political judgments are more immediate, direct, and personalistic. A third weakness is that theories about party identification focus primarily on national party images and organizations, not local politics. While machine politics on the local level still organize party identification and the vote in advanced democracies,[26] in Brazil party machines and personal contacts on the local and regional levels are especially important in determining popular affinities with parties and voter choice.

The problem with theories of civil society empowerment is the tendency to underestimate both the role of professional politicians and the emerging characteristics of mass electoral and party politics. By emphasizing the ability of civil society to oppose military rule and to establish new ethical parameters for democracy, this perspective conceals core problems of political organization and electoral politics. While new social movements in authoritarian Brazil were central to creating a new antimilitary/progovernment cleavage, the consolidation of this new cleavage requires building political organizations capable of competing in mass electoral politics. On the practical level, this means greater attention to mass electoral and party politics. On the theoretical level, this implies recognizing a new moment in the organization of social movements and democracy.

This chapter presented a third explanation for the development of partisan affinity among Brazilian voters in the transition period by emphasizing the context of plebiscitarian appeals and patronage machines. While the cognitive content and institutional context of party affinity in Brazil differ from party identification in advanced democracies, survey data suggest that direct popular appeals and patronage systems did indeed organize new Brazilian party images in recent years. The peculiar mixture of authoritarian and democratic politics and the protracted, elite-centered character of the Brazilian transition suggest that further analysis is required to understand these new trends in Brazilian public opinion and voter alignment.

— *Chapter 7* —

Plebiscitarian Issues and Local Concerns

Citizens in the advanced democracies tend to vote according to their positions on the national political issues of the day. The issue positions of individuals organize public opinion and voter align-ment because they converge along and reinforce the principal political cleavages, yet retain an autonomous influence on voter choice. Issue voting is a compelling theory of how aggregate-level rationality guides public opinion and determines voter choice.[1] By emphasizing how citizens perceive, evaluate, and vote on the basis of complex issues, these studies portray voters as considerably more capable and rational than previous social scientists had assumed. But the idea of issue vot-ing is based on more than liberal theory: the claim that mass publics vote rationally on the basis of positions on national issues is supported by retrospective analysis of survey data gathered over four decades.

For the first generation of electoral behavior analysts, the effect of issue positions on voter choice was overshadowed by an emphasis on party identification.[2] And while the party and class cleavages built during the Depression and New Deal dominated U.S. politics and issues until midcentury, the new issues of the 1960s—Vietnam, civil rights, student revolts—divided Americans and other advanced dem-ocratic publics in new ways. The rapid response of voters to new issues suggested that mass electorates were not constrained by long-term factors such as education, political socialization, and the limited

154

knowledge of "poorly endowed observers" nearly as much as empirical democratic theory had originally imagined. Instead, as Nie et al. claim, "It is exposure to politics, not attainment of higher levels of education and its accompanying cognitive capacity, that seems to lead to the greater coherence of citizen attitudes."[3] Indeed, the dealignment of modern, class-based politics throughout the advanced democracies in the 1970s has brought greater urgency to the task of understanding how issue positions inform voters' choices.[4]

Studies of issue voting in the advanced democracies contribute to an analysis of Brazilian voters in democratic transition for two reasons—one theoretical, one methodological. On the theoretical level, issue voting identifies a mechanism of electoral representation that is especially important during periods of change. When past definitions of party and class no longer convincingly apply to new political problems, voters tend to be directly influenced by discussion of political issues in electoral campaigns. Chapter 6 argued that popular appeals generated new party images and partisan affinities along a new anti-authoritarian-progovernment cleavage during the Brazilian transition. Theories of issue voting provide another theoretical perspective and an additional empirical dimension for examination of the content, context, and uneven development of mass belief systems among Brazilian voters.

On the methodological level, the concept of issue voting contributes to analysis of Brazilian voters by suggesting that structure in mass publics may appear only on the *aggregate* level in survey data as constellations of issue positions.[5] By master-coding respondents according to their political conceptualizations—immediate and personalistic—this analysis attempts to describe how individual Brazilians think about politics. However, because the political views of individuals often cut across social and political cleavages as well as the various conceptions of politics, this chapter analyzes intercorrelations between issue positions and other aggregate-level patterns. These patterns provide a more complex picture of mass opinion and reveal additional types of rationality among Brazilian voters.

Issue Voting among Brazilian Voters in
Democratic Transition

Did plebiscitarian appeals and patronage machines create new issue cleavages among Brazilian voters? The multiple regression estimates

presented in chapter 1 suggest that the views of Brazilian voters on national issues do indeed inform their choice of party and candidate. This chapter attempts to clarify the link between these views and voters' choices by analyzing two widely used measures of how issue positions organize public opinion and voter alignment. First, *issue voting* is measured by the degree to which a given set of issue positions correlates with voter choice. Second, *issue structure* is measured by the degree of constraint between issue positions (the degree to which issue positions intercorrelate according to the logic of existing cleavages).

The statistical attributes associated with issue voting do indeed appear among Brazilian voters after 1974. The Beta coefficients (B) from multiple regression analysis reported in table 7.1 permit comparison of the causal weight of national and local issue positions on voter choice. The coefficients were obtained by regressing scales of respondents' views on national and local issues on their intended vote for governor in the 1982 election. The scale of national issue positions explains approximately 15 percent of the variation in voter choice.[6]

While the statistical attributes associated with issue structure also appear in the survey data from the transition period, so do several

Table 7.1   Effect of National and Local Issues on Voter Choice, 1982

Influence on Choice of Candidate	Beta	Added R^2	B	SE B	T	Sig T
Positions on national issues	.39*	.15	.45	.03	12.6	<.001
Positions on local issues	.06	.00	.01	.00	1.9	.042
(Constant)			6.19	.24	25.0	.00
Adjusted R^2 = .15						

Source: 1982 electoral survey, southeast urban sample.

Note: Because only the PMDB and PDS seriously contested elections in the areas of the northeast and rural samples, the dichotomous dependent variable impedes multiple regression analysis. Logistic regression of national and local issue positions on intent to vote in these areas produced similar results, omitted for clarity. On the construction of national and local issue scales, see table 1.1, note.

differences between Brazilian voters and advanced democratic electorates. First, intercorrelations between issue position are found only
among respondents in the capital cities of the southeast region, and
even then at levels somewhat below those of advanced democratic
electorates (see table 7.2). The partial correlation coefficients (R) of
.23 reported for the southeast sample in table 7.2 mean that, given a
respondent's position on an issue, the likelihood of correctly predicting another issue position is .54. These patterns suggest that voters'
positions on national issues in the southeast capitals are logically constrained and interrelated.

The second difference between issue structures in Brazil and those
of advanced democracies is their extremely uneven development.
While the views of voters in the most advanced southeast capitals are
bound together, voters in the less developed northeast and rural areas
fail to exhibit the kinds of intercorrelated views or logical constraints
associated with issue cleavages. In sum, the new cleavage between
opposition to and support for the military government appears among
respondents in the southeast sample, but not among respondents
from the northeast and rural areas. Voter choice in these regions must
be explained by other factors relating to local politics and patronage.

How did the direct popular appeals of parties define voters' views
on national issues? How did patronage influence their perceptions of
local issues? The following sections address these questions to clarify
both the similarities and differences between issue voting in Brazil and
in advanced democracies and the uneven development of mass belief
systems across regions and between urban and rural areas.

Plebiscitarianism, National Issues, and Brazilian Voters

Brazilian voters in the period under study tended to base their political
views on either support of or opposition to military rule. Chapter 6
examined how this new cleavage defined new party images and political issues after 1974. Analysis of issue positions in the survey data
reveals two additional patterns among Brazilian voters in the period
of democratic transition. First, contrary to the prevailing view that
stresses a widespread opposition to authoritarianism, the survey data
suggest that a plurality of Brazilian voters supported the Brazilian military government on urgent national issues, and that levels of oppo-

Table 7.2 Structures of Positions on Issues Opposing or
Supporting the Military Government, 1982

	Restrict media campaigning?[a]	Military should leave government?[b]	Communist party should be legalized?[c]
Southeast			
Direct presidential elections?[d]	.06	.23	.07
Restrict media campaigning?[a]		.23	.22
Military should leave government?[b]			.21
Northeast			
Direct presidential elections?	.09	.09	.04
Restrict media campaigning?		.03	.08
Military should leave government?			.12
Rural area #1			
Direct presidential elections?	.00	.10	.00
Restrict media campaigning?		.08	.00
Military should leave government?			.00
Rural area #2			
Direct presidential elections?	.00	.13	.00
Restrict media campaigning?		.13	.00
Military should leave government?			.00

Source; 1982 electoral survey.

Note; Figures are partial correlation coefficients from logistic regression. The "Lei Falcão" (Decree # 6,639, July 1, 1976) limited electoral campaign messages on television and radio to the name, number, and party affiliation of the candidate, accompanied by a still photo in the case of television.

a. The question read: "Do you agree with the law against election campaigning on radio and TV?"

b. The question read: "Should the military leave the government?"

c. The question read: "Should the Communist party be legalized?"

d. The question read: "Should the next president be elected directly by the people?"

sition did not increase after 1978. Second, constellations of opposing positions were largely confined to the cities of the southeast. In comparison, rural voters seem concerned only with local services and infrastructure.

Public support for direct elections was the only national issue on which the opposition responses held a majority (see table 7.3). On all other issues—whether the military should leave power, restrictions on media coverage of campaigns, and legalization of the Brazilian Communist party—there was a consistent plurality of progovernment responses among survey respondents. Contrary to scholarly emphasis on opposition to authoritarianism, the plebiscitarian appeals during

Table 7.3 Respondents' Positions on National Issues, 1982
(percent)

Question Asked	Southeast	Northeast	Rural Areas
Should the next president be elected directly by the people?			
Yes	73.3	68.7	65.8
No	15.6	12.7	16.6
Should the military leave the government?			
Yes	39.5	34.3	18.6
No	39.5	41.2	54.8
Do you agree with the law against election campaiging on radio and TV?			
Yes	52.1	40.1	54.5
No	32.7	35.4	19.3
Should the Communist party be legalized?			
Yes	14.2	16.2	6.2
No	60.3	52.9	62.6
(N)	(2,463)	(1,860)	(481)

Source: 1982 electoral survey.

Note: "Not available" and "no response" categories are omitted to facilitate reading of the table. Including these categories, all responses would sum to 100 percent.

the transition period also produced broad support for the military government. Varying patterns of opposition and support among regions are also critical and confirm the hypothesis that opposition is concentrated in the southeast urban centers, while support of the military government is concentrated in the northeast and in rural areas.[7]

Furthermore, these levels of support for the government on current national issues remained high throughout the transition period. A plurality of Brazilian voters continued to favor military rule and censorship of media campaign coverage in 1978 and 1982 (see table 7.4). And while opposition attitudes increased from 1974 to 1978, they appear to have stabilized thereafter. Again, support for direct presidential elections is an important exception. A full 70 percent of Brazilian voters favored direct presidential elections while the proportion of those opposed fell to 15 percent by 1982.

Table 7.4 Respondents' Positions on National Issues in São Paulo and Porto Alegre, 1974–1982 (percent)

Question Asked	1974	1978	1982
Should the next president be elected directly by the people?			
Yes	59.3	68.7	69.6
No	31.5	18.2	15.6
Should the military leave the government?			
Yes	30.5	40.8	39.5
No	57.4	40.1	39.5
Do you agree with the law against election campaiging on radio and TV?			
Yes	—	54.1	52.1
No	—	32.6	32.7
(N)	(1,287)	(1,271)	(1,247)

Source: 1974, 1978, 1982 election surveys.

Note: Reported frequencies are averages between São Paulo and Porto Alegre. The surveys in the two cities were the only ones with comparable questions for all elections. "Not available" and "no response" are omitted to facilitate reading of the table. Including these categories, all questions would sum to 100 percent.

Are the issue positions of Brazilian voters informed by immediate and personalistic conceptions of politics? The survey data suggest that respondents who think about politics in personalistic and immediate terms not only vastly outnumber those who think in terms of ideology and group interest; they are also much more likely to form opinions on issues than voters at large and even slightly more than those with types of political conceptions found in the advanced democracies (see table 7.5). While the differences between types of conceptualization are small (2 to 9 percent), the differences among all three types of conceptualizations and the residual or control category (no response) are considerable (14 to 38 percent) and statistically significant (Chi-Square Pearson Value = 154.63). Furthermore, the absolute number of respondents with personalistic and immediate conceptualizations of politics is often fivefold the number who respond in terms of ideology or group interest.

Table 7.5 Types of Political Conceptualizations Among Voters Who Took Positions on National Issues, 1982 (cross-tabulation)

	Took Positions on Issues		
Type of Conceptualization	Yes	No	Total
Ideological or group interest	5.1	7.6	6.4
(N)	(57)	(1,010)	(158)
Immediate	7.4	14.5	11.2
(N)	(83)	(193)	(276)
Personalistic	26.2	41.6	34.6
(N)	(296)	(555)	(851)
None or no response	61.3	36.4	47.8
(N)	(692)	(486)	(1,178)
Total	45.8	65.2	100.0
(N)	(1,128)	(1,335)	(2,463)

Source: 1982 electoral survey.

Note: On the types of conceptualization, see Appendix 3. The scale of national issue positions was dichotomized to compare respondents who took one or more positions with those who expressed no views. Similar results were obtained in analysis of the northeast capitals and rural areas of the 1982 survey, but were not reported for ease of reading.

Respondents' positions on national issues also reveal characteristics associated with aggregate-level rationality in other mass publics. The left-right dimension is a widely accepted measure of underlying conceptions of substantive justice that is related to issue voting and structure. The fact that many repondents did not answer the question asking them to place themselves on a ten-point scale measuring their political tendencies, from *left* to *right* (71 percent did not respond in the southeast urban samples) has already been noted in chapter 1. Further research will be required to determine whether the left-right continuum becomes more prevalent among Brazilian voters in an era of fully democratic politics. Nonetheless, patterns in the 1982 electoral survey data suggest that this dimension, while not relevant to voters under hard-line military rule, did indeed inform Brazilian voters' views on national issues to an important degree (see table 7.6).[8]

Regressing the left-right self-placement of Brazilian respondents on their support of or opposition to the military government pro-

Table 7.6 Relation Between Positions on National and Local Issues and Respondents' Left-Right Self-Placement, 1982 (multiple regression)

Type of Position Taken	Beta	B	SE B	T	Sig T
Southeastern cities					
National issue	.45*	1.06	.08	11.8	<.001
Local issue	.13*	.06	.01	3.4	<.001
(Constant)		13.10	.61	21.2	<.001
Northeastern cities					
National issue	.34*	.89	.18	4.8	<.001
Local issue	.02	.01	0.3	.3	.736
(Constant)		11.87	1.28	9.2	<.001

Source: 1982 electoral survey.

Note: For information on how scales of national and local issues were constructed, see note to table 1.1. Starred coefficients are significant at <.001. Additional information for southeast model: multiple R = .47, R^2 = .22, adj. R^2 = .22, standard error = 2.31, F = 76.72, Sign. F <.001, minimum pairwise n = 532. Additional information for northeast model: multiple R = .34, R^2 = .12, adj. R^2 = .11, standard error = 2.54, F = 12.01, F = <.001, minimum pairwise n = 177.

duced statistically significant Beta coefficients of .34 and .45 in the northeast and southeast urban samples, respectively. These links between left-right self-placement and positions on national issues (and the weaker relation with views on local issues) provide additional evidence about the importance of direct popular appeals on the national level in Brazil. Contrary to what has been theorized about civil society empowerment, the 1982 data suggest that respondents' perceptions of local services and infrastructure are still only weakly related to their self-appointed location on a left-right continuum (Beta = .13) in the southeast urban sample, and the two are unrelated in the northeast urban sample. Again, the large number of missing responses suggests that further analysis is needed. But the data provide compelling evidence that Brazilians' conceptions of substantive justice influenced their views on national issues during the transition era, while this dimension remained largely unrelated to their perceptions of problems regarding local services and deficient local infrastructure. In sum, direct plebiscitarian appeals during the Brazilian transition appear to have created a new issue cleavage: whether one supports or opposes military government.

Patronage, Local Issues, and Brazilian Voters

"Public works win votes."
— *Ex-Vice President Aureliano Chaves, September 1985*

Inspired by theories about the empowerment of civil society, opposition movements and parties sought to link local issues to national issues during the Brazilian transition to democracy between 1974 and 1985.[9] New, independent union movements, neighborhood "base communities," progressive Catholic clergy, and opposition parties believed that local demands for public services could go hand in hand with the national struggle against authoritarianism.[10] Many Brazilian communities sorely lack basic services and infrastructure such as running water, sanitation, public transportation, and paved and illuminated streets; and simple amenities such as parks and leisure areas are rare. New opposition groups achieved impressive results by organizing local political demands. Indeed, the dynamism of civil society in national politics during the transition period was due in great part to these new autonomous social organizations.

However, the organization of local opposition and competing in mass elections are two very different types of collective action. In Brazil, voters' concerns about local problems have always been linked to national issues not because voters have opposed the Brazilian state but because they have been mobilized by professional politicians through patronage politics. Researchers studying PT electoral strategies during three months of participant observation in a peripheral neighborhood of São Paulo first reported, with surprise, the efficiency of professional politicians from the PTB and PMDB that appeared in the last weeks before the election.[11] Subsequent research has focused on the heavy politicization of local services and infrastructure, and the difficulty of social movements dislodging professional politicians.[12] During the period of competitive politics, from 1945 to 1964, clientelist and populist politicians constructed electoral bases in de facto districts and pursued national careers based on symbolic offerings of state-supported neighborhood facilities to the people. An entire generation of professional politicians won legislative and mayoral elections and built careers under military rule either by linking local improvements to the military ideology of national security and development, or exploiting the scant opportunities for advocacy and distribution of state services.[13]

The impact of local-level patronage on voters' choices can be seen in the statistical relations between respondents' perceptions of local services and infrastructure and their intended vote for governor in the 1982 survey (see table 7.7). Because views on local issues in the urban samples from the southeast and northeast remain unrelated to voter choice, the data are inconsistent with ideas that have been advanced regarding civil society empowerment: that concern with local problems should be linked to opposition to authoritarianism. Instead, urban voters seem not to take local issues into consideration when choosing parties or candidates.

The relation between voters' positions on local issues and their choices at the ballot box appears only in the two rural samples of the 1982 survey, and then only in support of the two major parties, PMDB and PDS.[14] One of the least appreciated aspects of Brazilian authoritarianism is the effectiveness of party organizations—both opposition groups and government parties—in the vast rural areas of Brazil.[15] Classic and contemporary works on clientelism in Brazilian politics stress the influence of local-level patronage on rural voters.

Table 7.7 The Effect of Perceptions About Local Services on Vote for Governor, 1982

Respondent's Party	Respondent's Views on Local Services					
	Running Water	Lighted Streets	Paved Streets	Sanitation	Public Transportation	Parks and Leisure Areas
Southeastern cities						
PDS	.00	.00	.00	.00	.00	.00
PMDB	.00	.00	.00	.00	.00	.00
PDT	.00	.00	.00	.00	.00	.00
PT	.00	.00	.00	.00	.00	.00
PTB	.00	.00	.00	.00	.00	.00
Northeastern cities						
PDS	.00	.00	.06	.00	.11	.06
PMDB	.00	.00	.06	.00	.11	.07
Rio Paranaiba						
PDS	.12	.10	.00	.00	.11	.00
PMDB	.11	.08	.00	.00	.00	.07
Rural area #1						
PDS	.03	.19	.20	.16	.11	.15
PMDB	.06	.18	.22	.16	.12	.19

Source: 1982 electoral survey.

Note: Partial correlation coefficients (R) from logistic regression measure relationships between dichotomous variables and represent the odds of predicting a respondent's intended vote for governor by party, given his or her position on a specific problem about local public services and infrastructure.

Indeed, the data on party images and issue positions given in this chapter and in chapter 6 suggest that highly organized parties and a strong state presence in rural areas of Brazil continued to take precedence over national issues and party images in voters' minds during the transition period. The following chapters will return to the impact of patronage and provincialism among rural voters.

Conclusion

During the period of hard-line rule in Brazil, voters' positions on issues failed to reflect existing political cleavages and remained statistically unrelated both to each other (indicating lack of logical constraint) and to voters' electoral choices.[16] After liberalization in 1974, the political views of Brazilians tended to coalesce around new issues either in opposition to or in support of the military government. Data from the urban southeast suggest that by 1982 this new issue cleavage was based on immediate and personalistic conceptions of politics, and, taken in isolation, explains approximately 16 percent of voters' choices. Comparing these patterns with analyses of public opinion under the preceding period of hard-line rule once again suggests that rapid change is possible in Brazil.

While these retrospective comparisons may offer grounds for optimism, several caveats are in order. First, intercorrelations between voters' views on issues are comparable to patterns in advanced democracies only among respondents in the southeastern capital cities. The scant evidence of issue structures in the northeastern cities, and the complete lack of intercorrelations in both rural samples of the 1982 survey, provide further evidence of the disparities between urban and rural areas and stress the importance of the different political contexts in which public opinion is formed.

Second, from 1978 through 1982 Brazilian voters exhibited surprisingly strong and stable progovernment attitudes on national issues. Despite an emphasis on opposition to military rule by most observers of the Brazilian transition, a convincing plurality of respondents *supported* the authoritarian government's decisions on national political issues throughout the transition period. Although the data analyzed here cover only the national elections from 1974 to 1982, returns from the 1986 and 1989 national elections (after the transition

to civilian rule in 1985) indicate that 35–40 percent of the electorate still held conservative views—even in the urban southeast, long considered a center of opposition to military rule.

Third, analysis of issue voting presents substantial evidence to counter the proposition that local opposition organizations effectively linked concern with local conditions to national political issues. Contrary to what recent theorists have said about civil society empowerment, the organization of local demands appears to be an inefficient means for getting out the opposition vote. Instead, the 1982 survey data suggest that local issues influence voters *only* in the rural areas, and then because patronage machines reinforce the particularism and provincialism of rural voters and deliver votes for the military government.

Finally, the uneven development of issue voting during the Brazilian transition provides further support for the central argument of this book: that direct plebiscitarian appeals, patronage, and the professionalization of politics were the predominant factors influencing Brazilian public opinion and voter alignment during the period under study. Chapter 6 argued that the direct popular appeals of national elections after 1974 gave parties new images, as either opposed to or supporting the military government. This chapter suggests that party competition in the national elections of the transition period also clarified national issues for a significant number of voters: both issue structures and issue voting increased during the transition period, according to standard measures of individual and aggregate-level mass belief systems. Meanwhile, rural voters focused primarily on matters of local services and infrastructure, tended to support the military government, and vote for whichever party controlled their municipality. To further examine the impact of direct plebiscitarian appeals and patronage politics on Brazilian voters in democratic transition, chapter 8 turns to the conceptual content and political context of voters' judgments about government performance.

— *Chapter 8* —

Government Performance and Accountability Voting

Liberal theories of democracy are built on the idea that periodic elections allow citizens to hold their leaders accountable for their decisions. The liberal conception of accountability in representative government has always been an ideal to be achieved through the interaction of various political institutions under conditions of fair competition. Social scientists have traditionally emphasized the importance of competitive elections, a free press, an informed public, disciplined parties, strong legislatures, and a responsive administration. In short, accountability is part of the liberal *gestalt* that pervades ideas about the impact of retrospective judgments on voting, party government, congressional representation, and democratic theory in general.[1]

Since the ground-breaking work of V. O. Key, a new, more restricted meaning of accountability has prevailed in analyses of public opinion and voter alignment.[2] Instead of a general component of democratic government, accountability became part of a theory of voter choice. Furthermore, since G. H. Kramer linked the electoral fate of incumbents to changing levels of inflation and unemployment over 100 years of U.S. history, scholars have focused on how public perceptions of a government's economic policies are primary determinants of voter choice.[3] Recent research recognizes other political, behavioral, and cognitive variables that also affect voters' choices, and

the methodological and theoretical debates in this burgeoning sub-field are complex.[4] G. Bingham Powell summarizes the field in the following four propositions:

1. The electoral popularity of incumbents is linked to the performance of the economy during their tenure.
2. The criteria by which voters judge incumbents for the economy's performance are unclear.
3. External factors (losing a war, scandal) and a tendency for incumbents to lose popularity once in office can have similar effects on voter alignment.
4. A viable electoral opposition, wide dissemination of information, and voters' perceptions of those who make economic policy *moderate* the impact of accountability voting.[5]

Scholars are still unable to fully explain short-term fluctuations in voter alignment. Perhaps further research can order the causal weight of variables, but so far theories about electoral accountability still remain only supplementary descriptions of the causes of voter alignment. By posing broader questions about "what moves public opinion," researchers depart from a strict concern with accountability voting in their research designs, in the sources of their data, in their statistical methods, and in their theoretical objectives.[6]

Theories of accountability are at the core of the liberal tradition and contribute to analysis of Brazilian voters because they stress the capacity of individuals to judge government performance rationally and to choose among parties on that basis. The idea that access to information and the existence of a viable opposition affect accountability voting seems especially relevant here. The fact that the word *accountability* cannot be translated directly into Portuguese suggests the distance between liberal theory and Brazilian politics. But this inquiry focuses on empirical evidence and the emerging characteristics of Brazilian public opinion and voter alignment—characteristics that appear to have outstripped meanings available in colloquial Portuguese.

Did the direct popular appeals and the patronage practices of Brazilian party-electoral politics produce accountability voting among Brazilian voters in democratic transition? The results form multiple regressional analysis presented in chapter 1 suggest that retrospective

judgments of executive performance did indeed affect Brazilian voters' choices in the 1982 elections. Further analysis of survey data from 1974 to 1982 suggests that Brazilian voters developed real opinions about executive performance, national progress, and the economic and social policies of the military government. The 1982 data also suggests that retrospective judgments of executive performance (presidential, gubernatorial, and mayoral) are more strongly linked to voters' choices than are other types of accountability, providing further evidence that direct popular appeals and immediate judgments by voters are critical in Brazilian politics and the shaping of public opinion.

Perceptions of Military Government Performance, 1974–1982

The survey data suggest that Brazilian voters became increasingly dissatisfied with the military government from 1974 to 1982; that their dissatisfaction was primarily general and influenced by social changes rather than pocketbook issues and individual motives; and that while economic policies were perceived negatively, the social policies of the military government were perceived positively. The first indication of dissatisfaction is evident in changing answers among southeastern urban respondents to the question "Has Brazil improved in the last 3– 4 years?" (see table 8.1). In 1974, 37.3 percent of survey respondents in the cities of São Paulo and Porto Alegre said no. Responses to the same question rose to 50.5 percent in the 1978 electoral survey and to 60.2 percent in 1982.

Further evidence suggests that dissatisfaction among Brazilian voters in the transition period was primarily a response to social change rather than based on pocketbook issues. While only 39.2 percent of respondents in urban areas acknowledged an improvement in their personal finances, 60.2 percent recognized the lack of economic progress in Brazil generally (see table 8.2).[7] Dissatisfaction among respondents in the southeast urban sample appears to be a collective judgment about the *nation*, not reactions to one's *individual* economic situation. Accountability voting in Brazil appears unrelated to a type of possessive individualism that links personal finances to political judgments.

Table 8.1 Perceptions of National Progress in São Paulo and Porto Alegre, 1974–1982 (percent)

Answers to the question, "Has Brazil improved in the last three to four years?"	1974	1978	1982
No	37.3	50.5	60.2
Yes	40.3	23.6	21.1
No response	22.4	25.9	38.7
Total	100.0	100.0	100.0
(N)	(1,287)	(1,271)	(1,247)

Source: 1974, 1978, 1982 electoral surveys.

Note: Reported frequencies are for São Paulo and Porto Alegre because they are the only cities with comparable questions in all surveys.

Table 8.2 Pocketbook Issues and Perceptions of National Progress, 1982 (percent)

Answers to the question, "Has Brazil improved in the last three to four years?"	Southeast	Northeast	Rural Areas
No	60.2	60.3	18.3
Yes	21.1	21.6	53.9
No response	38.7	38.1	27.8
Total	100.0	100.0	100.0
Answers to the question, "Has your personal economic situation improved?"			
No	29.7	33.6	13.7
Yes	39.6	39.4	59.9
No response	30.7	28.0	26.4
Total	100.0	100.0	100.0
(N)	(2,463)	(1,860)	(481)

Source: 1982 electoral survey.

Brazilian voters in the era of democratic transition present a rich case study for theories about accountability voting not only because dissatisfaction with the military government increased once contestation was permitted, but also because the 1982 survey was conducted during a severe economic recession. The adoption of restrictive policies by Economic Planning Minister Delfin Netto in late 1981 placed the issues of inflation and unemployment at the center of the 1982 campaign (expansionary policies from 1979 to 1981 aggravated inflation without producing growth). Indeed, public dissatisfaction with economic policies is considerably greater than dissatisfaction with social policy in the urban areas of Brazil. In the southeast capitals, dissatisfaction with the military government's economic policies against inflation, unemployment, and regressive income distribution ranks 40 percent higher than dissatisfaction with government policies regarding health, housing, and education (see table 8.3).

Urban respondents also rated the government poorly on both the structural problems of income distribution and the shorter-term problems of unemployment and inflation. Once again, disapproval of the military government's policies seems related to respondents' perceptions of collective social conditions, not how they are affected personally. In addition, both the total number of responses and degree of dissatisfaction with the government's economic policies were considerably lower among rural respondents. Assuming that both economic policy and the economy affect rural and urban voters equally, these urban-rural differences provide further evidence of the uneven development of mass belief systems in Brazil. Intense dissatisfaction with government economic policy is plausibly related to plebiscitary opposition voting, but appears only in cities. And whereas over 80 percent of those surveyed in urban areas responded to questions about government economic policies, roughly half of rural voters appear not to have formed an opinion.

It is also somewhat surprising that a significant number of voters—often a plurality of survey respondents—thought that the military government was, in fact, resolving social problems through health care, home financing, and basic education programs. While half of rural respondents had no opinion about economic policies, 72.8 percent responded favorably to questions about the military government's basic education policies. Over half of the respondents in the southeast capitals agreed. Approval of government policies on housing

Table 8.3 Evaluations of Government Economic and Social Policies, 1982 (percent)

Type of Problem	Is the Government Resolving This Problem?	Southeastern Cities	Northeastern Cities	Rural Areas
Regressive income distribution	No	73.3	65.0	30.7
	Yes	8.7	13.8	26.8
Unemployment	No	74.3	70.4	30.3
	Yes	7.4	10.1	19.2
Inflation	No	64.8	61.5	31.8
	Yes	12.4	14.1	21.3
Health services via INPS[a]	No	34.9	27.7	48.2
	Yes	33.6	38.3	15.1
Housing for the poor via BNH[b]	No	41.4	33.9	21.7
	Yes	24.9	27.6	13.4
Primary education	No	19.9	21.5	6.2
	Yes	50.1	21.5	72.8
		(n = 2,463)	(n = 1,860)	(n = 481)

Source: 1982 electoral survey.

Note: Questions were worded as follows: "Do you think that, in general, the government is resolving the problem of ___?" "No response" answers are omitted for legibility.

a. INPS = Instituto Nacional de Previdencia Social

b. BNH = Banco Nacional do Habitaçāo

and health was considerably lower. But the high ratings given to primary education facilities in the rural areas suggest that provision of social services was a fertile terrain for courting support via patronage during the transition period.

The Causal Logic and Uneven Development of Accountability Voting among Brazilian Voters in Democratic Transition

Survey answers that tapped perceptions of the government's accountability provide further evidence about how plebiscitarian voting and patronage practices influence Brazilian public opinion and voter alignment. Factor analysis of eleven questions about government policies and performance in the 1982 survey identified three underlying types of judgments: perceptions of government policies, retrospective judgments, and perceptions of executive performance. Multiple regression analysis suggests that broad judgments of executive performance take precedence over perceptions of specific government policies as explanations of respondents' intent to vote. These direct judgments of executive performance also appear to be structured and rational according to standard measures of mass belief systems: they appear to be both grounded in the voters' self-placement on a left-right continuum and in personalistic and unmediated conceptions of political figures. Finally, the greater constraint (or statistical correlation) between perceptions of accountability in the urban southeast provide additional evidence of the disparities in the development of mass beliefs between cities of the advanced southeast, those of the less-developed northeast, and rural areas.

These arguments differ considerably from existing accounts of how Brazilians perceive government policies and how they vote. Contributors to the first volume of Brazilian electoral sociology published after 1974 argued that perception of economic performance was a central cause of the unexpected surge of the MDB in 1974.[8] According to this publication, Brazilian voters focused on *income distribution* instead of inflation or unemployment in the 1974 election because a decade of growing income disparities under military rule had aroused voters' resentment over income inequality.[9] Nonetheless, this analysis of the 1982 electoral survey data suggests that direct plebiscitarian judgments of executive performance override specific evaluations of

economic and social policies. Given the primacy of direct popular evaluations and the diversity and complexity of Brazilians' judgments of
executive accountability in 1982, income distribution was probably
not of such overwhelming importance to voters in 1974, especially to
the extent that Faria and others claim.

On the impact of public perceptions of government economic
policies, the data suggest that few Brazilian voters were influenced
directly by economic matters alone (see table 8.4). Attitudes about
the success of military government policies against inflation, regressive
income distribution, and unemployment explained only 6 percent of
the variation in respondents' intended vote (adjusted R^2). The Beta
coefficients between .07 and .15 and adjusted R^2 coefficients less than
.05 in the southeast sample suggest that views of specific economic
policies (including perceptions of policies on income distribution) are
only slightly related to respondents' intention to vote.

Voters are more complex than they are portrayed by both recent
theorists of economic accountability and observers of Brazil's 1974
election. While the 1982 data suggests that Brazilian voters judged
the military government on the basis of economic and social policies,

Table 8.4 The Effects of Perceptions of Specific Economic Policies
on Voters' Choice for Governor, 1982

Types of Government Economic Policies Mentioned in Survey Questions	Beta	Added R^2	B	SE B	T	Sig T
Inflation	.15*	.04	.28	.05	5.2	.00
Regressive income distribution	.08*	.01	.17	.06	2.7	.00
Unemployment	.07*	.01	.16	.06	2.4	.01
(Constant)			2.39	.09	25.0	.00
Adjusted R^2 = .06						

Source: 1982 electoral survey.
Note: For wording of questions, see note to table 8.3. Because only two
parties competed in the northeast and in rural areas, intent to vote in these samples
is a dichotomous dependent variable requiring logistic instead of multiple regression analysis.

direct perceptions of executive performance provide a more powerful explanation of their intent to vote. Table 8.5 indicates the independent impact of these three types of perceptions on respondents' planned choice for governor in 1982. The scale measuring broad judgments of executive performance explains 16 percent of the variation in voter choice (adjusted $R^2 = .16$), while the scales measuring voters' perceptions of specific economic and social policies fail to increase the adjusted R^2. The precedence of broad judgments of executive performance—of the president, governor, and mayor—over specific perceptions of government policies once again suggests the influence of direct plebiscitarian appeals and immediate judgments in Brazilian public opinion and voter alignment.

Are these judgments of executive performance based on substantive political grounds? Three measures of mass belief systems provide evidence about the conceptual content and aggregate rationality of Brazilians' ideas about executive accountability. First, cross-tabulation of voters' perceptions of accountability with their political conceptualizations suggests that both unmediated and personality-based responses to candidates do indeed influence their perceptions of accountability (see table 8.6). Respondents who justify their intent to

Table 8.5 The Effects of Executive Performance and Perceptions of Social and Economic Policies on Voters' Choice for Governor, 1982

Influences on Voters' Choices	Beta	Added R^2	B	SE B	T	Sig T
Judgments of executive performance	.32*	.16	.17	.01	10.3	.00
Perceptions of social policies	.07*	.00	.05	.02	2.3	.01
Perceptions of economic policies	.09*	.01	.07	.02	2.8	.00
(Constant)			4.02	.23	16.8	.00
Adjusted $R^2 = .17$						

Source: 1982 electoral survey.
Note: For survey questions, see Appendix 2.

Table 8.6 Judgments About Executive Performance and Government Social Policies and Respondents' Political Conceptualizations, 1982

Type of Political Conceptualization	Took a Position on Executive Performance		Took a Position on Government Social Policies		All Respondents
	Yes	No	Yes	No	
Ideological or group interest	6.7	4.6	7.1	4.6	6.4
(N)	(142)	(16)	(127)	(31)	(158)
Immediate	12.3	4.9	13.0	6.5	11.2
(N)	(259)	(17)	(232)	(44)	(276)
Personalistic	36.9	20.6	37.8	25.8	34.6
(N)	(779)	(72)	(676)	(175)	(851)
None or no response	44.2	70.0	42.0	63.1	47.8
(N)	(933)	(245)	(751)	(427)	(1,178)
Total	85.8	14.2	72.5	27.5	100.0
(N)	(2,113)	(350)	(1,786)	(677)	(2,463)

Source: 1982 electoral survey, southeast urban sample.

Note: For survey questions, see Appendix 2. Chi², Pearson Value for executive performance = 81.84, Sign. = .00
Chi², Pearson Value for social policies = .89.18, Sign. = .00

vote in such terms tend to judge executive performance and government policies considerably more rigorously than do those in the control category of no response/no information. Furthermore, the absolute number of respondents with personalistic conceptions of politics is over five times the number of "ideologues," while the number of respondents with unmediated conceptions of politics is nearly double the number of ideologues. The data once again show that few Brazilian voters think about politics in terms of European ideologies or U.S. notions of group interest.

The extent to which Brazilian voters hold their leaders accountable for their actions and for the performance of the economy resembles aggregate-level rationality in other mass publics. The self-placement of respondents on a left-right scale from one to ten is a widely accepted measure of popular attitudes. The left-right self-placement of Brazilian voters was positively related to broad judgments of executive performance and specific perceptions of the government's social and economic policies in both the southeast and northeast urban samples (see table 8.7).[10]

Another accepted measure of aggregate-level mass belief is the degree to which specific survey responses are correlated with underlying factors. The statistical procedure of factor analysis was used to examine eleven questions in the 1982 survey that asked respondents about their perceptions of specific economic and social policies, general judgments of the mayor's, the governor's, and the president's performance, and their own financial well-being as well as that of the nation during the last few years. Analysis of the southeast urban sample extracted three underlying factors that are typical of accountability voting: citizens' perceptions of government policies, their judgments of their leaders in retrospect, and their evaluation of executive performance (see table 8.8).

Three factors were extracted obliquely through varimax rotation. The eigenvalue of 3.71 for factor 1 (government policies) accounts for 33.8 percent of the total variance. The eigenvalues of 1.26 for factor 2 (executive performance) explains an additional 11.5 percent of the total variance, and 1.1 for factor 3 (judgments of executive performance in retrospect) explains an additional 10.5 percent of total variance. The total variance among individual variables explained by the three factors is a substantial 55.8 percent.

Table 8.7 The Effect of Perceptions of Executive Performance and
the Government's Social and Economic Policies on
Respondents' Left-Right Self-Placement, 1982

Influences on Voters' Choices	Beta	Added R²	B	SE B	T	Sig T
Southeast						
Judgments of executive performance	.24*	.14	.26	.04	5.8	.00
Perceptions of social policies	.19*	.04	.26	.06	4.3	.00
Perceptions of economic policies	.10	.01	.17	.07	2.3	.01
(Constant)			5.53	.64	8.5	.00
Northeast						
Judgments of executive performance	.33*	.19	.42	.08	5.1	.00
Perceptions of social policies	.22*	.06	.30	.09	3.0	.00
Perceptions of economic policies	.08	.00	.13	.11	1.1	.23
(Constant)			7.03	.96	7.2	.00
Adjusted R² = .25						

Source: 1982 electoral survey.

Note: For survey questions, see Appendix 2. Unfortunately, the question of left-right self-placement was omitted from the rural surveys.

Factor analysis also provides further evidence of the great disparities in mass belief systems between the advanced southeast capitals and less-developed northeast cities and rural areas. The degree of autonomy and levels of constraint within the factors underlying perceptions of accountability are far greater among responses from the advanced southeast region than among voters in the latter two samples. While, in the southeast, perceptions of government policies, retrospective judgments, and executive performance can be distinguished as different reasons for voting, in the less-developed northeast capitals and rural areas, retrospective judgments of the nation's progress and

Table 8.8 Underlying Structure of Perceptions of Leaders'
             Accountability, 1982

	Factor		
	1: Government Policies	2: Executive Performance	3: Retrospective Judgments
National problems addressed by government policy			
Regressive income distribution	.74	.00	.12
Inflation	.72	.18	.15
Unemployment	.71	.02	.14
Housing	.59	.28	.04
Health care	.55	.25	.00
Education	.43	.45	.06
Perceptions of Executive Performance			
Mayor	.02	.81	.11
Governor	.16	.80	.10
President	.29	.52	.30
Opinions on personal and national economic progress in the past few years			
National	.05	.13	.81
Personal	.17	.09	.80

Source: 1982 electoral survey.

Note: Coefficients are the loadings of individual variables on underlying factors identified through varimax rotation. Three rotations identified the factors reported for the southeast sample, analysis of the northeast sample found three similar factors, while two rotations identified only two factors in the rural samples. The Kaiser-Meyer-Olkin measure of sampling adequacy (.83) suggests that the factor analysis is "meritorious," while Bartlett's test of sphericity is large and level of significance is zero.

one's own personal finances remained closely related to voters' perceptions of their leaders in the authoritarian state. This lack of autonomy among rural voters' retrospective judgments indicates the different bases for voting in rural Brazil.

Conclusion

This chapter presents compelling evidence that during the transition era voters' perceptions of government performance were constrained (statistically interrelated), were related to other political judgments such as a voter's self-image as "left" or "right," and were important causes of voters' choices. These patterns in the 1982 survey differ considerably from patterns in data available from the period of hard-line military rule only ten years before.[11] Cohen found support for the authoritarian government in 1972–1973 to be uncorrelated with other factors, while Lamounier found virtually no oppositional attitudes in a separate social survey of the northeast state of Bahia conducted during 1970–1971. The emergence of patterns commonly associated with accountability voting by 1982 confirms that rapid change occurred among Brazilian voters: public perceptions of executive performance and other evaluations of military government increasingly influenced Brazilian public opinion and increasingly determined voter choice during the transition to democracy.

While comparison of the 1982 survey data with similar data from a decade ago allows us to draw clear retrospective conclusions, at least two reasons counsel against generalizing about Brazil's future. First, while conclusions about changing patterns of accountability voting are based on data from 1974 to 1982, analysis is primarily based on the 1982 electoral survey. Because the 1982 elections were still held under restrictions on the media imposed by the military government, further research will be required to assess the durability of patterns found during democratic transition.

Even under the restrictive conditions of the 1982 election, voters' direct judgments about presidential performance and the state of the nation overruled their specific evaluations of government policies. In Brazil, accountability voting appears to focus strongly on direct public perceptions of executive performance. This analysis does provide evidence that judgments of executive performance are based on voters' attitudes about political and moral justice. But it must also be said that the high stakes of direct executive elections in the Brazilian presidential system leaves significant room for populist manipulation of public perceptions. Accountability voting will most likely continue to be plebiscitarian, and therefore somewhat unpredictable.

While this analysis of accountability voting in Brazil should not be used as a source for generalizations about voter alignment in es-

tablished democracies, several observations about "economic" theories of accountability are in order. First, to insist that citizens' perceptions of the economy are primary factors in voting in contemporary democracies is to underestimate the capacity of individuals to judge their leaders. Because citizens oppose or support their government for diverse reasons, analysis should focus on diversity and change in mass beliefs, not definitive causes of voters' choices.

Furthermore, the individual and collective impact of Brazilians' perceptions of accountability probably changed according to dramatically changing conditions during the transition itself. Placing too much emphasis on patterns in the 1982 data is unwarranted. The results of the analysis reveal emerging characteristics of Brazilian electoral behavior, not causes written in stone. The circumstances of future election campaigns and the evolution of democratic politics will determine which perceptions of accountability will prevail. Perhaps these findings are disturbing because no unilateral causes for voters' behavior can be established. But diversity, change, cross-cutting factors, and overdetermination are essential characteristics of mass belief systems in democratic electorates.[12] Complexity is essential to democratic politics.

Part of the problem is that stronger claims about the underlying motivations for voters' choices stray from the original purpose of theories of accountability. The original intent of "economic" theories of accountability was to explain short-term fluctuations in voter alignment above and beyond the widely recognized long-term sources of voter alignment such as an individual's class, party affiliation, positions on issues, and underlying political values. The original methodological contribution of "economic" theories was to compare official electoral results and economic statistics over extended periods of time by applying econometric modeling techniques. Given the original purpose and methodology of accountability theories, broader claims that seek to order the causes of voter behavior in subsequent research seem overstated. Accountability theory makes sense only in the context of other theories of class-based, party-based, issue-based, and value-based voting.

To isolate debates about accountability voting in a specialized subfield only distances electoral behavior research further from the liberal tradition. The classic liberal concept of accountability referred not only to the capacity of voters to pass judgment on government

policy, but also to the institutional mechanisms necessary to translate substantive public opinion into government policies and political action. This broader context has virtually disappeared from recent discussions of accountability. Granted, the liberal ideal of accountability is not easily measured. But the range of contemporary theories should equal that of the classic liberal interpretation of accountability—which refers both to mechanisms of citizen influence over the state *and* the efficiency and efficacy of state policies.

In conclusion, the emphasis on economic matters in recent theories of accountability voting seems inadequate on normative, theoretical, and empirical grounds. Normatively, theories of "economic" accountability reduce conceptions of voter rationality to far less than the core liberal and democratic belief that citizens are capable of evaluating their government. Theoretically, current analysts of accountability voting are determined to build a subfield of electoral behavior, in spite of the original objective of providing complementary explanations of short-term fluctuations. Finally, as an empirical description of Brazilian voters in democratic transition, recent accountability theories underestimate both the importance of direct plebiscitarian judgments of executive performance and the diverse perceptions of government policies that informed public opinion and voter choice.

— *Chapter 9* —

Participation: Corporatism, Civil Society Empowerment, or Electoral Politics in Mass Society?

In this mass democracy, the state has immediate contact with all its citizens. Indeed, all the important organizations functioning as mediators between the state and the individual are really entities connected with the state, rather than effectively autonomous organizations.

—Francisco Weffort

Classic liberal democratic theory holds that individual and group autonomy are both cause and consequence of a society's democratic practices. But more than a century has passed since John Stuart Mill and Alexis de Tocqueville argued that free association and political participation could produce both individual growth and collective empowerment. Today the complexity and personal anonymity of contemporary mass society present new challenges for the liberal tradition. Although much work has been done on participation in contemporary democracy,[1] social scientists have yet to equal the compelling normative and theoretical arguments of Tocqueville and Mill that linked social and political participation to the intellectual, moral, and political development of the people.

It may seem inappropriate to bring liberal expectations about association and participation to an analysis of Brazilian voters in dem-

ocratic transition. After all, Brazil's political system is far from liberal. Brazilian politics have long been described by both foreign and national observers as patrimonial, corporatist, clientelist, populist, and state-regulated.[2] As early as 1949, Victor Leal described how the clientelist organization of local power in rural areas impeded democratic forms of association and political participation.[3] For modernization theorists, the emergence of major urban areas in southeast Brazil by the 1950s created political environments that would certainly differ from the provincial rural areas dominated by clientelism. Here, it was expected that citizens' associations, parties, and ideology would reflect the organization of a society divided along class lines and separated into interest groups typical of modern politics.[4] However, by 1960 the impact of corporatist practices in Brazilian labor unions and other mass organizations developed during the postwar period was clearly evident.[5] Indeed, historians and social scientists agree that mass inclusion in Brazil took nonliberal forms: modern, class-based, ideological politics first emerged during the corporatist, authoritarian, nationalist, and populist Estado Novo of Getulio Vargas (1937–1945).

What was the impact of these state-centered and nonliberal legacies on political participation in Brazil? Labor unions are perhaps the most compelling and best documented example. Social science surveys of union members taken at the peak of hard-line military rule suggest that corporatist union structures continued to depoliticize the meaning of labor organization and social empowerment, despite widespread and frequent confrontations between labor and the state.[6] In 1971, members of Brazilian unions failed to value union membership and union autonomy as political means for securing workplace rights and expanding their powers of citizenship. Instead, members tended to perceive their unions as either welfare or service organizations. But corporatist unions not only altered the meaning of membership, they also depoliticized the views of members about the political world at large. In his analysis of social survey data from the peak of hard-line military rule (1972–1973), Youssef Cohen found that "workers not only placed little value on electoral politics, but also seemed to believe that such politics get in the way of good government."[7]

Did these realities change during the transition from military rule? Did new patterns of participation during the democratic transition inform public opinion and voter choice? Three theoretical perspectives present competing explanations about participation during the era of

transition. First, theories of civil society empowerment stress both the democratizing impact of an increasingly pluralistic Brazilian society and the critical role of new autonomous social organizations in galvanizing opposition to military rule.[8] Second, the more traditional perspective on Brazilian politics recognizes the changes that occurred during the transition period, but would suggest that the corporatist, clientelist, and state-centered character of Brazilian social organizations continue to keep most members and voters apolitical. Both theories of social empowerment and the recognition that Brazilian society retains corporatist elements describe critical aspects of political participation during the Brazilian transition. However, both perspectives tend to underestimate the emerging characteristics of mass electoral and party politics in Brazil.

This chapter develops a third explanation of political participation during the transition to democracy: that electoral politics and involvement in campaigns overshadowed both patterns of association emphasized by the above perspectives. Like the other dimensions of public opinion and voter alignment discussed in preceding chapters, the electoral survey data from 1974 to 1982 suggest that the direct popular appeals and patronage systems of Brazilian electoral campaigns were very influential.

There is little evidence in the survey data that new social organizations significantly politicized voters on the national level during the transition period. Indeed, no statistical relations appeared between membership in associations and patterns of political opposition. Instead, in the few cities and rural areas where membership was related to political matters, the political positions of association members tended to be determined by local factors and often favored the government. In short, instead of a changing civil society, the survey data suggest that Brazilian social organizations are still corporatist and that they still depoliticize their members. But contrary to both theories of civil-society empowerment and corporatism in Brazil, participation in *electoral* campaigns appears to have a considerable impact on Brazilian public opinion and voter alignment.

Compared to citizens of established democracies, many Brazilians participate in election campaigns, while few belong to social and community organizations (see table 9.1). Because voting is mandatory in Brazil, turnout levels are higher than in any country surveyed by Verba et al. except Austria.[9] And although suffrage was granted to illiterates

Table 9.1 Political Participation in Brazil and Four Other Countries (percent)

| | Brazil | | | | | | | |
| | | | Rural | | | | | United |
Type of Campaign Participation	Southeast	Northeast	Areas	Austria	India	Netherlands	States
Votes in national elections	78	76	73	96	59	—	72
Attends meetings or rallies	10	22	35	27	14	9	19
Contributes money to candidates	3	4	6	—	21	6	13
Displays campaign publicity	10	14	27	—	—	10	—
Belongs to community association	8	7	—	9	7	15	32

Sources: 1982 electoral survey; Verba, Nie, and Kim, *Participation and Political Equality*, p. 341.
a. Figures represent the percentage of registered voters. Voting is mandatory in Brazil.

only in the 1988 constitution, mandatory voting reduces dispropor-
tionalities in turnout based on education and income.[10] Attendance
at campaign meetings and campaign rallies is also comparable to levels
in other countries.

Two differences also appear in the comparative data. First, campaign contributions are considerably lower in Brazil than in India and
the United States. Second, campaign participation in the southeast
capitals remains considerably below that in the capital cities of the
less-developed northeast and in the two rural areas included in the
1982 survey. Although Nie et al. explain higher political participation
in rural and less-developed areas as evidence of a declining sense of
community in the cities, the present analysis suggests that in Brazil
political factors are more important: voters in developed and urban
areas tend to respond to the direct popular appeals of executive elections, while patronage systems prevail in the rural and less-developed
areas of Brazil—thus affecting the vote turnout.[11]

Social Organizations and Brazilian Voters in Democratic Transition

Did Brazilian social organizations become more politicized and influence public opinion and voter choice during the transition period?
With the exception of labor unions, little evidence of this influence
could be found; only 5.4 percent of survey respondents belonged to
neighborhood and professional associations, and they were no more
politicized than nonmembers or voters at large. The 1982 survey data
suggest that predictions of fundamental changes in social organizations and their power to politicize voters during the transition period
may be premature.

Table 9.2 presents the results of cross-tabulating respondents'
membership in social organizations and labor unions with their intention to vote in the 1982 gubernatorial election. Not only do very few
belong to community or professional organizations (5.4 in southeast
sample), but also there is little statistical difference between members
and nonmembers in their intention to vote or not in 1982. Indeed,
whereas 62.4 percent of nonmembers planned to vote for governor
by party, only 55.3 percent of members of social organizations declared such an intention.

Table 9.2 Intention to Vote Among Members of Social Organizations, Labor Unions, and Respondents in General, 1982 (percent)

	Member of Social Organization			Member of Labor Union			All Respondents
	Yes	No	NR/NA	Yes	No	NR/NA	
Intends to vote	55.3	62.4	55.8	66.5	53.6	35.5	56.1
(N)	(52)	(264)	(681)	(346)	(1,025)	(11)	(1,382)
Does not intend to vote	44.7	37.6	44.2	33.5	46.4	64.5	43.9
(N)	(42)	(159)	(540)	(174)	(887)	(20)	(1,081)
Total	5.4	24.3	70.3	21.1	77.6	1.3	100.0
(N)	(94)	(423)	(1,221)	(520)	(1,912)	(31)	(2,463)

Source: 1982 electoral survey.

Note: The figures for "all respondents" are not accurate row totals for social organizations because of the 725 missing cases.

Union membership is moderately related to respondents' intention to vote in the 1982 survey. The differences between union members and nonmembers is statistically significant: of the 520 southeast urban respondents who were union members (21.1 percent of the sample), 66.5 percent intended to vote, a moderate (but significant) 10.4 percent more than the 56.1 percent of respondents generally.

Cross-tabulation, presented in table 9.3, between membership in social organizations and labor unions with three types of political conceptualizations—that is, voting on the basis of (1) direct or unmediated, (2) personality-based, or (3) ideological or group-interest responses to political figures—suggest that community and professional organizations did not politicize voters in 1982. The proportion of social organization members who responded in terms of ideology or group interest is identical to the percentage of the total sample who responded in those terms (6.4 percent). And while the proportion of members in social organizations who justified their vote in "immediate" terms (17.0 percent) is greater than that of respondents generally (11.2 percent), their low number (16) suggests that this difference is most likely to be significant.

In sum, contrary to notions about civil society empowerment, members of social organizations in the survey data were no more likely to vote, and no more likely to explain their choice for governor in immediate, personality-based, or ideological/group interest terms, than were respondents at large. Further research may clarify the complex political realities connecting local politics to social organizations not revealed by the survey data. It is also possible that social organizations may have begun to politicize their members after the transition to civilian rule in 1985, or may do so in the future in a fully democratic Brazil. But survey results from the transition period provide no evidence of politicization among members of social and community organizations.

Labor unions appear to have been somewhat more influential. The survey data suggest that the members of labor unions differ from nonmembers, both because more intended to vote and because they tend to justify their vote on one of the above-mentioned criteria. Social scientists who have analyzed labor union politics during the Brazilian transition suggest that repression and persecution of unions by the authoritarian state reinforced corporatist factions within the unions and depoliticized the rank and file.[12] The problem *is not* that

Table 9.3 Types of Political Conceptualization Among Members of Social Organizations, Labor Unions, and Respondents in General, 1982 (percent)

Type of Political Conceptualization	Member of Social Organization			Member of Labor Union			All Respondents
	Yes	No	NR/NA	Yes	No	NR/NA	
Ideological or group interest	6.4	7.1	6.1	9.0	5.7	6.5	6.4
(N)	(6)	(30)	(75)	(47)	(109)	(2)	(158)
Immediate	17.0	13.7	11.9	12.9	10.9	3.2	11.2
(N)	(16)	(58)	(145)	(67)	(208)	(1)	(276)
Personalistic	27.7	36.6	32.9	40.6	33.1	22.6	34.6
(N)	(26)	(155)	(402)	(211)	(633)	(7)	(851)
None or no response	48.9	42.6	49.1	37.5	50.3	67.7	47.8
(N)	(46)	(180)	(599)	(195)	(962)	(21)	(1,178)
Total	5.2	24.3	70.3	21.1	77.6	1.3	100.0
(N)	(94)	(423)	(1,221)	(520)	(1,912)	(31)	(2,463)

Source: 1982 electoral survey.
Note: See Appendix 3. Column totals report the percent of total sample.

Brazilian workers are unorganized. In 1982 over 21 percent of survey respondents in the southeast capitals, 17 percent in the northeast capitals, and a full 46 percent in the two rural areas, were union members. Those who have studied labor unions during the transition era recognize the difficulties of transforming the corporatist character of Brazilian unions on the national level due to the sheer size and complexity of the country. Despite the presence of new, independent union movements in São Paulo and other southeast capitals, changing the corporatist structure of unions across Brazil would require profound legal and organizational changes in how labor unions relate to the state.[13]

Nonetheless, labor unionists clearly expressed a preference for left and center-left parties in the 1982 survey (see table 9.4). Three of the parties that emerged in the wake of the 1979 party reform directly targeted the labor vote in the 1982 election: the Workers party (PT) founded by the new independent unions; the Democratic Labor party (PDT), organized by Leonel Brizola after the Supreme Electoral Court denied him the logo of the pre-1965 populist labor party; and the Brazilian Labor party (PTB), which usurped the traditional logo sought by Brizola. Union members were significantly more likely to

Table 9.4 Union Members Among Those Intending to Vote for Governor, by Party, 1982 (percent)

	Left		Center-Left	Right		All Respondents
	PT	PDT	PMDB	PTB	PDS	
Union member	32.6	28.3	28.7	16.8	17.8	25.0
(N)	(42)	(77)	(141)	(18)	(68)	(346)
Nonmember	66.7	71.0	70.0	82.2	81.2	74.2
(N)	(86)	(193)	(347)	(88)	(311)	(1,025)
Total	9.3	19.7	35.5	7.7	27.7	100.0
(N)	(129)	(272)	(492)	(107)	(383)	(1,382)

Source: 1982 electoral survey.

Note: The "not available" or "no answer" category is not reported because only 1–4 cases were missing values.

express an intention to vote for the PT, PDT, and the opposition PMDB than for the more conservative PTB or PDS in the 1982 election.

The survey data also caution against inferring that Brazilian labor unions have had a broad progressive impact on voters during the democratic transition. Fewer union members in the northeast capitals and virtually none in the two rural areas of the 1982 survey were inclined to vote for left and center-left parties. Union members in the advanced southeastern cities were 14.9 percent more likely to vote for the PT than the PDS, and 11.0 percent more likely to vote for the PMDB than the PDS. In the capitals of the less-developed northeast, labor union members were only 6.8 percent more likely to vote for the PMDB than for the PDS. And in rural areas, the difference among labor union members of 1.3 percent is insignificant. In sum, the corporatist and clientelist practices of Brazilian labor unions still appear to have a depoliticizing effect in the rural and less-developed regions of the country.

Union membership also remained unrelated to all four underlying types of participation (campaign activity, voting, campaign information, social organization) identified by factor analysis of the sixteen measures of political participation (see table 9.7, below). While the 1982 data show a significant relation between union membership and intent to vote for center-left and left parties, union membership remained statistically unrelated to other dimensions of public opinion and voter alignment such as positions on local and national issues, perceptions of accountability, or other attributes of mass belief systems included in the survey data. Whereas the traditional perspective, which stresses the depoliticizing consequences of corporatist unions, still appears valid, the impact of other social organizations on public opinion and voter alignment fails to have materialized.[14]

Campaign Participation and Brazilian Voters in Democratic Transition

Although social organizations failed to politicize Brazilian voters and labor unions had only a moderate effect, participating in electoral campaigns had a substantial impact. The survey data provide strong evidence that involvement in electoral campaigns influenced Brazilian

public opinion and voter alignment during the transition period more pervasively and in fundamentally different ways from that predicted by those who study civil society empowerment and corporatism in Brazil. Politics for Brazilians during the protracted transition, 1974–1985, meant one electoral campaign after another, often in bewildering succession. Indeed, the experience of the transition period reaffirms that national elections are the principal collective political experience in Brazil.

Because voting is mandatory in Brazil, levels of participation in election campaigns during the transition period were extraordinary. While many have stressed the expansion of the Brazilian electorate before the military intervention of 1964, the dramatic extension of suffrage under military rule is less widely recognized. Suffrage did increase from 2.65 million voters under Getulio Vargas's Estado Novo in 1940 to 11.45 million in 1950 and 15.54 million in 1960 (see table 9.5). But the extension of suffrage continued under military rule, reaching to 28.96 million voters in 1970 and 50.61 million in 1982. Finally, the 1986 reregistration of voters conducted by the Brazilian Supreme Electoral Court after the transition to civilian rule widened the electorate even further, to over 82 million voters.

My experience as observer during both Fernando Henrique Cardoso's 1985 mayoral campaign and his 1986 Senate campaign overwhelmed a scholar accustomed to the more genteel routines of U.S. and European election campaigns. Brazilian literary critics have insightfully emphasized the *carnavalesco* quality of Brazilian electoral campaigns.[15] Elections during the period of democratic transition

Table 9.5 The Brazilian Electorate, 1940–1990

	1940	1950	1960	1970	1982[a]	1990[b]
No. of voters (in millions)	2.65	11.45	15.54	28.96	58.61	82.32
As % of population	6.45	22.05	22.18	31.10	49.26	56.77

Source: Instituto Brasileiro de Geografia e Estatística, *Estatísticas Históricas do Brasil*, p. 591.

a. Figures for 1982 are calculated on the basis of the 1980 census.

b. Figures for 1990 are based on preliminary estimates by the IBGE for the 1991 census, reported in *Istoe*, 15 January 1992.

called forth new civic pride and mass participation, both theretofore associated with the realities of military rule. Candidates were transformed overnight into media stars. Campaign news coverage and the two additional hours of air time per evening reserved for party programs often reached the upper levels of IBOPE scores. (IBOPE is the Brazilian broadcast rating company.) Campaign rallies, often organized by legislators in their de facto districts, drew vast numbers when leading candidates for governor and senator appeared. Electoral campaigns and rallies linked the broad appeal of executive races to the patronage machines of federal and state deputies—even in the public squares of the most remote villages. And because federal and state deputies from the same party competed on statewide proportional representation lists, at times only fistfights decided who would stand closest to the better-known candidates in majoritarian races for senator and governor. Finally, on election day, voters were virtually assaulted by competing *boca de urna* (literally, "ballot-mouth") canvassers organized by candidates and parties as they entered the voting booth.

Campaign participation in Brazil can mean anything from watching television to fulfilling traditional patronage obligations. However, the predominance of face-to-face types of participation in the less-developed northeast region and rural areas provide further evidence of the uneven development of mass politics in Brazil (see table 9.6). In the rural areas, 60.3 percent of respondents were personally contacted by party organizers getting out the vote (roughly double the number reported in urban areas); 35.1 percent of respondents in the rural surveys had attended campaign rallies (compared to 21.7 and 9.6 percent, respectively, in the northeast and in southeastern urban areas); and 27.8 percent had displayed campaign material at home or at work (compared to 14.5 and 10.4 percent in the urban areas).

In comparison, campaign participation in the most advanced cities of the southeast was largely confined to media exposure. In the southeast capitals, 76.7 percent of respondents had watched television and heard radio coverage of the campaign. While similar levels of media exposure were reported by respondents in the less-developed northeast capitals, only 58.9 percent of rural voters had seen media programming. Because people in developed countries and cities tend to be less directly involved in election campaigns, analysts have concluded that politics is somewhat peripheral to those who live in mod-

Table 9.6 Types of Campaign Participation, 1982 (percent)

Type of Campaign Participation	Southeast	Northeast	Rural Areas
Watched radio and TV programs	76.7	76.5	58.9
Was contacted personally by party or candidate	30.5	31.7	60.3
Attended campaign rally	9.6	21.7	35.1
Displayed campaign publicity	10.4	14.5	27.8
Attended party meeting	7.4	7.6	10.5
Served as volunteer	6.4	6.8	11.2

Source: 1982 electoral survey.
Note: Response categories were "yes/no," "no answer," and "no response." Negative responses and the latter two categories fluctuated between 0 and 3 percent and were omitted for readability.

ern urban areas, but important to rural voters. The primary explanation for these differences is the reduced sense of community and the social and political isolation characteristic of modern urban life.[16] However, the frequent personal contacts, willingness to display campaign materials, and heavy attendance at rallies in rural Brazil suggests that political factors are important: parties and patronage machines mobilized voters in less-developed areas.

The widespread face-to-face campaign participation reported in the 1982 election once again suggests that theories focusing on the empowerment of civil society and Brazil's state-centered character underestimate the nature of emerging mass politics in Brazil. The 1982 electoral survey was conducted in the two weeks preceding the election, well before the extensive personal contacts through *boca de urna* tactics on election day. Nonetheless, over 60 percent of rural voters and over 30 percent of city voters were personally contacted by campaign workers representing a political party or candidate.

In practical terms, this means that winning national elections requires intensive direct contacts with voters across Brazil. National election campaigns are the domain not of amateur organizations or civil associations that influence some voters, but of political parties or electoral alliances that organize support across diverse municipalities,

states, and regions. Local politics alone does not suffice. The extent of personal contact by parties and candidates suggests that, instead of emphasizing civil society empowerment and Brazil's state-centered government, mass participation must be analyzed on a broader level; to do otherwise is to risk the fallacy of composition. Assessing the impact of campaign participation on the mass public is fundamentally different from studying the impact of social organizations on their members.

What effect did campaign involvement have on Brazilian voters in the transition era? Rather than an indicator of how people would vote, participation can be seen as socializing voters and informing public opinion. The 1982 survey suggests that Brazilian voters in urban areas participated in campaigns in many of the same ways identified by Verba, Nie, and Kim in their analysis of seven established democracies.[17] Furthermore, specific types of participation among Brazilian voters appear to be interrelated in patterns typical of advanced democratic electorates, despite the protracted, elite-dominated, state-centered character of the Brazilian transition, and despite restrictions on media coverage and campaign programming in 1982.

Table 9.7 presents the results of factor analysis that identifies three underlying tendencies in participation among Brazilian voters in the southeastern capitals: (1) campaign activity, (2) voting, (3) campaign information, and (4) social organization. The total percentage of variance explained by the four factors is 45.5 percent, a high figure.[18]

Identifying four underlying types of participation among Brazilian voters in the transition era suggests that to understand electoral and party politics in Brazil, one must pay greater attention to the emergence of mass politics in that country. Discussions of civil society empowerment and Brazilian corporatism focus on the links between various types of participation and across various levels of collective action.[19] Both comparative analyses of mass participation and the present study suggest that anyone who attempts to connect types of social and political participation to political change in general must proceed with great care. The survey data provides no evidence linking membership in community and professional groups with other kinds of participation such as campaign involvement or voting. Again, theories of social empowerment and of state corporatism underestimate the emergent characteristics of mass participation in Brazil.

Table 9.7 The Underlying Structure of Political Participation, 1982

	Factor			
	1: Campaign Activity	2: Voting	3: Campaign Information	4: Social Organization
Type of Campaign participation				
Served as volunteer	.73	.03	.03	.02
Displayed campaign publicity	.66	.01	.01	.07
Attended party meeting	.63	.03	.14	.12
Attended campaign rally	.57	.00	.12	.00
Contributed money to candidate	.57	.04	.19	.04
Was personally contacted by party or candidate	.34	.21	.11	.07
Commitment to voting				
Voted for senator, 1978	.03	.80	.05	.00
Voted for senator, 1974	.04	.78	.02	.10
Intended to vote, 1982	.14	.62	.02	.16
Awareness of campaign information				
Listened to radio news	.06	.00	.70	.09
Watched TV debates	.06	.17	.67	.06
Read political news reports	.25	.02	.59	.02
Watched TV coverage	.03	.92	.56	.07
Membership in association or labor union				
Professional association	.05	.92	.00	.81
Community association	.05	.05	.01	.81
Labor union	.12	.27	.02	.09

Source: 1982 electoral survey.
Note: Coefficients are the loadings of individual variables on underlying factors identified through varimax rotation in SPSS/PC.

While further research is required to understand the causal logic, political consequences, and interrelationships among these types of participation, campaign involvement does indeed appear to have had a politicizing effect on Brazilian voters in 1974–1985. The extent to which respondents were active in campaigns and were informed about the 1982 election was significantly related to both their choice of party and their ability to justify their choice in more sophisticated terms.

Both involvement in a campaign and awareness of campaign publicity were related to respondents' intention to vote in 1982 (see table 9.8). While 56.1 percent of all respondents planned to vote, 67.1 percent of those highly informed about the election, and 69.7 percent of those participating in several types of campaign activity, expressed an intention to vote. In sum, significant and substantive relations exist between campaign participation, knowledge of campaign information, and intention to vote, a relation not found for membership in social organizations.

Furthermore, those who participate in campaigns and are aware of campaign publicity also tend to have more sophisticated approaches to politics. Once again, in 1982 not only did more respondents express personalistic and immediate conceptions of politics, they also participated in campaigns as often, or more often, than those who held ideological or interest-group concepts of politics (see table 9.9). Of the 1,194 respondents ranked as highly knowledgeable about the 1982 campaign in the southeast, only 5.4 percent justified their intent to vote for governor in terms of ideology or group interest. But 9.2 and 35.8 percent, respectively, of those who were active in campaigns justified their intention to vote for governor by party in "immediate" and personality-based terms. In sum, responses citing the latter two conceptions of politics are similarly sophisticated on the individual level and are far more numerous than those giving ideology and group interest as a basis for choice.

Conclusion

Since the mid-1970s, social scientists have argued that new, independent union movements, progressive neighborhood organizations, professional associations, and other social groups have mitigated the state-centered character of Brazilian society. In fact, political theory

Table 9.8 Relation Between Campaign Participation, Knowledge about the Campaign, and Intention to Vote, 1982 (percent)

	Degree of Campaign Participation			Level of Campaign Information			All Respondents
	High	Low	NA/NR	High	Low	NA/NR	
Intention to vote	69.7	55.3	44.6	67.1	55.2	23.4	56.1
(N)	(338)	(825)	(211)	(654)	(659)	(69)	(1,382)
No intention to vote	30.3	44.7	55.4	32.9	44.8	76.6	43.9
(N)	(147)	(666)	(262)	(320)	(535)	(226)	(1,081)
Total	19.8	60.9	19.3	39.5	48.5	12.0	100.0
(N)	(485)	(1,491)	(473)	(974)	(1,194)	(295)	(2,463)

Source: 1982 electoral survey.

Note: Columns are dichotomized scales constructed on the basis of all questions about participation and campaign information in the 1982 survey. A single control category (column total) for all respondents is reported because of the low number of missing values. Chi-Square Pearson estimates of 62.09 and 176.82 are significant at .00.

Table 9.9 Relation Between Types of Political Conceptualization and Levels of Campaign Participation and Information, 1982 (percent)

	Degree of Campaign Participation			Level of Campaign Information			All Respondents
	High	Low	NR/NA	High	Low	NR/NA	
Ideological or group interest	11.3	5.9	3.0	5.4	8.5	3.4	6.4
(N)	(55)	(88)	(14)	(65)	(83)	(10)	(158)
Immediate	16.1	10.0	10.1	9.2	15.6	4.7	11.2
(N)	(78)	(149)	(48)	(110)	(152)	(14)	(276)
Personalistic	36.9	35.6	28.5	35.8	39.2	13.9	34.6
(N)	(179)	(531)	(135)	(428)	(382)	(41)	(851)
None or no response	35.7	48.5	58.4	49.5	36.7	78.0	47.8
(N)	(173)	(723)	(276)	(591)	(357)	(230)	(1,178)
Total	19.8	60.9	19.3	48.5	39.5	12.0	100.0
(N)	(485)	(1,491)	(473)	(1,194)	(974)	(295)	(2,463)

Source: 1982 electoral survey.
Note: On the types of conceptualization, see Appendix 3. A single control category (column total) for all respondents is reported because of the low number of missing values.

and practice in Brazil increasingly focused on civil society—quite unusual in a nation with a traditionally strong state. Most agree that the empowerment of civil society played a fundamental part in delegitimizing Brazil's military rulers, bringing electoral change, and fostering democratization. Given such consensus, I expected to discover that community and professional associations politicized their members and organized Brazilian public opinion and voter alignment during the democratic transition. But I did not. With the important exception of labor unions, belonging to social organizations remained unrelated to voter choice or justifications of choice in more sophisticated terms. Particular local associations have undoubtedly politicized certain groups in Brazilian society, but this is not the broad link between social organization and national politics implied by received ideas about civil society empowerment.

Instead, the data suggest that campaign participation influences Brazilian public opinion and voter alignment. Quantitative methods may be crude instruments for describing the *carnavalesco* impact of national elections on Brazilian voters.[20] But far from identifying final causes or definitive underlying structures, this chapter seeks to identify emergent characteristics of campaign participation among Brazilian voters in democratic transition—in both a historical and theoretical sense. And the survey evidence indicates that direct popular appeals and patronage organized campaign participation and influenced Brazilian voters far more than would be expected according to new ideas about civil-society empowerment or older ideas about corporatist tendencies in Brazilian society.

— Chapter 10 —

Perceptions of Democracy and Democratic Institutions

Political stability and democratization depend on political culture.[1] Indeed, by returning to the basic concerns of Almond and Verba's ground-breaking *The Civic Culture*, political scientists have generated debates about political culture both during democratic transitions and in established democracies.[2] Guillermo O'Donnell, Philippe Schmitter, and Laurence Whitehead argue that experiences of repression, torture, and exile suffered under military rule may have pushed the political cultures of Latin American countries toward democracy.[3] But Howard Wiarda and Atilio Boron caution that the Hispanic cultural legacy contains authoritarian elements widely embraced by Latin American military leaders and antidemocratic movements.[4] Ronald Inglehart also argues that European and North American democracies still provide evidence for classic arguments that link culture to both economic development and the consolidation of democracy. Nonetheless, Seligson and Mueller present compelling evidence that Inglehart's claims about the link between political culture and democracy are amiss in Latin America.[5]

This chapter examines perceptions of democracy and democratic institutions among Brazilian voters in democratic transition both to address these questions and to clarify the similarities and differences between Brazilian voters and advanced democratic electorates. Earlier chapters have discussed how partisanship, positions on national issues,

perceptions of executive performance, and campaign participation rapidly organized public opinion and voter alignment during the Brazilian transition. Each of these dimensions also provides compelling evidence that immediate and personalistic conceptions of politics prevailed over European ideologies and U.S. notions of group interest. The survey data also suggest that these different conceptions of politics are both cause and result of the plebiscitarian appeals and patronage machines that dominate Brazilian party-electoral politics.

This chapter argues that party-electoral politics in Brazil after 1974 also generated values, beliefs, and judgments typically associated with political cultures in established mass democracies. However, three differences between Brazilian voters and those in advanced democracies are also critical. First, the causal weight of the left-right dimension and direct judgments of executive performance in the 1982 survey data suggest that direct, unmediated, plebiscitarian perceptions of government and conceptions of substantive justice influence Brazilian voters more than voters in the advanced democracies. Brazil's legacy of state-led development, state-centered populist inclusion, and the continued power of direct popular appeals and machine politics not only make Brazilian party-electoral politics fundamentally different; they also provide Brazilian voters with fundamentally different conceptions of politics.

The second critical difference between political culture in Brazil and that normally associated with advanced democratic electorates is the extremely uneven development of mass belief systems in Brazil. Differences between voters in urban and rural areas reflect not only the uneven development of the economy, society, and culture, but also the uneven development of mass politics.[6] Analysis of these differences is possible because the 1982 electoral survey was conducted simultaneously in seven capital cities of the advanced southeast region, three capitals of the less-developed northeast, and two rural areas in the southeast region. The survey data suggest that direct popular judgments tend to predominate over local concerns in urban areas, and that patronage machines tend to reinforce the conservatism and provincialism of rural voters.

Perceptions of Democracy among Brazilian Voters

Did the transition from military rule endow the idea of democracy with procedural and substantive meaning in Brazilian public opinion?

This section examines perceptions of democracy in Brazil, first as reflected in attitudes toward the political system in general, then in tolerance for political action, and finally in people's capacity to understand politics and political issues. Regarding general attitudes toward the political system, the data confirm the greater salience of politics and the state for rural voters.

More widespread interest in politics and greater satisfaction with the government among rural voters further indicate the uneven development of mass politics in Brazil. While only 10.8 and 8.5 percent of respondents in the surveys of southeast and northeast cities, respectively, declared themselves "very interested in politics," roughly three times that number among rural respondents (29.1 percent) expressed interest.[7] Belief that the government is attentive to people's needs is also significantly higher in rural areas: 17.2 percent of rural respondents reported such belief, compared to only 12.4 and 9.8 of southeast and northeast urban respondents. To understand how these attitudes translate into citizenship, further analysis is required.

Tolerance of political activism is another critical dimension of liberal and democratic attitudes in political culture.[8] The 1982 survey contained three questions that asked respondents if they approved or disapproved of the following types of political activity: circulating petitions, organizing labor strikes, and conducting sit-ins to demand redress from public agencies. Brazilians in the northeast and rural regions proved to be considerably less tolerant than their southeastern counterparts of such activities. Rural voters may express more interest in politics, but their notion of what constitutes acceptable political action is quite limited. Two or three times more southeastern and northeast urban respondents approved of writing petitions, conducting strikes, and the nonviolent occupation of public buildings, than rural respondents (see table 10.1). The rural intolerance of three traditional strategies of political action in Brazil confirms the underlying conservatism and passivity of rural political culture.

Whereas tolerance of dissent and contestation is critical for a political culture that values democracy, perhaps a more important indicator is how citizens perceive the act of voting. Responses to survey questions on the meaning and value of elections are also distributed in ways that suggest the uneven development of political culture and mass politics among Brazilian voters (see table 10.2). Southeastern city dwellers are more apt to believe that elections can better the lot

Table 10.1   Public Approval of Direct Political Action, 1982
              (percent)

	Southeastern Cities	Northeastern Cities	Rural Areas
Circulating petitions	80.4	76.2	46.3
Organizing labor strikes	45.1	50.5	19.1
Conducting sit-ins at public buildings	27.2	33.7	10.9
(N)	(2,463)	(1,860)	(481)

Source: 1982 electoral survey.
Note: Percentages for nonapproval and *no response* and *no answer* were omitted for readability.

Table 10.2   Views on the Value of Voting and Who Benefits from
              Voting, 1982 (percent)

	Southeastern Cities	Northeastern Cities	Rural Areas
Respondents who believe that the poor will benefit from the victory of their candidate for governor	23.0	16.2	9.9
Respondents who would vote, even if not required by law:			
As a duty	40.2	28.4	19.1
As a personal favor	1.5	2.4	15.0
(N)	(2,463)	(1,860)	(481)

Source: 1982 electoral survey.
Note: Other responses are omitted for readability.

of popular sectors: to the open question, "Who would benefit from the election of your candidate for governor?" 23.0 percent responded that the principal beneficiaries would be *o povo* (the people, popular

sectors). In comparison, only 16.2 percent of voters in northeast capitals and 9.9 percent of rural voters responded in similar ways. Elections appear to hold much less promise for voters in the northeast and rural areas of Brazil.

The greater number of respondents who believe that *executive* elections will better social conditions in the southeast urban samples also supports the argument that the plebiscitarian character of voting in Brazil tends to be concentrated in the more advanced urban areas. (Belief that the legislature could or would improve social conditions was roughly half as strong.) Other questions tapped the values that Brazilians ascribed to voting more directly. When asked if respondents would continue to vote, even if not required to by law, the most common unprompted positive explanation in urban areas indicated that voting represented a civic and democratic duty. In the southeast urban sample, 40.0 percent of respondents cited such reasons, but only 28.4 percent of voters in the northeast capitals and 19.1 percent of rural voters did so.

If any doubt remains about the central importance of patronage in rural Brazil, further evidence can be found in survey responses indicating why people would vote even if not required by law. Fifteen percent of rural respondents declared that they would still vote as a personal favor, or to *pagar uma promessa*. This debt is not religious, not otherworldly, but to meet personal political obligations to local political authorities. Only 1.5 and 2.4 percent of respondents from the capitals in the southeast and northeast responded in such terms.

The regional variations in Brazilians' perceptions of democracy have been examined, first regarding general attitudes toward the system, then toward democracy as an organizational and institutional process. The asymmetries in mass belief are even greater on the level of policy culture. Democratic policies can only be produced in a political culture in which citizens are aware of compelling national issues of the day and understand them to some extent; moreover, individual and aggregate opinions about these issues must display some degree of structure.[9] Table 10.3 displays the proportion of correct and coherent responses to open survey questions about important national issues and problems. Of the five policy questions included in the 1982 survey, rural voters were largely unable to define or explain their substantive content. The only policy question accurately described by survey respondents across Brazil, in rural as well as urban areas, con-

Table 10.3 Understanding of Political Issues, 1982 (percent)

	Southeastern Cities	Northeastern Cities	Rural Areas
Respondents who could describe the political *left* and *right*	24.7	21.7	8.8
Respondents who knew the meaning of direct elections	30.6	24.1	9.2
Respondents who could define *abertura* (political opening)	36.0	22.0	15.3
Respondents favoring legalization of the Communist party	12.7	14.8	1.7
Respondents opposing legalization of the Communist party	48.0	38.3	36.9
(N)	(2,463)	(1,860)	(481)

Source: 1982 electoral survey.
Note: Figures represent the percentage of coherent responses to open-ended questions describing each political issue or fact.

cerned the legalization of the Communist party. The sole contribution of military rule toward informing citizens and increasing the political and ideological sophistication of Brazilian voters was apparently to encourage anticommunism. On all other political issues, rural voters had little conception of the meaning of democracy or democratization.

The Left-Right Dimension

Inglehart argues that voters' self-definition regarding their placement on a left-to-right continuum summarizes underlying conceptions of substantive justice: "The core meaning of the left-right dimension is

whether one supports or opposes social change in an egalitarian direction."[10] Survey respondents from across the spectrum of political parties identified themselves as left or right in ways that confirm the significance of this dimension as described in chapter 1 (see table 10.4). The five parties that emerged from the 1979 party reform and that contested the 1982 election can be ranked from the PT and PDT on the left, the PMDB in the center-left, to the PTB and PDS on the right. Although the 1974 and 1978 national election surveys failed to ask about the left-right identification of respondents, the pre-1979 parties presented the public with an unusual two-party situation under authoritarian conditions: ARENA on the right, and the MDB on the center-left. Indeed, because the PT, PDT, and PTB remained weak outside southeast urban areas, a de facto two-party situation still existed in the 1982 election throughout the less-developed northeast and rural areas.

Table 10.4   Left, Center-Left, and Right Self-Placement and
            Respondents' Intended Vote for Governor, by Party,
            1982

Voters' Self-Identification	Left		Center-Left	Right	
	PT	PDT	PDMB	PTB	PDS
Southeast					
Left	56.7	36.8	33.7	8.0	2.3
Center-Left	43.3	56.6	58.6	56.3	64.8
Right	0.0	6.6	6.6	25.0	33.0
(N)	(30)	(76)	(92)	(16)	(88)
Northeast					
Left	—	—	33.3	—	2.3
Center-Left	—	—	61.5	—	64.8
Right	—	—	5.1	—	33.0
(N)	(1)	(4)	(39)	(6)	(27)

Source: 1982 electoral survey.

Note: Unfortunately, surveys in rural areas did not include questions about voters' left-right self-placement. No results are reported for the PT, PDT, and PTB in the northeast because there were too few cases to be statistically significant.

Further analysis of left-right self-identification among Brazilian voters will be required because 1,755 (71.3 percent) of the 2,463 respondents in the southeast urban sample did not place themselves on the left-right scale. As noted above, while McDonough, Pina, and Barnes also found that Spanish voters were reluctant to answer questions about their left-right self-identification early in the transition from authoritarianism, more were willing to do so in subsequent surveys taken in democratic Spain.[11] Furthermore, whether or not one answered the question about left-right self-placement in the 1982 survey appeared to be largely based on social class. Cross-tabulating left-right self-placement with per-capita family income and occupation shows considerable and statistically significant differences between those who took a stance on the left-right scale and those who did not (see table 10.5). While roughly half of respondents with manual occupations or low incomes ignored the question, only 14.1 percent of respondents with high incomes and 20.1 percent reporting nonmanual occupations did not respond. Further analysis of the left-right dimension in a fully democratic Brazil will be needed.

Immediate and Personality-Based Conceptions of Politics and Attitudes Toward Democracy

Do Brazilian voters who think about politics in ideological, immediate, and personality-based terms perceive and value democratic institutions differently from voters at large? This chapter has focused on the extent to which voters are informed about politics, the value they ascribe to democratic institutions, and their interest in politics. The survey data also suggest that Brazilian voters with personalistic and immediate conceptions of politics seem as capable of sustaining liberal and democratic politics as those who approach politics in terms of ideology or group interest.

Survey respondents who think about politics in personality-based or immediate terms not only vastly outnumber those with ideological and group-interest conceptions, they also tend to be equally interested in and informed about politics. They also value democracy and democratic institutions at the same level as those who think in terms of ideology and group interest (see table 10.6). Of the 1,194 respondents who demonstrated high political interest in the southeast sample

Table 10.5 Family Income, Occupation, and Left-Right Self-Placement, 1982

Type of Stance Taken	Per-Capita Family Income[a]			Occupation[b]		All Respondents
	High	Low	NR/NA	Nonmanual	Manual	
Left or right	85.9	52.4	76.8	79.9	50.3	70.5
(N)						(1,524)
None	14.1	47.6	23.2	20.1	49.7	29.5
(N)						(639)
Total	47.9	43.8	8.4	54.4	45.6	100.0
(N)	(1,035)	(947)	(181)	(865)	(725)	(2,163)

Source: 1982 electoral survey.
a. Chi² Pearson = 270.72, sign. = .00, missing n = 300.
b. Chi² Pearson = 154.29, sign. = .00, missing n = 873.

Table 10.6 Types of Conceptualization Among Respondents Interested and Informed About Politics and Committed to Democracy, 1982

Types of Conceptualization of Politics	Level of Political Interest[a]			Awareness of Political Information[b]		Commitment to Democratic Institutions[c]		All Respondents
	High	Medium	Low	High	Low	High	Low	
Ideological or group interest	9.9	6.4	2.1	8.0	6.2	6.3	7.2	6.4
(N)	(72)	(73)	(12)	(79)	(49)	(46)	(77)	(158)
Immediate	17.5	10.0	5.9	15.7	11.1	12.0	10.5	11.2
(N)	(127)	(114)	(33)	(155)	(88)	(87)	(113)	(276)
Personalistic	42.0	35.5	24.2	39.0	40.8	39.8	37.1	34.6
(N)	(305)	(404)	(136)	(386)	(323)	(289)	(398)	(851)
None or no response	30.6	48.1	67.9	37.4	41.8	41.9	45.3	47.8
(N)	(222)	(548)	(382)	(370)	(331)	(304)	(486)	(1,178)
Total	29.9	46.9	23.2	41.9	33.5	40.3	59.7	100.0
(N)	(726)	(1,139)	(563)	(990)	(791)	(726)	(1,074)	(2,463)

Source: 1982 electoral survey.

Note: A single control category (All Respondents) is reported at right because the distribution of types for each cross-tabulation was virtually identical, despite missing values for 35, 99, and 663 respondents. Columns are recoded scales. Political interest was measured by adding responses to questions about interest in politics and interest in the campaign. Political information was measured by combining five variables that asked respondents to name the gubernatorial candidates of the five parties. The value of democratic institutions was measured by combining responses to questions about whether people are capable of voting, whether parties help Brazil, and whether illiterates should be granted the vote.

a. Chi² Pearson = 193.21, sign. = <.001, missing n = 35.

b. Chi² Pearson = 212.56, sign. = <.001, missing n = 99.

c. Chi² Pearson = 3.25, sign. = <.001, missing n = 663.

of the 1982 survey, 9.9 percent justified their intention to vote for governor in terms of ideology or group interest (compared with 6.4 percent of all respondents). But 17.5 and 42.0 percent of those ranked high on the scale of political interest justified their intention to vote for governor by party in "immediate" and personality-based terms (versus 11.2 and 34.6 percent of all respondents).

In sum, because of the immediacy and personalism of Brazilian political beliefs, respondents do not justify their intent to vote in terms of ideology or group interest. Nonetheless, Brazilian voters appear to have not only judged parties, national issues, and executive performance, but also to have developed the beliefs and attitudes typical of the kind of political culture that scholars argue is critical for building democratic institutions and strengthening democracy.

Dimensions of Political Culture During the Era of Democratic Transition

The range and constraint of mass belief systems can also be examined on the aggregate level in survey data. Factor analysis seeks to identify theoretically plausible underlying dimensions of mass belief systems that are imperfectly measured by individual questions. This is accomplished by establishing the relative proximity of specific beliefs. Analysis of dichotomized responses to seventeen questions in the 1982 survey regarding what voters knew about and felt about democracy can be grouped into four classifications typical of constrained mass belief systems in mass democracies: (1) political information, or what voters know about the parties and candidates, (2) political interest, including attitudes about campaigns and voting, (3) tolerance of direct political action, such as strikes, sit-ins, and circulating petitions, and (4) attitude toward democratic institutions and to what extent they help the common people (see table 10.7).

Analysis of the survey data from the southeast capitals revealed autonomous underlying dimensions of voters' attitudes and behavior that are clearly consistent with descriptions of advanced democratic electorates. Each factor represents a distinctive type of knowledge or belief critical for building and deepening competitive mass democracy. Review of the relations among individual variables and underlying factors confirms their substantive conceptual content and theoretical

Table 10.7 Underlying Structure of Attitudes Toward Democracy
and Knowledge of Politics, 1982

	1: Political Information	2: Political Interest	3: Political Tolerance	4: Attitude Toward Democratic Institutions
Knowledge of parties and candidates				
PMDB party	.83	.04	.01	.00
PT party	.82	.06	.01	.05
PDS party	.82	.08	.00	.04
PDS candidate	.75	.03	.02	.00
PMDB candidate	.75	.04	.04	.03
PT candidate	.72	.11	.08	.09
PDT party	.69	.21	.09	.01
PDT candidate	.53	.15	.12	.08
Attitude toward politics and voting				
Interested in politics	.12	.73	.10	.01
Interested in campaign	.18	.70	.08	.04
Would vote if not mandatory	.08	.67	.07	.02
Approval of political action				
Labor strikes	.12	.08	.78	.01
Sit-ins of public buildings	.07	.04	.75	.05
Circulating petitions	.03	.03	.54	.01
Belief in democracy				
People are capable of voting	.08	.09	.03	.78
Parties help Brazil	.01	.32	.05	.56
Illiterates should have the vote	.04	.04	.23	.46

Source: 1982 electoral survey.

Note: Kaiser-Meyer-Olkin Measure of Sampling Adequacy = .88, Bartlett Test of Spericity = 7057.41, sign. = .00. Eigenvalues: Factor 1: 4.90, Factor 2: 1.68, Factor 3: 1.47, Factor 4: 1.10. Percent of variance explained: Factor 1: 28.8%, Factor 2: 9.9%, Factor 3: 8.7%, Factor 4: 6.5%. Total: 53.9%.

import. Only responses to questions about the names of parties and candidates were related in factor 1. Respondents' interest in politics and electoral campaigns, as well as their willingness to vote even if not required to by law made up factor 2. The three survey questions that measured whether respondents felt that petitions, strikes, and sit-ins were appropriate types of political action comprised factor 3. Finally, responses pertaining to people's ability to vote, suffrage for illiterates, and whether parties help Brazil made up the fourth factor, with the last variable touching on factor 2.

Analysis of this data also confirmed the uneven development of mass belief systems during Brazil's democratic transition. Identical factor analyses of the 1982 survey data from northeastern capitals and two rural areas failed to extract underlying dimensions similar to the southeast sample. While analysis of both the northeast and two rural samples identified political information as factor 1, additional underlying commonalities appeared among responses to questions that were designed to tap fundamentally different types of beliefs and values. On the statistical level, the extracted factors from the northeast and rural samples fail to establish autonomous underlying dimensions. Instead, several variables can be applied to more than one factor. On the conceptual level, the factors extracted from the northeast and rural samples fail to represent substantive categories in terms of the beliefs and capacities associated with political culture in mass democracy.

The links between these dimensions of mass belief systems are a critical problem for constructing a theory of political culture and democracy. Although this is complex terrain that requires further research, an apparent paradox among survey responses related to attitudes toward democracy during the period of hard-line military rule deserves comment.[12] In the 1972–1973 survey, as expected, highly educated respondents in nonmanual occupations not only were well informed about politics, but also seemed to believe that politics can bring about social change. However, respondents who valued liberal democratic institutions and procedures *were not* those generally associated with the upper levels of conceptualization (those with high education and nonmanual occupations). Instead, the belief that people are capable of voting wisely, and that political parties should have more power, both correlated with having little education and working in manual occupations (see table 10.8).

Table 10.8   Relation Between Social Class and Civic Culture
            Among Voters in Authoritarian Brazil, 1972

| Types of Democratic Political Culture | Social Class | |
	Nonmanual Occupation	High Level of Education
Belief in democratic institutions		
Believes people are capable of voting	−.21	−.23
Believes parties should have more power	−.16	−.16
Types of political conceptualization:		
(ideologial or group interest)	.30	.28
Belief that politics can change things	.21	.28
Awareness of campaign information:		
Can identify the president	.10	.16
Can identify the FGTS	.10	.08
Can identify the BNH	.18	.16
Can identify AI-5	.11	.11

Source: 1972–1973 survey, Representation and Development in Brazil.

Note: Reported correlations are Pearson's product-moment coefficients, significant at the .01 level. all variables are dichotomized. The correlations for low education (did not complete high school) and manual occupation are mirror images of those reported in the table.

Furthermore, these same demophile responses, which indicate the presence of civic culture even under military rule, were negatively correlated with having high education and nonmanual occupations. This distribution of civic culture among Brazilians in the military era is paradoxical because if one adopts the causal explanations of political sophistication and attitudes toward democracy in the tradition of Campbell and Converse (which emphasizes the importance of cognitive constraints and education), one might expect that highly educated and ideological voters would indicate a respect for democratic institutions. The opposite was true under military rule.

Although further analysis is needed, two explanations of this paradox are possible. First, perhaps the reverse distribution of responses under military rule may reflect Brazilians' longtime experience with democratic institutions. The dramatic periods of mass inclusion and

exclusion in modern Brazil may have given "the people" and democratic institutions clear political meanings. Because of populist and direct plebiscitarian appeals in Brazilian politics, the inclusionary aspirations of lower-class voters center, to an important degree, on the promises held out by democracy. But the exclusionary and antipopular fears of highly educated and affluent Brazilians also focus on democratic institutions and "the people." Hence, a positive attitude toward liberal and democratic institutions tends to be found among the lower classes, and antiliberal attitudes among the upper classes.

Second, while Brazil's civic culture differs from that found in advanced democratic electorates today, historians stress the antiliberal and antidemocratic attitudes of European and U.S. upper classes during other transitions to mass democracy.[13] From the eighteenth century through the early twentieth century, suffrage was extended and parliaments were democratized only under massive pressure from the lower and working classes, against the strong opposition of the more educated upper classes. In addition, other newly industrializing nations have witnessed this degree of support for democracy among lower classes and predominantly antidemocratic or antiliberal attitudes among the upper classes.[14]

Finally, this reverse distribution of democratic affect among Brazilians under military rule could very well be explained as the elite's having assimilated the dominant authoritarian values of their military rulers, an approach that has provided new perspectives on political culture in both the United States and Brazil.[15] Although Barbara Geddes and James Zaller provide evidence that several class segments did indeed assimilate authoritarian values under military rule in Brazil, more research is required to understand the changes of the transition period.[16] Nonetheless, one inference stands: approval for democracy among lower-class voters in authoritarian Brazil contradicts the idea that long-term political socialization and education are necessary for the development of a civic culture and a positive view of democratic institutions.

Conclusion

Competitive party and electoral politics not only informed public opinion and voter choice after 1974, it also produced the values, be-

liefs, and judgments that scholars believe permit democratization. The increased approbation for democracy and democratic institutions among Brazilian voters in the recent period of transition provides further evidence of rapid change, and once again counters the emphasis by empirical democratic theorists on long-term social, educational, and cognitive constraints on voters. Instead, like the other dimensions examined in chapters 6–9, the plebiscitarian appeals and patronage systems of Brazilian electoral politics appear to have educated voters and produced substantive change. Whereas the transition produced few ideologues and few voters who conceive of politics in terms of group interest, the 1982 data suggest that immediate and personalistic conceptions not only predominate among Brazilian voters; these conceptions of politics are bound together with the values, beliefs, and judgments that are typical of a civic culture. But the evidence also suggests the uneven development of mass politics and mass beliefs in Brazil concentrated in the urban centers of the advanced southeast surveyed in 1982.

These patterns imply that the recent near consensus on the merits of parliamentary institutions for new democracies should be carefully reconsidered. Juan Linz and others argue that presidential institutions tend to exacerbate the confrontational elements of political culture and that parliamentary institutions may therefore be preferable for democratic politics in Latin America and other world regions that have experienced transitions from authoritarian rule.[17] On the contrary, this analysis is based on the U.S. experience of party development and suggests that presidential elections generate direct popular appeals and enable executives to reorganize patronage machines through administrative nominations. In Brazil, these mechanisms rapidly organized new party images, informed voters about national issues, and produced clearer perceptions of executive performance. This final chapter also suggests that this alternative path of party development can indeed socialize voters, avert the excesses of confrontation, and generate a political culture that values democracy and democratic institutions.

Evidence that the plebiscitarian appeals of direct executive elections are critical for change and democratization, however passive it may be, suggests that the costs of averting crisis may be the immobilism long associated with parliamentary rule in Brazilian history. Parliamentary institutions were adopted twice in Brazil, first from 1824 to 1889 during the empire, and again in 1962, to reduce the presi-

dential powers of João Goulart and avert military intervention. It must be recognized that neither experience provides direct parallels for today. The Brazilian monarch dominated the imperial parliament, and the crises that produced a democratic breakdown in 1964 were well under way by the time parliamentary government was adopted. Nonetheless, both experiences suggest that parliamentary rule in Brazilian history significantly reduced the importance of direct popular appeals and reinforced the power of patronage machines.

Conclusion

While classic political theorists from Aristotle to Montesquieu argue that democracy is simply inappropriate for large nation-states, the dominant political philosophies of the twentieth century, liberalism and Marxism, and their expressions in political science were founded on greater optimism.[1] Theories of political development embodied this optimism by claiming that institutionalization, order, governability, and stable democracy could be achieved by democratizing competitive elections and party politics.[2] But after populist, nationalist, and socialist governments in Latin American produced confrontation and democratic breakdown rather than democratization in the 1960s and 1970s, this optimism fell from favor. The unexpected, unprecedented, and astounding series of transitions from authoritarian rule in Southern Europe, Latin America, Asia, Eastern Europe, and the former Soviet Union that occurred in the 1970s and 1980s will require a systematic reconsideration of democratic theory and practice into the next century. This analysis concludes with the hope that understanding the experiences of Brazilian voters in democratic transition may contribute not only to our knowledge of electoral behavior and party development, but also to the tasks of building, sustaining, and deepening democracy around the world.

Brazilian Voters, Electoral Behavior Research, and Democratic Theory

This analysis of Brazilian public opinion and voter alignment reaffirms the optimism inherent in major twentieth-century political doctrines

220

and counters the pessimism of empirical democratic theory. Substantial evidence from sequential electoral surveys suggests that the increasingly competitive nature of Brazilian politics after 1974 rapidly educated voters and influenced mass belief systems in ways typical of electorates in other mass democracies. Once the political constraints of military rule on information and contestation were liberalized, voters' evaluations of parties, positions on important issues, judgments of government accountability, and patterns of campaign participation increasingly organized public opinion and determined voter choice in Brazil. These patterns of diversity and change have several methodological and theoretical implications.

First, competitive theories of democracy in the Schumpeterian tradition must reconsider certain core assumptions about what brings about change in mass publics. Many still argue that change—and hence democratization—is constrained by voters' ignorance and that only gradual improvements in education and political socialization, which may require several generations, can alleviate the problem. But the rapid events of liberalization and transition after 1974 informed Brazilian voters, structured public opinion, and organized voters' choices in each dimension emphasized in studies of advanced democratic electorates.[3] The claim that democratization is constrained by long-term factors not only fails to account for the Brazilian case; it also ignores the bulk of current research about advanced democratic electorates, which now emphasizes complexity, diversity, and flux in mass belief systems.[4]

Second, existing typologies and scales of how individuals think about politics must be more open to cross-national differences. Brazilians rarely consider politics in terms of European ideologies or U.S. notions of group interest. But difference does not imply dysfunctionality. Brazilians' political beliefs must be understood in their historical, institutional, and political context. Brazilians' immediate and personalistic conceptions of politics originated during the national-populist period of mass inclusion from 1930 to 1945, were developed during the era of competitive politics between 1946 and 1964 and were reinforced by party and electoral politics after 1974. Far from being dysfunctional, these different conceptions of politics are related to the direct popular appeals, the party-electoral machines, and the direct state-society relations that characterize Brazilian mass politics. Far from irrational, the data suggest that these conceptions of politics

reflect broader ideas about substantive social and economic justice, inform voters' judgments of executive performance and their positions on national issues, and are cause and consequence of political participation and attitudes toward democratic institutions.

Third, the state-centered realities of Brazilian politics in the transition era suggests that we must consider the impact of direct democracy and state-led representation to fully understand electoral behavior in Brazil. The plebiscitarian character of direct popular appeals in Brazilian elections differs fundamentally from liberal descriptions of public opinion as a unidirectional, bottom-up expression of popular preferences and interests. Instead, these direct appeals in Brazil's state-centered politics creates state-led, top-down, populist discourses based on conceptions of justice that can be linked to Brazil's nationalist, populist, and democratic tradition. These direct links between the state and Brazilian voters also fail to conform to traditional explanations of voter choice. Both mediating factors such as class identity and political ideology and long-term factors such as political socialization and party identification simply do not explain much about Brazilian public opinion. Instead, the data suggest that conceptions of substantive justice, direct judgments of executive performance, and positions on national issues predominate among Brazilian voters (in the advanced southeast urban areas).

Brazil's state-centered political system has always puzzled liberal observers.[5] But economists have long recognized the state-led character of late development and the unparalleled extent of state intervention in Brazil.[6] Corporatist theories also cite Brazil as a paradigm of state-centered politics.[7] Accounts of Brazilian voters must confront not only the immediate and personalistic character of Brazilian public opinion, but also the impact of the state in its formation. Given the dominance of state-led representation in Brazil's history, and continued government intervention in economic, social, and political life, the liberal conception of representation as a unidirectional expression of interests and preferences fails to capture how direct democratic impulses in Brazilian public opinion and voter alignment link the state and society.

Fourth, broad syntheses of current knowledge about public opinion and electoral behavior are needed to meet the urgent tasks of building institutions of electoral representation and democracy in the many nations that have made transitions from authoritarian rule. But

this need arises just as the dealignment of modern, class-based politics throughout the advanced democracies has seriously impaired existing conceptions of electoral representation.[8] Neither classic ideas, nor demographic analysis, nor theories of party systems fully account for the diversity, complexity, and reciprocal relations currently found in advanced democratic electorates. This analysis has attempted to systematically clarify the similarities and differences between Brazilian voters and those in advanced democracies in each of the causal factors stressed by the major subfields of electoral behavior research. But the sum of contemporary research is assuredly greater than its parts. Integrating existing empirical knowledge about mass belief systems into broader models seems to be the most compelling means of constructing a positive theory of electoral representation.

Understanding how the various causes of public opinion and voter alignment interact to organize electoral representation certainly requires further analysis and research. But this synthesis is impeded not only by the extreme specialization of electoral behavior studies, but also by a clear tendency for scholars to emphasize statistical and methodological matters over theoretical concerns. Scholars are extremely sensitive to interactions between unspecified causes, to the possible existence of underlying causes that escape measurement, to poor question format, and to measurement error.[9] But they tend to describe these problems in statistical terms as the underestimation of causal models.[10] This conceals the fact that public opinion, voter alignment, and competitive elections are not determined. Only voters choose final causes. Determinacy appears only in retrospect. The relative and collective weight of the many causes of voter choice identified by scholars in five decades of empirical research is ordered differently in each election. Campaign managers know this, but political scientists building complex models of voter choice seem to have forgotten.

Finally, the Brazilian electoral surveys administered from 1974 to 1982 tap real individuals, avoid the ecological fallacy of drawing inferences from aggregate data such as censuses and official electoral statistics, and provide exceptional opportunities to address core problems of democracy in a Latin American setting. But we must recognize methodological constraints common to all analyses of survey data. Even slight changes in the wording of survey questions can produce dramatic fluctuations in response.[11] The need to translate finely honed questions designed to tap complex aspects of public opinion from

English into Portuguese invites greater measurement error. In addition, this study of Brazilian voters relies on secondary analysis of data in which open responses have already been master-coded. Although this was not possible for the survey data from 1974 to 1982, more careful analysis of raw uncategorized responses in new survey data may shed further light on the content and context of Brazilian voting. In sum, complex recursive theories are easy to formulate but difficult to test.[12] It is extremely difficult to measure causal direction and weight accurately. Models describing the causes of voter choice are always tainted by significant measurement error and unspecified causes, and those presented herein are no exception.

Presidential Institutions, Party Development, and Democracy

The emerging characteristics of party-electoral politics during Brazil's democratic transition also suggests that comparative analysts of political parties must be more open to national differences. Lipset and Rokkan first noted how European social cleavages from the 1920s had been frozen into voting patterns that still endure today.[13] But their use of the metaphor of frozen cleavages suggests that the assumptions of Parsonian sociology that informed their path-breaking analysis also precluded a full explanation of party system consolidation.[14] Indeed, the development of mass parties and party systems cannot be explained by sociological variables alone.[15] Without detailed analysis of the different sequences of parties and the formation of party systems, Stein and Rokkan recognize that "we simply cannot make sense of variations in current alignments."[16] The formation of competitive party systems must be analyzed not only on a sociological level, but also on an explicitly political level in historical and comparative perspective. Formal models of European party systems inspired scholars to suggest almost thirty years ago that mass parties could resolve central problems in Latin America.[17] Experience should have taught us that competitive party systems cannot be imposed on polities simply by borrowing from theories of organization and retaining a bias toward order.[18]

This analysis suggests that party development in the American presidential and federal system provides a powerful historical, theo-

retical, and comparative reference for analyzing party-electoral politics in Brazil. In a process strikingly similar to the nineteenth-century U.S. experience, which is normally described as exceptional, Brazil's directly elected executives (and military leaders) quickly negotiated electoral alliances with local and regional party machines by distributing administrative appointments during the transition era. This process of party development runs counter to that described in recent critiques of presidential systems, casts doubt on the view of Brazilian party politics as underdeveloped, calls for a shift of comparative focus from Europe to the United States, and poses tough normative and theoretical problems that Max Weber eloquently captured with the concept of passive democratization. Analysts often describe the lack of ideology, spurious party programs, complex legislative and electoral alliances, and capricious organizational structure among Brazilian parties as evidence of party system underdevelopment. These views seem entirely too similar to the naive liberalism that flourished among U.S. scholars in the 1950s, who lamented the lack of ideology, meaningless party programs, lack of congressional discipline, and widespread patronage and corruption in their own country.[19] The power of subsequent interpretations of U.S. parties and American democracy by Key, Schattschneider, Chambers, Burnham, Lowi, and others may indicate the extensive possibilities for understanding parties and democracy in Brazil awaiting those willing to undertake a similar conceptual shift.[20]

This reassessment of presidential institutions, party development, and democratization must include a careful reconsideration of democratic theory. Recent debates about party development and mass inclusion in the United States seem unable to separate empirical assertions from normative positions.[21] By contrast, Weber not only clearly identifies new mechanisms of political change; he also sharply poses their normative implications by provocatively juxtaposing passivity with democratization. Furthermore, by using minimal and descriptive definitions to restate central postulates of classic democratic theory as empirical research problems, he overcomes the false dichotomy between participatory theories of change and mainstream competitive theories of stasis. While democracy and democratization are complex and, as Connolly suggests, "essentially contested" concepts, contemporary democratic theory lacks an agenda that clearly links empirical research on public opinion and party development to democratic ideals.

By placing parties and elections at the core of Brazilian politics, this analysis builds on several trends in social science. Many scholars agree that the relation between the state and society in Brazil is best described as coexisting tendencies of state bureaucracies to dominate society and the private use of the state by social groups.[22] But this amalgam of opposing tendencies cannot be unraveled if state-society relations are posed in dichotomous or zero-sum terms. Instead, analysis must focus on the concrete political mechanisms that *link* state and society. Alfred Stepan argues that concern with specific sectors of civil society has failed to explain either bureaucratic politics within the state or the sphere of political society proper.[23] Indeed, studies of state agencies, ministries, and government social policies under military rule illuminate the complex links between state and society and explore the implications of these patterns for democracy in Brazil.[24] This study of Brazilian voters and party-electoral politics is indebted to these works and pursues their concerns by focusing squarely on questions of democratic theory and practice.

In conclusion, analysts of liberal institutions in Brazil have long noted the incompatibility of Brazilian society with competitive electoral politics.[25] But democracy in Brazil is not dysfunctional because some voters are ignorant or poorly educated, because change is limited by long-term constraints, or because political parties are weak. Instead, the threats to democracy in Brazil lie in the tension between politics based on direct popular appeals to substantive economic and social justice and the political and economic constraints on change in dependent capitalist society. Abundant survey evidence from 1974–1982 and recent interpretations of party and electoral politics in pre-1964 Brazil support these assertions. Political crisis and military intervention occurred in 1964 because competitive politics brought substantive democratic issues to the fore.[26] This book suggests that the mechanisms of passive democratization—links between plebiscitarian appeals and party-electoral machines through distribution of administrative appointments by directly elected executives—will prevail in a democratic Brazil. The Brazilian voter is far more informed and capable than either empirical democratic theory or prevailing views suggest. What remains unclear is whether Brazil's politicians can work within an increasingly complex and competitive international context abroad and increasing opportunities for demagoguery at home.

Appendixes
Notes
Bibliography
Index

Appendix 1
The Electoral Surveys: Sampling and Application Procedures

The Surveys

The data used in this study were obtained from pre-electoral surveys conducted by major Brazilian social science institutes and universities during the two weeks prior to quadrennial national elections—1974, 1978, and 1982—during the period of Brazil's transition from military to civilian rule. In 1974, pre-electoral surveys were conducted in the southeast cites of Belo Horizonte (directed by Professor Fabio Wanderley Reis at the Universidade Federal de Minas Gerais), São Paulo (directed by Professor Bolivar Lamounier at CEBRAP, Centro Brasileiro de Análise e Planejamento), and Porto Alegre (directed by Professor Marcello Baquero at the Universidade Federal de Rio Grande do Sul). In 1978, surveys were applied in the above cities by these same researchers, as well as Rio de Janeiro (directed by Amaury de Souza at IUPERJ, Instituto Universitario de Pesquisa do Rio de Janeiro). In 1982, an identical electoral survey was conducted in all four of the above southeastern state capitals, as well as capital cities of the northeast: Salvador, Bahia; Fortaleza, Ceara; and Recife, Pernambuco (all applied by researchers at the respective federal universities). In addition, the 1982 survey was applied in two rural zones: one comprising the municipality of Rio Paranaiba in the interior of Rio de Janeiro State, the other comprising three rural municipalities on the border between Espirito Santo and Minas Gerais states (directed by the staff of IUPERJ, Rio de Janeiro).

The questionnaires were modeled on standard surveys of U.S. and European electorates and modified for the Brazilian case. Furthermore, the 1982 questionnaire was pretested in all cities, so that the final version could be discussed and altered as needed before appli-

cation. The 1982 questionnaire contained 226 closed questions (including information about the interview) and 34 open questions. For analysis in this study, comparable questions in the 1974 and 1978 surveys were recoded and reorganized along the categories and coding standards of the 1982 survey.

The Sample

For all three surveys, the sample population was chosen in a three-stage process. First, sectors for the 1974 and 1978 surveys were randomly selected, based on the 1970 Instituto Brasileiro de Geografia e Estatística (IBGE) census, and for the 1982 survey sectors were chosen according to the 1980 census. Second, residences were randomly selected after verification of their current use as residences. The third stage involved the selection of individuals at the chosen residences.

On the basis of the IBGE censusus, the population was divided between *urban* or *rural*, with an additional category for those living in *poor urban* areas (*favelas*). After the relevant population within each given municipality was defined, sectors were defined proportionally by population, with ten residences to be interviewed per sector.

Regarding the second stage of sample selection, residences to be interviewed were chosen by the method proposed by Marques and Berquo. This method establishes ten groups from among currently occupied residential units, whereupon residences are chosen at systematic intervals from within each group.

For the selection of individuals, lists were obtained of all voting-age adults (eighteen years of age and older). These lists were then ordered from eldest to youngest male, then eldest to youngest female, in each residence. Then, from this list of individuals, persons were chosen for interviews according to random tables supplied by Marques and Berquo.

Application of the Questionnaire

The first phase of field research was to list and number the residences chosen for the sample. In all surveys, 1974, 1978, 1982, the final list was compiled in August and September by research assistants rigorously instructed about the sample procedure. The final list was compiled after on-site verification of each residence by researchers supplied

with maps and addresses of those residences chosen for the sample. After all currently occupied residences were examined, the final list was used to correct the census-based list of residences for each sector.

Approximately thirty-five interviewers for each city or rural zone were recruited from university graduate social science departments. In addition to receiving a briefing and training session, each interviewer applied a test questionnaire before undertaking the actual survey. Interviewers applied the questionnaire to ten respondents per sector. Interviewers were not allowed to make substitutions; the list of alternates remained with those directing research and interviewers could make substitutions only after consultation. (This facilitated control of the interview method by the research directors.) Targeted individuals were substituted only after two unsuccessful attempts to conduct the interview and only in the following cases: (1) the residence was not occupied when the questionnaire was applied; (2) the respondent refused to respond; (3) other reasons such as health problems. Finally, 10 percent of all residences interviewed were visited by assistant research directors to verify that individuals were selected adequately and the questionnaire was applied properly. Of all interviews, 95 percent were used in the final data sets. The principal reason for not including an interview was lack of time: interviews were conducted during the two weeks prior to an election, and those still incomplete by election day were not included in the data.

Composition of Regions in Official Election Results

Regions were composed as follows: *Southeast*: Espirito Santo, Minas Gerais, Rio de Janeiro, and São Paulo; *Northeast*: Alagoas, Bahia, Ceara, Maranhão, Paraiba, Pernambuco, Piaui, Rio Grande do Norte, and Sergipe; *South*: Parana, Rio Grande do Sul, and Santa Catarina; *Center-west*: Goias, and Mato Grosso; *North*: the states of Acre, Amazonas, and Para and the territories of Rondonia, Amapa, and Roraima.

Appendix 2
Additional Information on the Multiple Regression Model: Frequency Distribution of Variables and Scales

Left/Right Self-Placement

This scale measures respondents' self-description of their political inclinations along a ten-point scale ranging from "left" to "right." The question in Var170 reads as follows: "Now let's suppose that on this scale [show card] number one corresponds to the left and number ten to the right. As you can see, a very left person would be on number one, a very right person on number ten. Where would you place yourself?"

National Issues

Views on national issues were measured on a four-point scale tapping opposition to or support for the military government on four national concerns. Specific questions about issues included the following:

1. "Speaking further about elections, some say that the best solution for Brazil is that the next president (to be elected in 1985) should be elected by the people in a direct election. What do you think?" [coded *favors/opposes*]
2. "In the 1974 election political campaigns were mounted live on radio and television. In the current 1982 election a law prohibits candidates from speaking directly on radio or appearing live on television. Do you think this restriction is a good one?" [coded *yes/no*]
3. "What do you think about the military in government? Some say that they should leave the government and permit election

Table A.1 Frequency Distribution of Left-Right Affinity

	Value	Frequency	Percent	Valid Percent	Cum Percent
Left	1	54	2.2	7.6	7.6
	2	27	1.1	3.8	11.4
	3	61	2.5	8.6	20.1
	4	71	2.9	10.0	30.1
	5	164	6.7	23.2	53.2
	6	99	4.0	14.0	67.2
	7	41	1.7	5.8	73.0
	8	64	2.6	9.0	82.1
	9	26	1.1	3.7	85.7
Right	10	101	4.1	14.3	100.0
	99	1,755	71.3	Missing	
Total		2,463	100.0	100.0	

Note: Valid N = 708; missing N = 1,755

Table A.2 Scale of National Issues

	Frequency	Percent	Valid Percent	Cum Percent
Supports government on four issues	126	5.1	9.4	9.4
Supports government on three issues	348	14.1	26.1	35.5
Supports or opposes government on two issues	456	18.5	34.2	69.7
Opposes government on three issues	268	10.9	20.1	89.7
Opposes government on four issues	137	5.6	10.3	100.0
Not Applicable/no response	1,128	45.8	Missing	
Total	2,463	100.0	100.0	

Note: Valid N = 1,335; missing N = 1,128

of a civilian for president. Others say that the military are still needed in government and that a civilian president would not be convenient. What is your opinion?" [coded *yes/no*]

4.   "Some say that the Communist party should be legalized, that it should have the same rights as other parties. Are you in favor or opposed to the legalization of the Communist party?" [coded *favors/opposes*]

Executive Performance

This was measured by three questions asking respondents to rank the performance of the president, their state governor, and their mayor along a five-point scale. The question read: "Do you think current President João Figueiredo is performing (1) very well, (2) well, (3) more or less, (4) poorly, or (5) terribly." The question was restated for governor and mayor.

Table A.3 Scale of Executive Performance

	Value	Frequency	Percent	Valid Percent	Cum Percent
Low	3	44	1.8	2.1	2.1
	4	49	2.0	2.3	4.4
	5	125	5.1	5.9	10.4
	6	310	12.6	14.7	25.0
	7	302	12.3	14.3	39.3
	8	314	12.7	14.8	54.1
	9	410	16.6	19.4	73.5
	10	183	7.4	8.7	82.2
	11	257	6.4	7.4	89.6
	12	76	3.1	3.6	93.2
	13	89	3.6	4.2	97.4
	14	22	.9	1.0	98.4
High	15	348	14.1	Missing	
Total		2,463	100.0	100.0	

Note: Valid N = 2,115; missing N = 348

Intention to Vote

This question asked respondents how they intended to vote in the 1982 gubernatorial election, recoded by party from left to right. The question read: "For whom do you intend to vote for governor?" [Interviewer read names of candidates.]

Table A.4 Intention to Vote

	Value	Frequency	Percent	Valid Percent	Cum Percent
PT	1	129	5.2	9.3	9.3
PDT	2	272	11.0	19.7	29.0
PMDB	3	491	19.9	35.5	64.5
PTB	4	107	4.3	7.7	72.3
PDS	5	383	15.6	27.7	100.0
NR/NA/intends to annul	9	1,081	43.9	Missing	
Total		2,463	100.0	100.0	

Note: Valid N = 1,382; missing N = 1,081

Appendix 3

The Types of Political Conceptualizations and Original Master Codes for Variable 235

Var235: "Why do you intend to vote for [respondent's candidate for governor]"?

CODE/Category	Freq	Percent	Valid Percent	Cum. Percent
00 (No information)	5	.2	.2	.2
10 *Voto vinculado* (electoral legislation requiring straight party voting by ticket)	17	.7	.7	.9
20 Affect: personal preference, the one favored by friends and relatives	150	6.1	6.1	7.0
21 Popularity: "because he's the best known"; "everyone is going to vote for him"; "he's the most talked about"	43	1.7	1.7	8.7
30 Past performance: "for what he has done"; because "he has experience"	224	9.1	9.1	17.8
31 Expectations: (without allusion to political ideology) "he's going to be good"; "he'll improve things"	436	17.7	17.7	35.5
40 Party: because "he's of my party"	75	3.0	3.0	38.6

CODE/Category	Freq	Percent	Valid Percent	Cum. Percent
41 Opposed to government: because "he's opposition," "authentic," "combative"	72	2.9	2.9	41.5
42 In favor of government: "defends the revolution"; "he can accomplish something because he is in government"	68	2.8	2.8	44.3
50 Group affiliation: community, professional, labor union, religious association	9	.4	.4	44.6
51 Class interest: social groups or the bases he represents	57	2.3	2.3	46.9
52 Ideology of candidate: "because he's socialist"; "because he's right (or left)"	17	.7	.7	47.6
60 Mixed responses: complex explanations not categorizable in the above	136	5.5	5.5	53.1
61 State-level responses: problems or reasons particular to a state	14	.6	.6	53.7
77 Not applicable: because respondent doesn't favor candidate or is not a voter	1,082	44.1	44.1	97.7
88 NS	42	1.7	1.7	99.4
99 NR	14	.6	.6	100.0
Total	2,463	100.0	100.0	100.0

Types of Conceptualization Represented in Questionnaire
Categories

Value Label	Freq	Percent	Valid Percent
Converse's Types: (ideology, group interest)			
(40, 50, 51, 52 = 1) (Else = 0)	158	6.4	12.3
Immediate Type: (41, 42, 60 = 1)			
(Else = 0)	276	11.2	21.5
Personalist Type: (20, 21, 30, 31 = 1)			
(Else = 0)	851	34.6	66.2
	1,178	47.8	—
Total	2,463	100.0	

Valid N = 1,285, Missing N = 1,178

Notes

Introduction

1. Recent research on electoral behavior is reviewed in Benjamin I. Page and Robert Y. Shapiro, *The Rational Public* (Chicago: University of Chicago Press, 1992), pp. 1–37; and Herbert Asher, "Voting Behavior Research in the 1980s: An Examination of Some Old and New Problem Areas," in *Political Science: The State of the Discipline*, ed. Ada Finifter (Washington, D.C.: American Political Science Association, 1983).

2. On how elections served as a mechanism for the transition to democracy, see Bolivar Lamounier, "Authoritarian Brazil Revisited: The Impact of Elections on the Abertura," in *Democratizing Brazil*, ed. Alfred Stepan (New York: Oxford University Press, 1989), pp. 43–79.

3. See Asher, "Voting Behavior Research in the 1980s"; and G. Bingham Powell, "Comparative Voting Behavior: Cleavages, Partisanship, and Accountability," *Research in Micropolitics* 2 (1987): 233–64.

4. Recent examples of such studies include Page and Shapiro, *The Rational Public*; and Samuel Popkin, *The Reasoning Voter* (Chicago: University of Chicago Press, 1991). On the trend toward recognizing complexity, rationality, and change in mass publics, see Donald Kinder, "Diversity and Complexity in American Public Opinion," in *Political Science: The State of the Discipline*, ed. Finifter, pp. 389–425.

5. Angus Campbell, Phillip Converse, Warren Miller, and Donald Stokes, *The American Voter* (New York, John Wiley, 1960), p. 255. Self-declared mainstream scholars of democratic theory continue to stress informational, educational, and long-term constraints on change in mass publics. See Giovanni Sartori, *The Theory of Democracy Revisited* (Chatham: Chatham House, 1987), pp. 103–10.

6. On public opinion in Brazil from 1965 to 1974, see Youssef Cohen, *The Manipulation of Consent: State and Working Class Consciousness in Brazil* (Pittsburgh: University of Pittsburgh Press, 1989); and Bolivar Lamounier, "Ideology and Authoritarian Regimes: Theoretical Perspectives and a Study of the Brazilian Case." Ph.D. diss., University of California, Los Angeles, 1974.

7. Scales of political conceptualizations are typologies of how individuals think about politics. After Campbell et al., *The American Voter*, and Philip Converse's ground-breaking work, "The Nature of Belief Systems in Mass

Publics," in *Ideology and Consent*, ed. David Apter (New York: Free Press, 1964), pp. 206–56, conventional levels of conceptualization are as follows: (1) ideologue, (2) near ideologue, (3) group interest, (4) nature of the times, and (5) no content.

8. For reviews of methodological problems in survey analysis, see Christopher Achen, "Toward Theories of Political Data," in *Political Science: The State of the Discipline*, ed. Finifter; and Herbert Asher, *Causal Modeling*, rev. ed. (Beverley Hills: Sage, 1983).

9. Adam Przeworski suggests that the unpredictability of democracy is its essential characteristic. See "Democracy as a Contingent Outcome of Conflicts," paper prepared for the seminar "Issues on Democracy and Democratization: North and South," University of Notre Dame, November 1983.

10. These surveys, modeled on international electoral surveys and modified for the Brazilian case, have been financed by the Ford Foundation, FAPESP, and FINEP in Brazil since 1974. Appendix 1 describes sampling procedures and application of the questionnaire.

11. See Kinder, "Diversity and Complexity in American Public Opinion." On causal complexity, see Benjamin Page and Calvin Jones, "Reciprocal Effects of Policy Preferences, Party Loyalites, and the Vote," *American Political Science Review* 73 (1979): 1071–89.

12. The traditional model is based largely on Campbell et al., *The American Voter*. On the continued influence of this model in current research, see Asher, "Voting Behavior Research in the 1980s."

13. For a careful conceptual analysis, see Hanna Pitkin, *The Concept of Representation* (Berkeley and Los Angeles: University of California Press, 1968).

14. On change and structure in public opinion, see Ronald Inglehart, "Aggregate Stability and Individual Level Flux in Mass Belief Systems: The Level of Analysis Paradox," *American Political Science Review* 79 (1985): 97–116.

15. On the emergence and consolidation of party systems, see Giovanni Sartori, *Parties and Party Systems* (Cambridge: Cambridge University Press, 1976).

16. For example: Kinder, "Diversity and Complexity in American Public Opinion." On reciprocal relations between dimensions of mass beliefs, see Benjamin Page, *Choices and Echoes in Presidential Elections* (Chicago: University of Chicago Press, 1978).

17. Karl Deutsch presents a rather bucolic model of elite influence as a series of cascading pools in *The Analysis of International Relations* (Englewood Cliffs, N.J.: Prentice-Hall, 1968), pp. 101–10; other theories of elite influence according to competitive theories of democracy are noted in Sartori, *The Theory of Democracy Revisited* 1:92–102.

18. Theodore Adorno et al., *The Authoritarian Personality* (New York: Harper and Row, 1950); Robert Lane, *Political Ideology* (New York: Free

Press, 1962); Elizabeth Noelle-Neumann, *The Spiral of Silence* (Chicago: University of Chicago Press, 1984).

19. For example, Michael Margolis and Gary Mauser, *Manipulating Public Opinion: Essays on Public Opinion as a Dependent Variable* (Pacific Grove, Calif.: Brooks/Cole, 1989); Benjamin Ginsberg, *The Captive Public: How Mass Opinion Promotes State Power* (New York: Basic Books, 1986).

20. On parties in contemporary Brazil and Latin America, see Scott Mainwaring, "Political Parties and Democratization in Brazil and the Southern Cone," review article, *Comparative Politics* 21 (1988): 91–120.

21. Walter D. Burnham, *Critical Elections and the Mainsprings of American Politics* (New York: Norton, 1970), p. 10.

22. See Paul Kleppner, "Beyond the 'New Political History': A Review Essay." *Historical Methods Newsletter* 6 (1972): 17–26. Central contributions to the "new political history" include Walter D. Burnham, *The Current Crisis in American Politics* (New York, Oxford University Press, 1982); Phillip E. Converse, "Change in the American Universe," in *The Human Meaning of Social Change*, ed. Angus Campbell and Phillip E. Converse (New York: Sage, 1973); Paul Kleppner, *The Cross of Culture: A Social Analysis of Midwestern Politics, 1850–1900* (New York: Free Press, 1970); Richard Jensen, *The Winning of the Midwest: Social and Political Conflict, 1888–1896* (Chicago: University of Chicago Press, 1971).

23. On differences between European and U.S. political development, see Samuel Huntington, *Political Order in Changing Societies* (New Haven: Yale University Press, 1968), chap. 2.

24. Max Weber makes this argument in both "Politics as a Vocation" in *From Max Weber*, ed. H. H. Gerth and C. Wright Mills (New York: Oxford University Press, 1946), and in "Parliament and Government in a Reconstructed Germany," *Economy and Society* (Berkeley and Los Angeles: University of California Press, 1978), 2:1381–1462. See also M. I. Ostrogorski, *Democracy and the Organization of Political Parties in the United States and Great Britain* (Garden City, N.Y.: Doubleday, 1964); and James Bryce, *The American Commonwealth* (New York: Macmillan, 1907).

25. Oliveira Vianna, *Instituições Políticas Brasileiras* (Rio de Janeiro: Editora Nacional, 1949), p. 296.

26. Weber discusses the passive element in the organization of U.S. politics in "Politics as a Vocation," p. 113, and in "Parliament and Government in a Reconstructed Germany," pp. 1398–1402.

27. The resurrection of civilian society under authoritarianism and during transitions to democracy is described in Guillermo O'Donnell and Phillipe Schmitter, "Transitions From Authoritarian Rule: Tentative Conclusions," in *Transitions From Authoritarian Rule: Prospects for Democracy*, ed. Guillermo O'Donnell, Phillipe Schmitter, and Laurence Whitehead (Baltimore: Johns Hopkins University Press, 1986).

28. The increasingly pluralistic character of Brazilian society and the emergence of social organizations with greater autonomy from the state are

important developments for Brazilian democracy. See Scott Mainwaring and Eduardo Viola, "New Social Movements, Political Culture, and Democracy: Brazil and Argentina in the 1980's," *Telos* 61 (Fall 1984); Wanderley G. dos Santos, "A Pós-Revolução Brasileira," in *Brasil: Sociedade Democrática*, ed. Hélgio Trindade (Rio de Janeiro: José Olympio, 1985); and Alfred Stepan, "State Power and the Strength of Civil Society in the Southern Cone of Latin America," in *Bringing the State Back In*, ed. Peter Evans et al. (Cambridge: Cambridge University Press, 1985), pp. 317–46.

29. On the importance of new social contexts in the 1974 election, see Fernando H. Cardoso and Bolivar Lamounier, eds., *Os Partidos e as Eleições no Brasil* (Rio de Janeiro: Paz e Terra, 1975).

30. For a critique of conceptions of opposition voting prevailing in the late 1970s, see Wanderley G. dos Santos, *Poder e Política: Uma Crônica do Autoritarismo no Brasil* (São Paulo: Alfa Omega, 1979). For a suggestive attempt to differentiate and conceptualize voting patterns, see Fabio W. Reis, "Conclusão: Em Busca da Lógica do Processo Eleitoral Brasileiro," *Os Partidos e o Regime* (São Paulo: Símbolo, 1978), pp. 289–303.

31. On professional politicians during the 1946–1964 period, see Barry Ames, "The Congressional Connection: The Structure of Politics and the Distribution of Public Expenditures in Brazil's Competitive Period," *Comparative Politics* (1987): 147–71; on the authoritarian era, see Eli Diniz, *Voto e Máquina Política: Patronagem e Clientelismo no Rio de Janeiro* (Rio de Janeiro: Paz e Terra, 1982). See also Maria D. G. Kinzo, *An Opposition Party in an Authoritarian Regime: The Case of the MDB (Movimento Democrático Brasileiro) in Brazil, 1966–1979* (New York: St. Martin's, 1989). On *cabos eleitorais*, see Tereza Caldeira, "Electoral Struggles in a Neighborhood on the Periphery of São Paulo," *Politics and Society* 15 (1986–1987): 43–66.

32. Interview with Senator Fernando Henrique Cardoso, 4 November 1986.

33. Juan Linz, "The Perils of Presidentialism," *Journal of Democracy* 1 (1990): 51–69; Scott Mainwaring, "Presidentialism in Latin America," review article, *Latin American Research Review* 25 (1990): 157–79.

34. Brazilian political parties achieved neither the ideals of liberal representation, nor the criteria of ideological party systems. The classic liberal interpretation of the dysfunctionality of parties in Brazilian society is Raymundo Faoro, *Os Donos do Poder* (Porto Alegre: Globo, 1958), pp. 315–30. See also Bolivar Lamounier and Rachel Meneguello, *Partidos Políticos e Consolidação Democrática: O Caso Brasileiro* (São Paulo: Brasiliense, 1986).

Chapter 1. Brazilian Voters, Party Development, and Passive Democratization

1. See Sartori, *The Theory of Democracy Revisited*.

2. Carol Pateman, *Participation and Democratic Theory* (Cambridge: Cambridge University Press, 1970); Peter Bachrach, *The Theory of Democratic Elitism* (University Press of America, 1967).

3. See William E. Connolly, *The Terms of Political Discourse* (Princeton: Princeton University Press, 1974).

4. Much of contemporary political science can be described as dealing with this core problem. See Robert Dahl, *Polyarchy* (New Haven: Yale University Press, 1971).

5. Joseph S. Schumpeter, *Capitalism, Socialism, and Democracy* (New York: Harper and Row, 1942), pp. 243, 269.

6. On the link between Schumpeter's conception of democracy and theories of retrospective voting, see Asher, "Voting Behavior Research in the 1980s."

7. Emphasis added. I find this distinction between minimal and descriptive definitions helpful to demarcate problems inherent in the concept of democracy. Giovanni Sartori seems to reserve this distinction for simpler, subsystemic, and (in the context of this discussion) less contested concepts (*Parties and Party Systems*, p. 63).

8. For example, Dahl (*Polyarchy*, p. 16) poses the central question about polyarchies as a question of change: "What circumstances significantly increase the mutual security of government and opposition and thereby increase the chances of public contestation and polyarchy?" In broad terms, this also characterizes the research agenda of theorists who stress participation, suggesting the need to revise the perception that competitive and participatory theories are incompatible.

9. Weber, *Economy and Society*, p. 985.

10. Among important exceptions are Asher, "Voting Behavior Research in the 1980s"; and Powell, "Comparative Voting Behavior."

11. See Jean Campbell, *Survey Research in the United States: Roots and Emergence 1890–1960* (Berkeley and Los Angeles: University of California Press, 1987).

12. Philip E. Converse, "Of Time and Partisan Stability," *Comparative Political Studies* 2 (1969), estimated that durable party identification required party loyalty within the family over three generations. See also *New Views of Children and Politics*, ed. Richard G. Niemi (San Fransico: Jossey-Bass, 1974).

13. Among the important exceptions, see V. O. Key, *The Responsible Electorate: Rationality in Presidential Voting 1930–1960* (Cambridge: Harvard University Press, 1966); and Lane, *Political Ideology*.

14. See Norman H. Nie, Sidney Verba, and John Petrocik, *The Changing American Voter* (Cambridge: Harvard University Press, 1980).

15. In 1964, U.S. voters at large appeared to exhibit levels of cognitive constraint (intercorrelated views on issues) that *exceeded* that of congressional candidates in 1958. The proportion of voters who thought about politics in terms of ideology and group interest also increased during the 1960s. Nie et al. conclude that "the way in which citizens conceptualize the political realm is dependent on the political context to which they are exposed" (ibid., p. 121).

16. Instead, the rigidities of mass belief systems came to be seen as the consequence of generational experiences and described with more open categories such as political immunization. William McPhee and Nathan Ferguson, "Political Immunization," in *Public Opinion and Congressional Elections*, ed. McPhee and Nathan Glaser (New York: Free Press, 1966); Nie et al., *The Changing American Voter*, p. 76.

17. Critics suggest that the findings of increased ideological conceptualizations and issue voting during the 1960s may have been simply caused by changes in research design and method. Technical problems, such as changes in question wording and the use of already coded protocols instead of raw data, may explain the increase of ideological responses reported by Nie, Verba, and Petrocik. Furthermore, both the primacy of centrist voters and the adoption of ideological language by survey respondents without much accompanying logical constraint appears to explain much of the rise in ideological conceptualizations of politics among U.S. voters. See Christopher Achen, "Mass Political Attitudes and the Survey Response," *American Political Science Review* 69 (1975): 1218–31.

18. Asher, "Voting Behavior Research in the 1980s"; Powell, "Comparative Voting Behavior."

19. For an excellent summary of demographic cleavages in the Brazilian electorate, see Fabio W. Reis, ed., *Os Partidos e o Regime* (São Paulo: Símbolo, 1978).

20. The traditional model of public opinion and voter choice in advanced democracies relies on the following causal sequence: long-term factors such as political socialization, class-based identities, and party identification moderate short-term shifts in public opinion caused by voters' perceptions of economic performance, candidate personality, and new political issues. See Campbell et al., *The American Voter*. On the continued importance of this traditional model in current research, see Asher, "Voting Behavior Research in the 1980s."

21. On the problem of few responses to survey questions during periods of transition from authoritarian rule, see Peter McDonough, Antonio López Piña, and Samuel H. Barnes, "The Spanish Public in Political Transition," *British Journal of Political Science* 11 (January 1981): 49–79. On the problem of missing values in survey data generally, see Roderick Little and Donald B. Rubin, "The Analysis of Social Science Data With Missing Values," in *Modern Methods of Data Analysis*, ed. John Fox and J. Scott Long (Beverly Hills: Sage, 1990).

22. On voters' inability or unwillingness to place themselves on the left-right continuum and demographic variables, see chapter 10.

23. Samuel Barnes, Peter McDonough, and Antonio López Piña, "The Development of Partisanship in New Democracies: The Case of Spain," *American Journal of Political Science* 29 (1985): 695–720.

24. The factors of participation and political culture are considered separately from those introduced in the causal model because they do not de-

termine voter choice. The patterns of mass participation that inform public opinion and the attributes of political culture associated with the durability of mass democratic politics are discussed at length in chapters 9 and 10. Immediate—that is, unmediated or transparent—and personality-based conceptions of candidates are discussed below as a critical and unique feature of Brazilian public opinion within *each* causal dimension.

25. See discussion in chapter 5.

26. Three matters were critical. First, the question about left-right self-placement was omitted from survey of rural areas. Second, because minor parties failed to mount successful campaigns in both northeast cities and the rural areas, it became impossible to recode the dependent variable of intent to vote for governor by party from left to right. Finally, even statistical procedures designed to compare causal weight in situations where the dependent variable is dichotomous such as Logit and Probit, estimates were less reliable because there were so many missing cases on some variables in the northeast and rural samples.

27. Aziz Simão, "O Voto Operario em São Paulo." *Revista Brasileira de Estudos Políticos* 1 (1956): 130–41.

28. Oliveiros Ferreira, "Comportamento Eleitoral em São Paulo." *Revista Brasileira de Estudos Políticos* 8 (1960): 162–228.

29. Francisco Weffort, "Raízes do Populismo em São Paulo," *Revista Brasileira da Civilização Brasileira* 2 (1965).

30. "The large number of candidates for the legislature . . . depoliticizes the election. The elector ends up voting for a candidate recommended by someone, who is generally a canvasser [*cabo eleitoral*]" (Paul Singer, "A Política das Classes Dominantes," in *Política e Revolução Social no Brasil*, ed. Octavio Ianni [Rio de Janeiro: Civilização Brasileira, 1965], p. 91).

31. For review of studies on local-level party politics, see Jose M. Carvalho, "Estudos de Poder Local no Brasil," *Revista Brasileira de Estudos Políticos* 25 (1968): 231–48.

32. Victor N. Leal, *Coronelismo, Enxada, e Voto* (Rio de Janeiro: Forense, 1949).

33. Glaucio D. Soares, *Sociedade e Política no Brasil* (São Paulo: Difel, 1973).

34. Maria C. C. Souza, *Estado e Partidos Políticos no Brasil, 1930–1964* (São Paulo: Alfa Omega, 1976), pp. 52–56.

35. For the original formulations of the levels-of-conceptualization scales, see Campbell et al., *The American Voter*, pp. 218–23; and Converse, "The Nature of Belief Systems in Mass Publics," p. 208.

36. Eric Smith, "The Levels of Conceptualization: False Measures of Ideological Sophistication," *American Political Science Review* 74 (1980): 685–96; Achen, "Mass Political Attitudes and the Survey Response."

37. On the diverse meanings of "the people" in democratic discourse, see Sartori, *Democratic Theory Revisited*, p. 22.

38. On the democratic content of populist discourse, see Michael Conniff, ed., *Latin American Populism in Comparative Perspective* (Albuquerque: University of New Mexico Press, 1982).

39. Chaps. 6–10 review the distribution of the types of political conceptualization in each of the dimensions of public opinion and voter alignment.

40. Cardoso, introduction to *Os Partidos e as Eleições no Brasil*, ed. Cardoso and Lamounier.

41. Inglehart, "Aggregate Stability and Individual Level Flux in Mass Belief Systems."

42. The classic example of master coding is Converse's levels-of-conceptualization scale (see "The Nature of Belief Systems in Mass Publics," p. 218).

43. Inglehart, "Aggregate Stability and Individual Level Flux in Mass Belief Systems," pp. 97–116.

44. Sartori, *Parties and Party Systems*, p. 20.

45. Weber, "Politics as a Vocation," in *From Max Weber: Essays in Sociology*, Maurice Duverger, *Political Parties* (Cambridge, Mass.: Metheun, 1954); Hans Daalder, "Parties, Elites, and Political Developments in Western Europe," in *Political Parties and Political Development*, ed. Joseph LaPalombara and Myron Weiner (Princeton: Princeton University Press, 1966), pp. 43–78.

46. On the meaning of these changes in representation, see Sartori, *Parties and Party Systems*, p. 27.

47. E. E. Schattschneider, *Party Government* (New York: Rinehart, 1941); Richard Rose, *The Problem of Party Government* (New York: Macmillan, 1974).

48. Weber's treatment of the consequences of modernity for democratic ideals is encyclopedic and his considerations on mass parties are "as penetrating as they are inumerable" (Sartori, *Parties and Party Systems*, p. 24).

49. Weber, *Economy and Society*, p. 985.

50. Weber writes that parallels between bureaucratization and democratization must not be exaggerated, however typical it may be (ibid.).

51. Ostrogorski, *Democracy and the Organization of Political Parties*, Bryce, *The American Commonwealth*.

52. Weber recognizes the value of Tocquevillian factors in U.S. society ("Politics as a Vocation," in *From Max Weber*, p. 110).

53. Ibid., p. 91.

54. Weber, *Economy and Society*, p. 1400.

55. Weber, "Politics as a Vocation," in *From Max Weber*, p. 108.

56. Ibid., p. 103.

57. See Nathan Glazer and Daniel P. Moynihan, *Beyond the Melting Pot* (Cambridge: MIT Press, 1971), cited in Martin Shefter, "Party and Patronage: Germany, England, and Italy," *Politics and Society* 7 (1977): 451.

58. Weber, "Politics as a Vocation," p. 108.

59. On the impact of Progressive-era reforms on the organization of U.S. parties, see Burnham, *Critical Elections and the Mainsprings of American Politics*, pp. 74–90.

60. For interpretations of the dysfunctionality of parties in Brazilian society, see Faoro, *Os Donos do Poder*, pp. 315–25 and Lamounier and Meneguello, eds., *Partidos Políticos e a Consolidação Democrática: O Caso Brasileiro*.

61. Douglas A. Chalmers, "Parties and Society in Latin America," in *Friends, Followers and Factions*, ed. Steffen W. Schmidt et al. (Berkeley and Los Angeles: University of California Press, 1977), p. 418.

Introduction to Part II

1. The clearest statement of this reformist liberalism is the special report, "Toward a More Responsible Two Party System," *American Political Science Review* 44 (1950), supplement.

2. Burnham, *The Current Crisis in American Politics*.

3. Theodore J. Lowi, "Party, Policy, and Constitution in America," in *The American Party Systems: Stages of Political Development*, ed. William N. Chambers and Walter D. Burnham (New York: Oxford University Press, 1967).

4. Samuel Hays, "Political Parties and the Community-Society Continuum," in ibid., pp. 152–81.

5. Daalder, "Parties, Elites, and Political Developments in Western Europe." On party building after the establishment of modern state bureaucracies, see Shefter, "Party and Patronage."

6. Daalder writes: "In France and Germany powerful bureaucracies were built up as social control mechanisms long before non-bureaucratic social groups had learned to use the weapon of political organization to secure influence. Ever since, parties have had difficulty in obtaining full control. . . . In Britain, on the other hand, the build-up of the modern civil service occured after non-official social groups were securely in political control; ever since, the civil service has loyally accepted control by party ministers ("Parties, Elites, and Political Developments in Western Europe," p. 46).

7. See Giovanni Sartori, preface to *Partidos e Sistemas Partidarios* (Rio de Janeiro: Zahar, 1982).

8. Souza, *Estado e Partidos Políticos no Brasil*, p. 57.

9. This comparison should not be taken too far. To fully explain the differences among Latin American party systems, one would have to conduct a more detailed historical and comparative analysis of the different sequences of parties and party system formation, without which, as Sartori notes, "we simply cannot make sense of variations in current alignments."

10. On party politics in Colombia, see Jonathan Hartlyn, *The Politics of Coalition Rule in Colombia* (Cambridge: Cambridge University Press, 1988).

11. On the early consolidation of competitive party systems in Chile and Argentina, see Karen Remmer, *Party Competition in Argentina and Chile: Political Recruitment and Public Policy, 1890–1930* (Lincoln: University of Nebraska Press, 1984); and Manuel A. Garreton, *The Chilean Political Process* (Boston: Unwin Hyman, 1988).

12. On party politics in Venezuela, see Daniel H. Levine, *Conflict and Political Change in Venezuela* (Princeton: Princeton University Press, 1973); and Michael Coppedge, "Strong Parties and Lame Ducks: A Study of the Quality and Stability of Venezuelan Democracy," Ph.D. diss., Yale University, 1988.

13. Chalmers, "Parties and Society in Latin America," p. 418, emphasis added.

14. For this view of Brazilian party politics before 1964, see Souza, *Estado e Partidos Políticos no Brasil*, chap. 6.

15. See Juan Linz and Alfred Stepan, eds., *The Breakdown of Democratic Regimes, Latin America* (Baltimore: Johns Hopkins University Press, 1978).

16. Michael Conniff, *Urban Politics in Brazil: The Rise of Populism, 1925–1945* (Pittsburgh: Pittsburgh University Press, 1982); and Gino Germani, *Authoritarianism, Fascism, and National Populism* (New Brunswick, N.J.: Transaction Books, 1978).

17. The clearest statement of Latin American populism as a multiclass front against imperialism can be found in Haya de la Torre, *El Anti-Imperialismo y el APRA*, 45th ed. (Lima: Amauta, 1972), cited in Fernando H. Cardoso, *Autoritarismo e Democratização* (São Paulo: Paz e Terra, 1975). pp. 167–71.

18. The concept of misplaced ideas is from Roberto Schwartz's analysis of European cultural genres in Brazil. Brazilian historians, sociologists, and political scientists have emphasized the utility of Schwartz's argument on the distance and dysfunctionality of European and American ideas in Brazil (*Misplaced Ideas: Essays on Brazilian Culture* [New York: Verso, 1992]).

19. Faoro, *Os Donos do Poder*, pp. 315–25.

20. Lamounier and Meneguello, *Partidos Políticos e Consolidação Democrática*, chap. 1.

Chapter 2. The First Party System

1. Richard Graham, *Patronage and Politics in Nineteenth Century Brazil* (Stanford: Stanford University Press, 1990).

2. José M. Carvalho, "Political Elites and State Building: The Case of Nineteenth-Century Brazil," *Comparative Studies in Society and History* 24 (1982): 378–99.

3. Paula Beiguelman, *A Formação Política do Brasil* (São Paulo: Pioneiro, 1967); and *Pequenos Estudos de Ciência Política* (São Paulo: Pioneiro, 1973); principal works of Oliveira Vianna on nineteenth-century Brazilian electoral sociology are: *As Instituições Políticas Brasileiras* (Rio de Janeiro: Editora Nacional, 1954; *O Ocaso do Império* (Rio de Janeiro: José Olympio, 1959; *Problemas da Política Objetiva* (São Paulo: Editora Nacional, 1947).

4. On liberalism in nineteenth-century Brazil, see Wanderley G. dos Santos, *Ordem Burguesa e Liberalismo Político* (São Paulo: Duas Cidades, 1978).

5. Leslie Bethell and José M. de Carvalho, "Brazil from Independence to the Middle of the Nineteenth Century," in *The Cambridge History of Latin America*, ed. Bethell (Cambridge: Cambridge University Press, 1985), pp. 679–746; Stanley Stein, "Historiography of Brazil, 1808–1889," *Hispanic American Historical Review* 15 (1969): 346; Kenneth Maxwell, "The Generation of the 1790's and the Downfall of the Luso-Brasilian Empire," in *Colonial Roots of Modern Brasil*, ed. Aldin Dauril (Berkeley and Los Angeles: University of California Press, 1973), pp. 107–44; and Célia Barros Barreto, "O Movimento Maçônico na Independência," in *Historia Geral da Civilização Brasileira*, ed. Sérgio B. Holanda and Boris Fausto (São Paulo: Difel, 1973).

6. The rural, parliamentary, and, provocatory anti-Portuguese bias of the 1823 Constitutional Assembly led to its suspension by the emperor—not its inherently threatening democratic character. See Caio Prado, Jr., *A Evolução Política do Brasil* (São Paulo: Brasiliense, 1986), p. 60.

7. On the influence of Benjamin Constant on the 1824 consitution, see *História Geral da Civilização Brasileira*, ed. Holanda and Fausto, 3:257–62; and João Cruz Costa, *A History of Ideas in Brazil* (Berkeley and Los Angeles: University of California Press, 1964).

8. "The *poder moderador* can call whomever he wishes to organize the Cabinet: this person then organizes the election because it must be done; the election then produces the [parliamentary] majority. This is the representation system of our country!" Joaquim Nabuco, *Um Estadista do Império* (São Paulo: Editora Nacional, 1936), p. 205.

9. Oliveira Lima writes, "The memory of the conflicts between the Emperor and the Consitutional Assembly poisened the relations between the two powers during the entire reign of Dom Pedro I and caused his departure in the face of revolts" (*O Império Brasileiro* [Brasília: Editora da Universidade de Brasília, 1981], p. 71).

10. Afonso A. M. Franco, *História e Teoria dos Partidos Políticos no Brasil*, 2d ed. (São Paulo: Alfa-Omega, 1974).

11. On the electoral system during the Empire, see Maria D. G. Kinzo, *Representação política e Sistema Eleitoral no Brasil* (São Paulo: Símbolo, 1980).

12. Beiguelman, *A Formação Política do Brasil*, pp. 123–27.

13. Weber, "Politics as a Vocation," p. 87.

14. Holanda and Fausto, eds., *Historia Geral da Civilização Brasileira*, 5:88.

15. On the freezing of social cleavages into party systems, see Seymour M. Lipset and Stein Rokkan, *Party Systems and Voter Alignment* (New York: Free Press, 1967), chap. 1.

16. Faoro, *Os Donos do Poder*, pp. 315–35; Nestor Duarte, *A Ordem Privada ca Organização política Nacional* (São Paulo: Ed. Nacional, 1939), no. 172.

17. Prado, *A Evolução Política do Brasil*, p. 87, writes: "The governments after 1841 all have the same character. Even if they differ because as to their label of liberal or conservative, all evolved in the same manner without this differnt name retaining the least significance."

18. The most influential Marxist interpretation of political change in the Second Empire remains the final chapter of Prado, *A Evolução Política do Brasil*.

19. For an argument against seeing a direct correlation between newer forms of capital and progressive politics, see Beiguelman, *A Formação Política do Brasil*, p. 22. For example, on the regional alliance for abolition of slavery: "The axis of abolitionist agitation was articulated between the area without slaves (West São Paulo) which could afford salaried labor, and the area in decline (Northeast Brazil) for which the maintainance of slaves was a burden."

20. Oliveira Vianna is often cited as a cogent critic of liberal political institutions on Brazilian soil and an erudite spokesman for the Brazilian tradition of instrumental authoritarianism. However, respect for his insightful political sociology does not imply agreement with his authoritarian conclusions. See Vianna, *Instituições Políticas Brasileiras, O Ocaso do Império*; and *Problemas da Política Objetiva*.

21. Beiguelman, *A Formação Política do Brasil* and *Pequenos Estudos de Ciência Política*.

22. Caio Prado, Jr., *The Colonial Heritage of Modern Brazil* (Berkeley and Los Angeles: University of California Press, 1967).

23. Leonard Krieger, *The German Idea of Freedom* (New York: Columbia University Press, 1957) links the political conceptions and policies of German princes to the character of German premodern rural society. An equally broad historical perspective is helpful in accounting for the political conceptions of rural Brazilian political elites in the nineteenth century.

24. On suffrage and income requirements in imperial Brazil, see Graham, *Patronage and Politics in Nineteenth Century Brazil*, pp. 103–09.

25. Vianna, *Instituições Políticas Brasileiras*, p. 296.

26. Notes Vianna: "This code, with its municipal democracy, obliged, indeed forced, these rural gentleman into understandings and alliances to elect local authorities such as: *juízes de paz* (justices of the peace) with police

functions; municipal judges (criminal judges); municipal council members; and National Guard officials. These offices were elected in this period and were empowered with functions of police and the maintenance of order. . . . It was this private motive of defense or egoism that obliged the feudal chiefs to congregate in a syncretic moment, forging solidarities (parties) on the municipal level (ibid., p. 282).

27. Ibid., p. 290.

28. The 1836 Additional Act was a compromise between preparty factions, the *restauradores* (by maintaining the lifetime Senate) and the *exaltados* (by confering greater powers to the provincial assemblies). The Second Empire centralized control over justice, police, and the nomination of provincial presidents on December 3, 1841.

29. Beiguelman, *A Formação Política do Brasil,* p. 243.

30. Ibid., pp. 243–46.

31. The Liberal party clearly stood for progressive electoral legislation during the latter decades of the empire. See Beatriz W. C. Leite, *O Senado nos Anos Finais do Império: 1870–1889* (Brasília, D.F.: Imprensa do Senado, 1979). The landslide victory of the Liberals in the 1860 election has been cited as the party realignment that never was. See Lima, *O Império Brasileiro,* p. 43.

32. On the end of the empire, see Frank Colson, "On Expectations—Perspectives on the Crisis of 1889 in Brazil," *Journal of Latin American Studies* 13 (1981): 265–92.

33. José M. Carvalho, "A Composição Social dos Partidos Políticos Imperiais," *Cadernos DCP* 2 (1974): 1–34. Carvalho is primarily concerned with the general processes of homogeneous elite formation and Brazilian state building. Consequently, he stresses the *social* composition of imperial political parties and the shared socialization experiences of the Brazilian elite. The existence of unified patterns of elite socialization do indeed help to explain the remarkable stability of the Brazilian Empire compared to other Latin American nations in the nineteenth century. However, because of a concern with general patterns of social continuity, Carvalho seems to ignore patterns of political change.

34. This, of course, is Huntington's definition and operationalization of institutionalization. See *Political Order in Changing Societies,* p. 12.

35. The argument on state bureaucratic domination of imperial politics can be found in Faoro, *Os Donos do Poder,* and Fernando Urococheia, *O Minotauro Imperial* (São Paulo: Difel, 1981).

36. Emilia V. Costa, *The Brazilian Empire: Myths and Histories* (Chicago: University of Chicago Press, 1985).

37. John Henry Schultz, "The Brazilian Army in Politics: 1850–1894," Ph.D. diss., Princeton University, 1973; William Dudley, "Institutional Sources of Officer Discontent in the Brazilian Army: 1870–1889," *Hispanic American Historical Review* 45 (1975): 44–65.

38. Colson, "On Expectations—Perspectives on the Crisis of 1889 in Brazil."

Chapter 3. Devolution in the Second Party System

1. On the influence of U.S. federalism on Brazil's 1891 consitution, see Maria C. C. Souza, "O Processo Político-Partidário na Primeira República," in *Brasil em Perspectiva*, ed. Carlos G. Mota (São Paulo: Difel, 1969).

2. Thomas Skidmore, *Politics in Brazil: An Experiment in Democracy* (Oxford: Oxford University Press, 1967), p. 331.

3. Comparative studies of the major Brazilian states are Joseph Love, *Rio Grande do Sul and Brazilian Regionalism.* (Stanford: Stanford University Press, 1971); Joseph L. Love, *São Paulo in the Brazilian Federation, 1889–1937* (Stanford: Stanford University Press, 1980); Robert M. Levine, *Pernambuco in the Brazilian Federation, 1889–1937* (Stanford: Stanford University Press, 1978); John D. Wirth, *Minas Gerais in the Brazilian Federation, 1889–1937* (Stanford: Stanford University Press, 1977).

4. A renaissance of historical research occurred after military intervention in 1964, when Brazilian scholars turned to less controversial periods such as the Old Republic. See Eduardo Kugelmas, "Dificil Hegemonia: Um Estudo Sobre São Paulo na Primeira República," Ph.D. diss., Universidade de São Paulo, 1986.

5. For example, see Edgar Carone, *A República Velha (Evolução Política)* (São Paulo, Difel, 1971). A classic account of *coronelismo* that focuses on the Old Republic period is Leal, *Coronelismo, Enxada e Voto.*

6. See Kugelmas, "Dificil Hegemonia."

7. On the concept of *Política dos Governadores*, see Paula Beiguelman, "A Primeira República no Período de 1891 a 1909," appendix to *Pequenos Estudos de Ciência Política*; and Souza, "O Processo Político-Partidário na Primeira República."

8. Peter Flynn writes in *Brazil: A Political Analysis* (Boulder: Westview Press, 1978), p. 30: "In November 1894, a Paulista president, Prudente de Morais, was able to take over the government, followed by two more paulista Presidents, Campos Salles (1898) and Rodrigues Alves (1902–1908), in a pattern of Paulista domination which continued unchallenged until 1930."

9. Love, *São Paulo in the Brazilian Federation*, p. 86. Celso Furtado, *The Economic Growth of Brazil: A Survey from Colonial to Modern Times* (Berkeley and Los Angeles: University of California Press, 1963), also stresses the centrality of coffee oligarchs (read São Paulo elite) in the Old Republic and argues that the central elements of state policy, such as currency devaluations and subsidy programs, socialized the losses of the coffee sector. But Kugelmas offers several reasons why industrial expansion and coffee interests were, in fact, quite compatible. The short-term interests of the coffee sector

did indeed determine whether inflationary or deflationary policies were adopted by the government. But the consequences for other economic sectors were not always perverse. First, coffee price support programs and import taxes actually stabilized internal markets and encouraged local industry. Second, the currency devaluations that tended to favor coffee exporters also favored industrial exporters as well as commercial and financial interests. In sum, on the level of state policy, agrarian, commercial, and industrial interests were not incompatible: industrial and coffee interests were *not* as irreconcilable as supposed by previous accounts. The broad interventionist policies of the 1906 Taubaté agreement would not have been possible if they simply socialized the losses of the coffee sector. See Kugelmas, "Difícil Hegemonia," chap. 1.

10. Mauricio A. Font, *Coffee, Contention, and Change in the Making of Modern Brazil* (New York: Basil Blackwell, 1990). For other perspectives on interests and policies in the Old Republic, see: João M. C. Mello, *O Capitalismo Tardio* (São Paulo: Brasiliense, 1982); and Love, *São Paulo in the Brazilian Federation.*

11. Beiguelman, "A Primeira República no Período de 1891 a 1909"; and Souza, "O Processo Político-Partidário na Primeira República."

12. Fernando Henrique Cardoso, "Dos Governos Militares a Prudente-Campos Salles," in *História Geral da Civilização Brasileira*, Tomo III, no. 1, ed. Holanda and Fausto (São Paulo: Difel, 1973).

13. Leal, *Coronelismo, Enxada e Voto.*

14. Vianna notes this displacement of local autonomy in his introduction to the 1920 census. Cited in Font, *Coffee, Contention, and Change*, p. 131.

15. Ibid., p. 135.

16. Ibid., p. 136.

17. Ibid.; Kugelmas, "Difícil Hegemonia"; and Elisa P. Reis, "The Agrarian Roots of Authoritarian Modernization in Brazil, 1880–1930," Ph.D. diss., Massachusetts Institute of Technology, 1980.

18. In the case of Minas Gerais State, see Frances Hagopian, "The Politics of Oligarchy: The Persistence of Traditional Elites in Contemporary Brazil," Ph.D. diss., Massachusetts Institute of Technology, 1986.

19. Font, *Coffee, Contention and Change*, p. 130, argues that during the Old Republic "bureaucratization soon led to centralization and a policy-making style less directly bound to narrow private interests." Indeed, Font suggests that an "autonomous entrepreneurial vision of statemaking" emerged in São Paulo during the implementation of large-scale projects from 1900 to 1920 such as immigration programs, railroad construction, and foreign debt management.

20. James Malloy, *The Politics of Social Security in Brazil* (Pittsburgh: University of Pittsburgh Press, 1979).

21. Font notes, "The 1920s provide much evidence of a growing collaboration and coalition among immigrant industrialists, immigrants in gen-

eral, and the PRP" (Mauricio Font, "Coffee, Planters, Politics, and Development in Brazil: An Alternative Scenario," *Latin American Research Review* 22 [1983]: 79).

22. Boris Fausto, *A Revolução de 1930: Historiografia e História* (São Paulo: Brasiliense, 1970).

23. On the link between the traditional *Paulista* coffee elite and opposition to the PRP and the Old Republic, see Font, *Coffee, Contention, and Change*, chap. 8.

24. Ibid., p. 151.

25. Ibid., p. 158.

26. Font notes: "As party politics became key channels of open political contention, associations began to play a relatively circumspect representational role" ("Coffee, Planters, Politics, and Development in Brazil, p. 76).

27. On the turn to opposition, Font notes that: "The PD projected a progressive or leftist image and therefore expected to draw support from the "popular" sectors and to form the mass movement deemed necessary to overthrow the PRP" (ibid., p. 79).

28. Ibid., p. 84.

29. For an explanation of political change in the 1920s in Brazil that focuses primarily on social and economic forces, see Huntington, *Political Order in Changing Societies*, pp. 220–24.

30. On the integration of coffee with subsequent mercantile, industrial, and financial capital, see Mello, *O Capitalismo Tardio*.

31. Souza, "O Processo Político-Partidário na Primeira República," pp. 219–26.

32. For this comparison between Argentina and Brazil, see Boris Fausto, "Pequenos Ensaios da História da República, 1889–1945," *Cadernos Cebrap* 10 (1972).

33. For two opposing perspectives on the importance of Rui Barbosa's 1910 election campaign, see Hélgio Trindade, "Bases da Democracia Brasileira: Lógica Liberal e Práxis Autoritária," in *Como Renascem as Democracias*, ed. Alain Rouquie et al. (São Paulo: Brasiliense, 1985); and Vianna, *Problemas da Política Objetiva*, p. 65.

Chapter 4. Mass Inclusion in the Third Party System

1. On the spoils system from 1945 to 1964, see Ames, "The Congressional Connection."

2. Literature reviews by Fábio Wanderley Reis and Bolivar Lamounier compare the diverse theories and methods used to analyze party politics, political polarization, and democratic breakdown in 1964. This section is largely based on Lamounier and Meneguello, *Partidos Políticos e Consolidação Democrática*; and Fábio W. Reis, "O Econômico, O Institucional, e o Polí-

tico na Literatura Brasileira Recente," appendix to *Política e Racionalidade*, spec. ed. no. 37 (Belo Horizonte: Revista Brasileira de Estudos Políticos, 1984).

3. Juan Linz and Alfred Stepan, eds., *The Breakdown of Democratic Regimes: Latin America* (Baltimore: Johns Hopkins University Press, 1978).

4. J. Samuel Valenzuela, *The Breakdown of Democratic Regimes: Chile* (Baltimore: Johns Hopkins University Press, 1978).

5. Alfred Stepan, "Political Leadership and Regime Breakdown: Brazil," in *The Breakdown of Democratic Regimes: Latin America*, ed. Linz and Stepan.

6. On the idea of a party system in Brazil, see Giovanni Sartori, preface to *Partidos e Sistemas Partidarios* (Rio de Janeiro: Zahar/Universidade de Brasilia, 1982).

7. Lamounier and Meneguello, *Partidos Políticos e Consolidação Democrática*.

8. For discussion of politics in pre-1964 Brazil from this perspective, see Huntington, *Political Order in Changing Societies*, p. 224.

9. Lamounier and Meneguello, *Partidos Políticos e Consolidação Democrática*, p. 36.

10. On the events leading to the abandonment of structural economic reforms and increasing confrontation between President Goulart and the business community, see Thomas Skidmore, *The Politics of Military Rule in Brazil, 1964–1985* (New York: Oxford University Press, 1988).

11. The most influential interpretation from this perspective remains, Guillermo O'Donnell, *Modernization and Bureaucratic Authoritarianism* (Berkeley: Institute of International Studies, 1973).

12. Other works that take this approach are Olavo Brasil, Jr., "The Brazilian Multi-party System: A Case for Contextual Rationality," Ph.D. diss., University of Michigan, 1980; and Lúcia Hippólito, *PDS: De Raposas e Reformistas* (Rio de Janeiro: Paz e Terra, 1985).

13. Wanderley G. dos Santos, "The Calculus of Conflict: Impasse in Brazilian Politics and the Crisis of 1964," Ph.D. diss., Stanford University, 1979.

14. See also Youssef Cohen, "Democracy from Above: The Political Origins of Military Dictatorship in Brazil," *World Politics* 40 (1987): 30–54.

15. Souza, *Estado e Partidos Políticos no Brasil*, p. 140.

16. The structure of Souza's argument (ibid.) is quite similar to Max Weber's account of how Senate-based patronage systems were reorganized by the plebiscitary impulses of presidential elections in the United States. See the discussion in chap. 1.

17. Souza follows Theodore Lowi, *The End of Liberalism*, 2d ed. (New York: Norton, 1979) in distinguishing between redistributive, regulatory, and distributive policies.

18. On the irresponsibility of party leaders and career patterns before 1964, see Souza, *Estado e Partidos Políticos no Brasil;* and Lamounier and Meneguello, *Partidos Políticos e Consolidação Democrática.*

19. On the organization of labor politics and mass inclusion as critical junctures in Brazil and Latin America, see Ruth Collier and David Collier, *Shaping the Political Arena* (Princeton: Princeton University Press, 1991).

20. On the difference between exclusionary and inclusionary corporatism, see: Alfred Stepan, *State and Society: Peru in Comparative Perspective* (Princeton: Princeton University Press, 1978).

21. For a review of the literature on the 1945 transition, see Stanley Hilton, "The Overthrow of Getúlio Vargas in 1945: Intervention, Defense of Democracy, or Political Retribution?" *Hispanic American Historical Review* 67 (1987): 1–37.

22. For discussion of the turn to democratic mechanisms by authoritarian leaders in 1974, see chap. 5.

23. Juan Linz, "The Future of an Authoritarian Situation or the Institutionalization of an Authoritarian Regime: The Case of Brazil," in *Authoritarian Brazil,* ed. Alfred Stepan (New Haven: Yale University Press, 1973).

24. See Fernando H. Cardoso, *Autoritarismo e Democratização* (Rio de Janeiro: Paz e Terra, 1975), p. 175.

25. This review of party and electoral legislation relies on Souza, *Estado e Partidos Políticos no Brasil.*

26. The 1945 Electoral Code was based on the postrevolutionary Electoral Code of 1932—without the features of functional representation. The core principle of the code combined proportional representation for legislative offices and majoritarian elections for executive posts. This system attempts to separate the plebiscitarian tendencies of majoritarian elections from legislative races and is based on Assis Brasil's classic *Democracia Representiva* (Rio de Janeiro, 1931). See Kinzo, *Representação Política e Sistema Eleitoral no Brasil.* This hybrid electoral system has remained in effect until today and was used even during authoritarianism, 1965–1985, despite cancellation of direct elections for the presidency, governorships, and mayorships of capitals and cities declared national security zones.

27. On the declaration of presidential candidacies in the 1945 transition, see Maria V. M. Benevides, *A UDN e o Udenismo: Ambiguidades do Liberalismo Brasileiro* (Rio de Janeiro: Paz e Terra, 1981). Requirements for party registration were quite liberal in 1945. Only 500 signatures and 10,000 votes were needed across five states. However, the clause that allowed the Tribunal Superior Eleitoral (TSE, Supreme Electoral Court) to ban antidemocratic parties and President Dutra's raising the threshold in 1946 from 10,000 to 50,000 voters made it easy to manipulate the process. In 1945, the União da Juventude Comunista (UJC, Union of Communist Youth) was banned and the Partido Communista Brasileiro (PCB, Brazilian Communist party) followed in 1947.

28. Souza, *Estado e Partidos Políticos no Brasil,* p. 119.

29. Figures for the percentage of ex-officio registrations among total registered voters in other states are: 54 percent in the Federal District, 33 percent in São Paulo state, 31 percent in Rio de Janeiro, 21 percent in Rio Grande do Sul and Pernambuco, 17 percent in Minas Gerais, and 15 percent in Bahia. ibid. p. 121.

30. The computerized records of the 1986 reregistration of voters are available at the Processamento de Dados do Senado (PRODASEN, Data Processing Service of the Brazilian Senate).

31. This summary of the organization of parties during the 1945 transition is based on Souza, *Estado e Partidos Políticos no Brasil.*

32. John French, "Workers and the Rise of Adhemarista Populism in São Paulo, Brazil 1945–1947," *Hispanic American Historical Review* 68 (1988): 1–43; and Regina Sampaio, *Adhemar de Barros e o PSP* (São Paulo, Global, 1982).

33. The memoirs of Amaral Peixoto, *Memórias de um Político* (Rio de Janeiro: Alfa Omega, 1985), are an excellent source on the transformation of the organizational and political resources of an interventor in Rio de Janeiro into lasting personal and PSD support in the state.

34. For an account of opposition in the Estado Novo and the organization of the UDN, see Benevides, *A UDN e o Udenismo.*

35. See John W. F. Dulles, *Vargas of Brazil: A Political Biography* (Austin: University of Texas Press, 1967); and Paulo Brandi, *Vargas, da Vida para a Historia* (Rio de Janeiro: Zahar, 1985).

36. Lamounier and Meneguello, *Partidos Políticos e Consolidação Democrática,* pp. 48–50.

37. Souza, p. 140.

38. Both Souza, *Estado e Partidos Políticos no Brasil,* and Brasil, "The Brazilian Multi-party System," agree that the critical pre-1964 trend in elections is not a shift to minor parties, but to party alliances of the most diverse sort.

39. Lamounier and Meneguello, *Partidos Políticos e Consolidação Democrática,* p. 50.

40. Souza, *Estado e Partidos Políticos no Brasil,* p. 152.

41. Ibid., p. 152.

42. See Albert O. Hirschman, "The Turn to Authoritarianism in Latin America and the Search for Its Economic Determinants," in *The New Authoritarianism in Latin America,* ed. David Collier (Princeton: Princeton University Press, 1979), pp. 68–98; and Maria da Conceição Tavares, "Rise and Decline of Import Substitution in Brazil," *Economic Bulletin from Latin America* 9 (1964): 1–65.

43. Fernando H. Cardoso, "Associated Dependent Development: Theoretical and Practical Implications," in *Authoritarian Brazil,* ed. Stepan.

44. Skidmore, *Politics in Brazil, 1930–1964;* and Flynn, *Brazil: A Political Analysis.*

45. Stepan, "Political Leadership and Regime Breakdown: Brazil."
46. Skidmore, *Politics in Brazil, 1930–1964*, p. 328.
47. On conservative political action groups before 1964, see Rene Dreifuss, *A Conquista do Estado* (Petrópolis: Vozes, 1981).
48. On recent proposals for parliamentary government in Latin America, see Arend Lijphart, *Parliamentary versus Presidential Government* (New York: Oxford University Press, 1992).

Chapter 5. Toward the Fourth Party System

1. On the transition period, see Skidmore, *The Politics of Military Rule in Brazil*. The complex mixture has led to diverse claims. Some argue that more open electoral contests would promptly lead to the demise of military rule (M. J. Sarles, "Maintaining Control Through Political Parties: the Brazilian Strategy," *Comparative Politics* 15 [1982]: 41–72). Others suggest that electoral and party activity during liberalization would increase and perhaps institutionalize authoritarian state control (Maria H. M. Alves, *The Formation of the National Security State: The State and Opposition in Military Brazil* [Austin: University of Texas Press, 1985]). Juan Linz describes the unusual combination of directly elected opposition governors within an authoritarian regime after 1982 as a situation of diarchy ("The Transition from Authoritarianism to Democracy in Spain: Some Thoughts for Brazilians," unpublished MS, Yale University, 1983).

2. O'Donnell, *Modernization and Bureaucratic Authoritarianism.*

3. On the ESG in Brazilian politics, see Alfred Stepan, *The Military in Politics: Changing Patterns in Brazil* (Princeton: Princeton University Press, 1971)

4. During 1980 I reviewed over seventy transcripts, working papers, and special project reports on public opinion, social communications, and public relations in the Superior War College library. See Kurt von Mettenheim, "Media-State Relations in Brazil: 1955–1980," unpublished MS, Columbia University, 1982.

5. On the public relations groups of political action groups before 1964, see Dreifuss, *A Conquista do Estado.*

6. Otavio Costa, "Governo e Comunicação Social," Conference, Escola Superior de Guerra, Rio de Janeiro, 1970.

7. Cohen, *The Manipulation of Consent.*

8. See Lamounier, "Ideology and Authoritarian Regimes." The distribution of immediate and personalist conceptualizations is not reported because no adequate recoding procedure was encountered to compare the 1972/1973 social survey data to subsequent electoral survey data. However, because Converse's incomplete typology of how voters think about politics informs existing accounts of public opinion in authoritarian Brazil, survey respondents are dichotomized between a very large unpoliticized mass and a

very small portion of citizens able to think ideologically, perceive group interests, and value democratic institutions. Given the typological problems discussed in chapter 1, this characterization of the Brazilian public seems to rule out the possibility of more sophisticated mass *opposition* to authoritarianism.

9. Linz, "The Future of an Authoritarian Situation."

10. On the void between state and society in bureaucratic authoritarianism, see Guillermo O'Donnell, "Tensions in the Bureaucratic Authoritarian State and the Question of Democracy," in *The New Authoritarianism in Latin America*, ed. Collier.

11. Skidmore, *The Politics of Military Rule in Brazil.*

12. Linz, "The Future of an Authoritarian Situation."

13. Douglas Chalmers and Christopher Robinson, "Why Power Contenders Choose Liberalization Strategies," *International Studies Quarterly* 26 (1982): 3–36.

14. Alfred Stepan, "Paths Toward Redemocratization: Theoretical and Comparative Considerations," in *Transitions from Authoritarian Rule*, ed. O'Donnell et al.

15. Thomas Skidmore, "Brazil's Slow Road to Democratization: 1974–1985," in *Democratizing Brazil*, ed. Stepan.

16. On the origins and development of Brazilian military theory, see Stepan, *The Military in Politics.*

17. On the tradition of instrumental authoritarianism in Brazil, see Lamounier, "Ideology and Authoritarian Regimes."

18. On President Geisel and liberalization, see Skidmore, *The Politics of Military Rule in Brazil*, pp. 163–64. President Geisel's speeches marking the liberalization of the military government were printed in the daily papers, and organized in the opposition weekly, *Movimento*, September 2, 1974.

19. G. Golbery do Couto e Silva, *Conjuntura Política Nacional: O Poder Executivo e Geopolítico do Brazil* (Rio de Janeiro: José Olympio, 1981).

20. "National objectives" is a military concept that refers to the goals of national security and development.

21. Golbery, *Conjuntura Política Nacional.*

22. In the first major social science volume devoted to electoral and party politics in contemporary Brazil, Bolivar Lamounier and Fernando Cardoso emphasize the *plebiscitarian* character of the 1974 election, and cite several explanations for the unexpected strength of opposition voting: the presence of a new generation of young, first time voters; the response of voters to economic crisis and negative income distribution; and the symbolic role of the MDB as a protest vote against the regime: *Os Partidos e as Eleições no Brasil*, ed. Cardoso and Lamounier. For further discussion, see chaps. 6 and 8.

23. ARENA swept all governorships in October 1974 because they were chosen in restricted state-level electoral congresses.

24. Santos, *Poder e Política*, p. 128.

25. On the 1976 municipal elections, see Reis, ed., *Os Partidos e o Regime*. The strength of ARENA in the less populated municipalities can be seen by the translation of votes into offices. While the national vote in the 1976 municipal elections was 15.2 million for ARENA and 12.7 million for the MDB, ARENA retained control of 83 percent of the nation's mayorships and a majority in most municipal assemblies.

26. On military dissent and presidential succession in the Geisel government, see W. Goes, *O Brasil do General Geisel* (Rio de Janeiro: Nova Fronteira, 1978).

27. In June 1979, prior censorship of the mass media ended. See Joan Dassin, "Press Censorship in Brazil: How and Why," *Index on Censorship*, vol. 8 (London: Oxford University Press, 1979). During 1980, a restricted and reciprocal amnesty was granted to virtually all exiled and banned political figures. The meaning of reciprocity was that it also applied to military personnel which overstepped the law in the war against subversion. Henceforth, no military personnel could be charged for crimes committed before July 1980. On the amnesty in Brazil, see Skidmore, *The Politics of Military Rule in Brazil*, p. 217. Finally, Labor Minister Murilo Macedo instituted semestral wage readjustments which, although short of labor demands, protected real wage levels by linking readjustments to inflation (ibid., p. 222).

28. Golbery, *Conjuntura Política Nacional*, p. 28.

29. The mandatory vote by party list, called the *sublegenda* legislation (Art. 92, Código Eleitoral 1965, law no. 4,737 of July 17, 1965) was first adopted for the 1966 elections, and was meant to reconcile the candidacies of the UDN, PSD, and PTB in the new government party, ARENA.

30. See the interview with ex-President Figueiredo in *Veja*, October 14, 1984.

31. The Brazilian electoral calendar normally holds national and state elections every four years, with municipal elections in between.

32. The *voto vinculado* (literally, linked vote), extended the sublegenda legislation to majoritarian offices, forcing voters to choose one party in all contested offices. See Skidmore, *The Politics of Military Rule in Brazil*, p. 113.

33. Linz, "The Transition from an Authoritarian Regime to Democracy in Spain."

34. The *Jogo de Bicho* leaders of suburban Rio de Janeiro were once closely affiliated with the death squads and police repression during the 1970s.

35. It appears that the vice-president had alienated several military ministers, especially SNI Minister Octavio Medeiros, by, for example, defending constitutional succession rules during President Figueiredo's hospitalizations in 1981 and 1983.

36. On the Paulo Maluf campaign, see the special edition of *Veja*, November 14, 1984.

37. On the discussions between Tancredo Neves and Thales Ramalho, as well as other PDS members, see the special edition of *Veja*, January 16, 1985.

38. On the labor, social, and opposition movements and parties in the campaign for direct elections, see Margaret Keck, *The Workers' Party and Democratization in Brazil* (New Haven: Yale University Press, 1992), pp. 219–20.

39. Cited in ibid., p. 220.

40. On May 1, 1981, a bomb exploded in the parking lot of the Rio-Centro stadium during a concert and celebration by left groups and political parties. Two plainclothes sergeants from the information services were killed while preparing the bomb—for disruptive purposes. The subsequent military investigation was widely denounced in the press as a coverup. From the perspective of the military, the trial was a public relations disaster that delegitimized hard-line groups in the intelligence services and tipped the scales against a pro-coup alliance within the military.

41. The lists submitted by regional party leaders to Tancredo Neves for appointments to executive agencies and state companies were published by *Veja*, July 17, 1985, pp. 20–27.

42. On the difference between popular mobilization in the direct elections campaign and the sickness and death of Tancredo Neves, see Marlyse Meyer and Maria L. Montes, *Redescobrindo o Brasil: A Festa na Política Brasileira* (São Paulo: T. A. Queiroz, 1985).

43. *Fisiológico* literally means of the corpus, and refers to a politician whose career and power bases lie in state bureaucratic politics.

44. Interview with Senator Fernando Henrique Cardoso, November 20, 1985.

45. Ibid.

46. James Sundquist, *Dynamics of the Party System*, 2d ed. (Washington, D.C.: Brookings, 1983), p. 11.

47. Interview with Senator Fernando Henrique Cardoso, November 4, 1986.

48. MDB *historicos* were national leaders of the party dating from its role as opposition party under military rule and democratic transition.

49. Interview with Fernando Gasparian, PMDB federal deputy from São Paulo, March 1991.

50. See also Diniz, *Voto e Máquina Política*; Kinzo, *An Opposition Party in an Authoritarian Regime*; and Caldeira, "Electoral Struggles in a Neighborhood on the Periphery of São Paulo."

51. On September 29, 1992, the Brazilian Chamber of Deputies voted 441 to 38 to suspend Fernando Collor de Mello from office and initiate a formal trial in the Senate. In December 1992, 76 of 81 senators voted for

impeachment. See Kurt Weyland, "The Rise and Fall of President Collor and Its Impact on Brazilian Democracy," *Journal of Interamerican Studies and World Affairs* 35 (1993): 1–37.

52. See Bolivar Lamounier and Dieter Nohlen, eds., *Presidencialismo ou Parlamentarismo* (São Paulo: Loyola, 1993) and José Serra, ed., *Reforma Política no Brasil, Parlamentarismo x Presidencialismo* (São Paulo: Siciliano, 1993).

53. O'Donnell, "Tensions in the Bureaucratic Authoritarian State," pp. 288–91.

Introduction to Part III

1. For reviews of Brazilian electoral sociology, see Bolivar Lamounier, ed., *Voto de Desconfiança* (Petrópolis: Vozes, 1980); and Reis, ed., *Os Partidos e o Regime*.

2. Giovanni Sartori, "From the Sociology of Politics to Political Sociology," in *Politics and the Social Sciences*, ed. Seymour M. Lipset (Oxford: Oxford University Press, 1969).

Chapter 6. Plebiscitarian Appeals and Patronage Machines

1. Cardoso, introduction to *Os Partidos e as Eleições no Brasil*, ed. Cardoso and Lamounier, p. 11.

2. Bolivar Lamounier, "O Voto em São Paulo, 1970–1978," in *Voto de Desconfiança*, ed. Lamounier (Petrópolis: Vozes, 1980), p. 80.

3. For a recent review, see Mainwaring, "Political Parties and Democratization in Brazil and the Southern Cone."

4. For review of the literature on Brazilian parties and party identification, see Lamounier and Meneguello, *Partidos Políticos e Consolidação Democrática*.

5. The odds of an event occurring are defined as the ratio of the probability that it will occur to the probability that it will not occur (*SPSS/PC Advanced Statistics 4.0* [Chicago: SPSS, 1990], p. B-43).

6. Comparative analysis of party identification focuses less on long-term factors. See Ian Budge, Ivor Crew, and David Farlie, eds., *Party Identification and Beyond* (New York: Wiley, 1976).

7. The idea that stable democracy requires stable party identification can be traced to Duverger's concern with "flash parties." See Duverger, *Political Parties*, pp. 312–24; Seymour M. Lipset, *Political Man: The Social Bases of Politics* (New York: Doubleday, 1960), pp. 148–79; William P. Shiveley, "Party Identification, Party Choice, and Voting Stability: The Weimar Case," *American Political Science Review* 56 (1972).

8. On the literature on party identification, see Budge, Crew, and Farlie, eds., *Party Identification and Beyond*.

9. The link between collective experiences under authoritarianism and the transformation of political culture has been made by Mainwaring and Viola, "New Social Movements."

10. Joaquim F. Assis Brasil, *Democracia Representativa: Do Voto e do Mode de Votar* (Rio de Janeiro: Imprensa Nacional, 1931).

11. Interview with Senator Fernando Henrique Cardoso, November 4, 1986.

12. Converse, "Of Time and Partisan Stability."

13. Barnes et al., "The Development of Partisanship in New Democracies: The Case of Spain."

14. Maria D. G. Kinzo, "Novos Partidos: O Início do Debate," in *Voto de Desconfiança*, ed. Bolivar Lamounier (Petrópolis: Vozes, 1980).

15. The classic accounts of Brazilian politics correctly stress the passivity of its society and the patrimonial-bureaucratic character of its state. These contexts for partisan affinity in Brazil are quite distant from liberal ideals. However, ideal conceptions of how electoral representation works tend to overlook the consequences of plebiscitarian and patronage politics, and the effects of these different historical experiences on the way Brazilian citizens think about politics and vote.

16. Cardoso and Lamounier, eds., *Os Partidos e as Eleições no Brasil*; Santos, "As Eleições e a Dinâmica do Processo Político Brasileiro," in *Poder e Política: Uma Crônica do Autoritarismo no Brasil* (São Paulo: Alfa Omega, 1979); Reis, ed., *Os Partidos e o Regime*.

17. Santos, *Poder e Política*, p. 104.

18. Correlations Between Pre-1964 Party Identification and Post-1965 Party Identification, Porto Alegre, 1972–1978:

| | Post-1964 Party Identification | | | | | |
| | 1972 | | 1974 | | 1978 | |
Pre-1964 Identification	*Arena*	*MDB*	*Arena*	*MDB*	*Arena*	*MDB*
União Democático Nacional	.12	—	.47	—	.25	—
Partido Social Democrático	.15	—	.20	—	.16	—
Partido Trabalhista Brasileiro	—	.28	—	.57	—	.38

Source: 1972 Social Survey, Porto Alegre Electoral Surveys, 1974, 1978. Reported corelations are Pearson's product-moment coefficients, significant at the level of .01.

Note: The reported data is from the Municipality of Porto Alegre because it was the only city with comparable survey questions over time. Porto Alegre is perhaps the most politicized city in Brazil, but even here the decreasing importance of pre-1964 affinity holds.

19. On partisanship in Chile and Argentina, see Garreton, *The Chilean Political Process*, J. Samuel Valenzuela and Arturo Valenzuela, "Party Oppositions Under the Chilean Military Regime," *Military Rule in Chile: Dictatorship and Oppositions* (Baltimore: Johns Hopkins University Press, 1986); Edgardo Catterberg, *Argentina Confronts Politics: Political Culture and Public Opinion in the Argentine Transition to Democracy* (Boulder, Colo.: Lynne Rienner, 1991).

20. Unfortunately, the differences between survey questions asked about parties and issues between the cities of the 1978 survey (as well as with the 1974 and 1982 surveys) do not allow analysis of the structural content of the new party images and identifications that appeared after 1974.

21. Linz, "The Transition from an Authoritarian Regime to Democracy in Spain."

22. On conservative forces in recent Latin American politics, see Atilio Boron, Maria C. Souza, and Douglas Chalmers, *The Right and Democracy in Latin America* (Westport, Conn.: 1991).

23. Indeed, this link between differentiation and organization in Brazilian public opinion is consistent with theories of political development: differentiation is cited as a central variable of political institutionalization.

24. On the diverse types of political sophistication in mass publics, see Kinder, "Diversity and Complexity in American Public Opinion." On the historicity of the left-right dimension, see Ronald Inglehart, "The Changing Structure of Political Cleavages in Western Society," in *Electoral Change in Advanced Industrial Democracies: Realignment or Dealignment?* ed. Russell Dalton et al. (Princeton: Princeton University Press, 1983); and Giovanni Sartori and Giacomo Sani, "Polarization, Fragmentation, and Competition in Western Democracies," in *Western European Party Systems*, ed. Hans Daalder and Peter Mair (Beverly Hills: Sage, 1983).

25. Scholars now tend to emphasize issue positions, postmaterialist value orientations, retrospective judgments, and other causes of voter alignment that grant considerably greater rationality to voters than the idea of durable family-based party identification.

26. Esther Fuchs and Robert Shapiro, "Government Performance as a Basis for Machine Support," *Urban Affairs Quarterly* 18 (1983): 537–50.

Chapter 7. Plebiscitarian Issues and Local Concerns

1. The classic statement on the increased importance of issue voting remains Nie et al., *The Changing American Voter*. On the implications of issue voting for theories of public opinion and voter alignment, see Inglehart, "Aggregate Stability and Individual Level Flux in Mass Belief Systems."

2. For example, Duverger, *Political Parties*, and Campbell et al., *The American Voter*.

3. Nie et al., *The Changing American Voter*, p. 155. Compare this perspective to the original formulations in Campbell et al., *The American Voter*, p. 255: "Whatever the depths of a person's political involvement, there are rather basic limitations on cognitive capacities which are likely to make certain of the most sophisticated types of content remain inaccessible to the poorly endowed observer."

4. Russell Dalton, Scott Flanagan, and Paul Beck, *Electoral Change in Advanced Industrial Democracies: Realignment or Dealignment?* (Princeton: Princeton University Press, 1983).

5. Inglehart, "Aggregate Stability and Individual-Level Flux in Mass Belief Systems"; Ronald Inglehart, *The Silent Revolution* (Princeton: Princeton University Press, 1977).

6. The causal weight of issues on voter choice in the advanced democracies normally explains 15–30 percent of voter choice. See Ronald Inglehart and Hans Klingemann, "Party Identification, Ideological Preference, and the Left-Right Dimension among Western Publics," in *Party Identification and Beyond*, ed. Budge, Crew, and Farlie.

7. On the geographic distribution of opposition and support during the transition period, see the conclusion to Reis, ed., *Os Partidos e o Regime*.

8. Although over 70 percent of respondents failed to answer the survey question about left-right self-placement, the regression analysis model remains compelling because of the large number and wide distribution of valid cases, the primarily demographic character of differences between respondents who did and did not answer, and the experience of other analysts with low response rates to surveys conducted early in periods of democratic transition.

9. Ruth C. L. Cardoso, "Movimentos Sociais Urbanos: Balanço Crítico," in *Sociedade e Política no Brasil Pós-1964*, ed. Bernardo Sorj and Maria H. T. de Almeida (São Paulo: Brasiliense, 1984).

10. Antonio Flávio de Oliveira Peirucci, "Democracia, Igreja, e Voto: O Envolvimento dos Padres de Paróquia de São Paulo nas Eleições de 1982," Ph.D. diss., Universidade de São Paulo, 1985.

11. Caldeira, "Electoral Struggles in a Neighborhood on the Periphery of São Paulo."

12. On the empowerment of the PT in municipal governments, see Keck, *The Workers' Party and Democratization in Brazil*. On municipal politics in the industrial suburbs of São Paulo, see Maria T. Souza, "Concentração Industrial e Estrutura Partidária: O Processo Eleitoral no ABC, 1966–1982," Ph.D. diss., Universidade de São Paulo, 1984.

13. Diniz, *Voto e Máquina Política: Patronagem e Clientelismo no Rio de Janeiro*.

14. The relation between perceptions of local services and infrastructure and intent to vote for the PMDB in rural areas is stronger in the rural areas

because the opposition party PMDB actually controlled municipal executives and chambers in two of the four rural municipalities where the electoral surveys were applied.

15. Maria G. Rua, "O Comportamento Político de Eleitorado Rural: Uma Análise Comparada," M.A. thesis, Instituto Universitário de Pesquisas do Rio de Janeiro, 1984.

16. On the absense of issue intercorrelations during the period of hardline rule in authoritarian Brazil, see Cohen, *The Manipulation of Consent*, pp. 40–46; and Lamounier, "Ideology and Authoritarian Regimes."

Chapter 8. Government Performance and Accountability Voting

1. Morris Fiorina, *Restrospective Voting in American Elections* (New Haven: Yale University Press, 1981); Schattschneider, *Party Government*. On accountability as a characteristic of representation, the classic work is Warren E. Miller and Donald E. Stokes, "Constituency Influence in Congress," *American Political Science Review* 57 (1963): 45–56. On accountability in contemporary democratic theory, see Sartori, *The Theory of Democracy Revisited*, p. 233.

2. Key, *The Responsible Electorate*.

3. G. H. Kramer, "Short Term Fluctuations in United States Voting Behavior, 1864–1964," *American Political Science Review* 65 (1971): 131–43.

4. Robert Shapiro and Bruce M. Conforto, "Presidential Performance, The Economy, and the Public's Evaluation of Economic Conditions," *Journal of Politics* 42 (1980): 49–81; Howard Bloom and Douglas Price, "Voter Response to Short Run Economic Conditions: The Assymetric Effect of Prosperity and Recession," *American Political Science Review* 69 (1975): 1240–54.

5. Powell, "Comparative Voting Behavior."

6. Benjamin Page, Robert Shapiro, and Glen Dempsey, "What Moves Public Opinion," *American Political Science Review* 81 (1987): 23–43.

7. On sociotropic and pocketbook voting, see Donald Kinder, "Presidents, Prosperity, and Public Opinion," in *Public Opinion Quarterly* 45 (1981): 1–21; Heinz Eulau and Michael Lewis Beck, *Economic Conditions and Electoral Outcomes: The U.S. and Western Europe* (New York: Agathon Press, 1985).

8. Vilmar Faria's analysis of opposition voting tendencies in the 1974 election refers to Hirschman's idea of a changing tolerance for income inequality in the course of economic development. See Faria, "As Eleições de 1974 em São Paulo: Uma Análise das Variações Inter-Regionais," in *Os Partidos e as Eleições no Brasil*, ed. Cardoso and Lamounier, p. 238.

9. Even President Medici, who led Brazil through both the economic miracle and period of hard-line rule (1969–1973), commented that while the economy was going well, the Brazilian people most certainly were not.

10. Unfortunately, the question about left-right self-placement was omitted from the surveys of rural areas. Again, although over 70 percent of respondents failed to answer the survey question about left-right self-placement, the regression analysis model remains compelling because of the large number and wide distribution of valid cases, the primarily demographic character of differences between respondents who did and did not answer, and the experience of other analysts with low response rates to surveys conducted early in periods of democratic transition.

11. Cohen, *The Manipulation of Consent*; Lamounier, "Ideology and Authoritarian Regimes."

12. On the theoretical level, diverse types of public evaluations of government are central to democratic patterns of voter alignment. On the methodological level, recent research suggests that core characteristics of mass belief systems are complexity, flux, and multidimensionality. See Kinder, "Diversity and Complexity in American Public Opinion"; and Inglehart, "Aggregate Level Stability and Individual Level Flux in Mass Belief Systems."

Chapter 9. Participation

1. Perhaps the most influential works on participation in political science are: Sidney Verba, Norman H. Nie, and Jae-on Kim, *Participation and Political Equality: A Seven Nation Comparison* (Chicago: University of Chicago Press, 1978); and Pateman, *Participation and Democratic Theory.*

2. On corporatism in Brazil, see Philippe Schmitter, *Interest Conflict and Political Change* (Stanford: Stanford University Press, 1971). On the predominance of nonliberal politics during apparently liberal periods of Brazilian history, see Trindade, "Bases da Democracia Brasileira." On patrimonialism in Brazilian politics, see Simon Schwartzman, *Bases do Autoritarismo Brasileiro* (Rio de Janeiro: Campus, 1982). On state-regulated citizenship, see Wanderley G. dos Santos, *Cidadania e Justiça: A Política Social na Ordem Brasileira* (Rio de Janeiro: Campus, 1979).

3. Leal, *Coronelismo, Enxada, e Voto.*

4. See Soares, *Sociedade e Política no Brasil.*

5. See Kenneth P. Erickson, *The Brazilian Corporative State and Working Class Politics* (Berkeley and Los Angeles: University of California Press, 1977).

6. Leôncio Martins Rodríguez, *Industrialização e Atitudes Operárias: Estudo de um Grupo de Trabalhadores* (São Paulo, Brasiliense, 1970).

7. Cohen, *The Manipulation of Consent*, p. 39.

8. Theories of civil society empowerment are discussed in chap. 1.

9. Verba, Nie, and Kim, eds., *Participation and Political Equality*, p. 341.

10. Illiterates could not vote in the 1982 election, but this restriction was abolished in 1985 and suffrage for Brazil's illiterates was definitively granted by the 1988 constitution. On the equalizing effect of mandatory voting, see ibid., p. 7.

11. On the importance of regional and urban-rural cleavages in Brazil, see Glaucio D. Soares, "The Politics of Uneven Development: The Case of Brazil," in *Party Systems and Voter Alignment*, ed. Lipset and Rokkan, pp. 467–96.

12. On labor politics during the Brazilian transition, see Keck, *The Workers' Party and Democratization in Brazil.*

13. Erickson, *The Brazilian Corporative State*; and Margaret Keck, "The New Union Movement in the Brazilian Transition," in *Democratizing Brazil*, ed. Stepan, pp. 252–96.

14. These conclusions are based on data from the 1982 survey. Subsequent political developments during democratic transition may have changed these patterns. See Keck, *The Workers' Party and Democratization in Brazil.*

15. Meyer and Montes, *Redescobrindo o Brasil: A Festa na Política Brasileira.*

16. See: Verba, Nie, and Kim, *Participation and Political Equality*, pp. 270–75.

17. On the modes of participation, see ibid., pp. 310–39.

18. The Kaiser-Meyer-Olkin measure of sampling adequacy (.72) suggests that the factor analysis is "meritorious," while Bartlett's test of sphericity is large and its level of significance is zero. The hypothesis that the population correlation matrix between variables is an identity can be rejected.

19. On the need to recognize different attributes on different levels of collective action, see Mancur Olson, *The Logic of Collective Action: Public Goods and the Theory of Groups* (Cambridge: Harvard University Press, 1965).

20. Meyer and Montes, *Redescobrindo o Brasil.*

Chapter 10. Perceptions of Democracy and Democratic Institutions

1. See Gabriel Almond, "The Intellectual History of the Civic Culture Concept," in *The Civic Culture Revisited*, ed. Almond and Sidney Verba (Boston: Little, Brown, 1980).

2. Gabriel Almond and Sidney Verba, *The Civic Culture: Political Attitudes and Democracy in Five Nations* (Princeton: Princeton University Press, 1963); Atilio Boron, "Authoritarian Ideological Traditions and Transition Towards Democracy in Argentina," *Papers on Latin America*, no. 8, Columbia University, Institute of Latin American and Iberian Studies; Ronald Inglehart, *Culture Shift in the Advanced Democracies* (Princeton: Princeton University Press, 1990).

3. O'Donnell et al., eds., *Transitions from Authoritarian Rule: Southern Europe and Latin America.*

4. Howard Wiarda, ed., *Politics and Social Change in Latin America: The Distinct Tradition* (Amherst: University of Massachusetts Press, 1974); Boron, "Authoritarian Ideological Traditions and Transition Towards Democracy in Argentina."

5. Ronald Inglehart, *Culture Shift* (Princeton: Princeton University Press, 1991); Edward Mueller and Mitchell Seligson, "Insurgency and Inequality," *American Political Science Review* 81 (1987): 425–51. Also see Mitchell Seligson, "Political Culture and Democratization in Latin America," in *Latin American and Caribbean Contemporary Record*, vol. 7, ed. James Malloy and Eduardo Gamarra (New York: Holmes and Meier, 1989).

6. See Soares, "The Politics of Uneven Development: The Case of Brazil."

7. Total N for the southeast sample = 2,463; northeast sample = 1,860; and rural areas = 481.

8. See Herbert McClosky and Arida Brill, *Dimensions of Tolerance: What Americans Believe about Civil Liberties* (New York: Russell Sage Foundation, 1983); John Sullivan, James Pireson, and George Marcus, *Political Tolerance and American Democracy* (Chicago: University of Chicago Press, 1982).

9. This operationalization of policy culture can be found in Campbell et al., *The American Voter*, p. 15.

10. Inglehart, "The Changing Structure of Political Cleavages in Western Society." p. 37.

11. Barnes et al., "The Development of Partisanship in New Democracies: The Case of Spain."

12. Data is taken from the survey, "Representation and Development" (of 1,314 residents in southeast Brazil during 1972–1973) conducted by the Center for Political Studies of the Institute for Social Research of the University of Michigan and IUPERJ, Rio de Janeiro.

13. Thanks to Larry Peterson for this historical perspective on the class distribution of attitudes toward democratic institutions.

14. For example, see Henry Hart, "The Indian Constitution: Political Development and Decay," *Asian Survey* 20 (1980): 428–51.

15. Herbert McClosky and James Zaller, *The American Ethos: Public Attitudes Toward Capitalism and Democracy* (Cambridge: Harvard University Press, 1985).

16. Barbara Geddes and John Zaller, "Sources of Popular Support for Authoritarian Regimes," *American Journal of Political Science* 33 (1989): 319–47.

17. Juan Linz, "The U.S. Constitution Abroad: The Failure of Presidentialism," prepared for the annual meeting of the American Political Science Association, Chicago, 1987.

Conclusion

1. The Marxist tradition contains sustained debates on the possibilities for democratization and social transformation within competitive electoral politics. See Adam Przeworski, *Paper Stones* (Cambridge: Cambridge University Press, 1989). After military intervention in many advanced Latin American countries in the 1960s and the defeat of Chile's electoral road to socialism in 1973, Marxist theory was forced to reconsider the political-economic constraints on change through competitive electoral politics in capitalist society. But this turn to authoritarianism in Latin America did not produce a revival of revolutionary strategies among left parties and theorists. Instead, Marxists in Latin America increasingly recognized the importance of competitive elections for producing change. In the Brazilian case, both Marxist parties and leading intellectuals in the Marxist tradition now speak of competitive elections and political democracy as a universal value. See Carlos N. Coutinho, *A Democracia Como Valor Universal* (Rio de Janeiro: Salamandra, 1984); and Francisco Weffort, "Why Democracy?" in *Democratizing Brazil* (New York: Oxford University Press, 1989).

2. For a critical overview of the liberal assumptions that informed theories of political development, see Robert Packenham, *Liberal America and the Third World* (Princeton: Princeton University Press, 1973).

3. As noted above, the idea that democratization is constrained by long-term factors is inconsistent not only with the findings presented herein, but also with current research on diversity and flux in democratic electorates. See Kinder, "Diversity and Complexity in American Public Opinion."

4. Inglehart, "Aggregate Stability and Individual Level Flux in Mass Belief Systems."

5. For a review of liberal interpretations of Brazilian politics, see Santos, *Ordem Burguesa e Liberalismo Político*.

6. Werner Baer, *Industrialization and Economic Development of Brazil* (Chicago: Homewood, 1989).

7. Schmitter, *Interest Conflict and Political Change in Brazil*.

8. Russell Dalton et al., *Electoral Change in the Advanced Industrial Democracies: Realignment or Dealignment?*

9. See Pamela J. Conover and John L. Sullivan, "Methodology in Voting Research," *Research in Micropolitics* 2 (1987): 265–88.

10. Achen, "Toward Theories of Political Data"; Asher, *Causal Modeling*.

11. Achen, "Mass Political Attitudes and the Survey Response."

12. New statistical procedures such as LISREL which integrate both structural causes and short-term effects are promising. See Achen, "Toward Theories of Political Data."

13. Lipset and Rokkan, eds., *Party Systems and Voter Alignment*. Meanwhile, Robert Dahl, *Political Oppositions in Western Democracies* (New Ha-

ven: Yale University Press, 1966), seeks to explain the consolidation of party systems in the tradition of pluralist political sociology. According to Dahl, since perfectly cross-cutting cleavages do not exist empirically, one would expect that the most salient cleavages at the time of mass incorporation or the expansion of suffrage would be institutionalized in patterns of party competition.

14. Parsons claimed that a science of politics was impossible because political outcomes could not be isolated from their social and economic contexts. Nonetheless, authors and contributors to *Cleavages, Ideologies and Party Systems*, ed. E. Allardt and Y. Littunen (Helsinki: Westermarken, 1964) wrote central works on the development and consolidation of mass politics and mass parties.

15. Sartori, "From the Sociology of Politics to Political Sociology."

16. Lipset and Rokkan, *Party Systems and Voter Alignment*, p. 2, cited in ibid., p. 89.

17. On parties as mechanisms for political development in Latin America, see Robert Scott, "Political Parties and Policy-Making in Latin America," in *Political Parties and Political Development* (Princeton: Princeton University Press, 1966), pp. 331–68. On parties in developing countries generally, see Huntington, *Political Order in Changing Societies*, chap. 7.

18. Huntington frames empirical research by transposing the *ideal* characteristics of organizations to the analytic level of party systems. But Sartori argues that the structures of consolidated party systems are *not* analogous to those of bureaucratic organizations. Indeed, the epistemological status of a party system *qua system* is resolved quite prematurely by recourse to theories of organization. See Sartori, *Parties and Party Systems*, p. 267.

19. APSR, "Toward a More Responsible Two Party System." Supplement, *American Political Science Review* 44 (1950).

20. E. E. Schattschneider, *The Semi-Sovereign People* (New York: Rinehart, 1960); Key, *The Responsible Electorate*; Lowi, "Party, Policy, and Constitution in America."

21. See the exchanges between Burnham, Converse, and Rusk in the *American Political Science Review*: Walter D. Burnham, "Theory and Voting Research: Some Reflections on Converse's "Change in the American Electorate" and "Rejoinder to 'Comments' by Philip Converse and Jerrold Rusk"; Philip Converse, "Comment on Burnham's 'Theory and Voting Research' "; and Jerrold G. Rusk, "Comment: The American Electoral Universe: Speculation and Evidence," *American Political Science Review* 68 (1974): 1002–57.

22. Bolivar Lamounier and Fernando H. Cardoso, "A Bibliografia de Ciência Política Sobre o Brasil (1949–1974)," *Dados* 18 (1978): 4.

23. Alfred Stepan, *Rethinking Military Politics: Brazil and the Southern Cone* (Princeton: Princeton University Press, 1988), pp. 4–6.

24. Malloy, *The Politics of Social Security in Brazil*; Ben Schneider, *Politics within the State: Elite Bureaucrats and Industrial Policy in Authoritarian Brazil* (Pittsburgh: University of Pittsburgh Press, 1991); and Hagopian, "The Politics of Oligarchy."

25. For a history of Brazilian ideas on liberal institutions, see Santos, *Ordem Burguesa e Liberalismo no Brasil*.

26. Souza, *Estado e Partidos Políticos no Brasil*, chap. 6.

Bibliography

Achen, Christopher. "Mass Political Attitudes and the Survey Response." *American Political Science Review* 69 (1975): 1218–31.

Achen, Christopher. "Toward Theories of Political Data." In *Political Science: The State of the Discipline*, ed. Ada Finifter. Washington, D.C.: American Political Science Association, 1983.

Adorno, Theodore, et al. *The Authoritarian Personality.* New York: Harper and Row, 1950.

Alford, R. *Party and Society: The Anglo American Democracies.* Chicago: University of Chicago Press, 1963.

Almond, Gabriel, and Sidney Verba. *The Civic Culture.* Princeton: Princeton University Press, 1963.

Almond, Gabriel, and Sidney Verba, eds. *The Civic Culture Revisited.* Boston: Little, Brown, 1980.

Altman, Werner, et al., eds. *El Populismo en America Latina.* Mexico City: 1983.

Alves, Maria H. M. *State and Opposition in Military Brazil.* Austin: University of Texas Press, 1985.

Amaral, Azevedo. *O Estado Autoritario e a Realidade Nacional.* Brasília: Editora da Universidade de Brasília, 1981.

American Political Science Association. "Toward a More Responsible Two-Party System." *American Political Science Review* 44 Supplement (1950).

Ames, Barry. "The Congressional Connection: The Structure of Politics and the Distribution of Public Expenditures in Brazil's Competitive Period." *Comparative Politics* 20 (1987): 147–71.

Ames, Barry. *Rhetoric and Reality in a Militarized Regime: Brazil since 1964.* Beverly Hills: Sage Publications, 1973.

Ames, Barry. *Strategies of Survival.* Berkeley: University of California Press, 1988.

Asher, Herbert. *Causal Modeling*, rev. ed. Beverly Hills: Sage, 1983.

Asher, Herbert. "Voting Behavior Research in the 1980s: An Examination of Some Old and New Problem Areas." In *Political Science: The State of the Discipline*, ed. Ada Finifter. Washington, D.C.: American Political Science Association, 1983.

Bachrach, Peter. *The Theory of Democratic Elitism*. Boston: Little, Brown, 1967.

Baer, Werner. *Industrialization and Economic Development of Brazil*. Chicago: Homewood, 1989.

Barnes, Samuel, Peter McDonough, and Antonio López Piña. "The Development of Partisanship in New Democracies: The Case of Spain." *American Journal of Political Science* 29 (1985): 695–720.

Baquero, Marcello, ed. *Abertura Política e Comportamento Eleitoral nas Eleições de 1982 no Rio Grande do Sul*. Porto Alegre: Editora da UFRGS, 1984.

Barros Barreto, Célia. "O Movimento Maçônico na Independência." In *História Geral da Civilização Brasileira*, ed. Sérgio B. Holanda and Boris Fausto. São Paulo: Difel, 1973.

Beiguelman, Paula. *Formação Política do Brasil*. São Paulo: Pioneiro: 1976.

Beiguelman, Paula. *Pequenos Estudos de Ciência Política*. São Paulo: Pioneiro: 1973.

Benevides, Maria V. *A UDN e o Udenismo*. Rio de Janeiro: Paz e Terra, 1981.

Berger, Suzanne D., ed. *Organizing Interests in Western Europe*. Cambridge: Cambridge University Press, 1981.

Bethell, Leslie, and Jose M. de Carvalho. "Brazil from Independence to the Middle of the Nineteenth Century." In *The Cambridge History of Latin America*, ed. Leslie Bethell. Cambridge: Cambridge University Press, 1985.

Binder, Leonard. "The Natural History of Development Theory." Paper prepared for the annual meeting of the American Political Science Association, Chicago, 1983.

Bloom, Howard, and H. Douglas Price. "Voter Response to Short-Run Economic Conditions: The Assymetric Effect of Prosperity and Recession." *American Political Science Review* 69 (1975): 1240–54.

Boron, Atilio. "Authoritarian Ideological Traditions and Transition Towards Democracy in Argentina." *Papers on Latin America*, no. 8. Institute of Latin American and Iberian Studies, Columbia University.

Boron, Atilio, Maria C. Souza, and Douglas Chalmers. *The Right and Democracy in Latin America*. New York: Praeger, 1992.

Brasil, Assis. *Democracia Representativa*. Rio de Janeiro: 1931. Brasil, Olavo L., Jr. "The Brazilian Multi-Party System: A Case for Contextual Rationality." Ph.D. diss., University of Michigan, 1980.

Bryce, James. *The American Commonwealth*. New York: Macmillan, 1907.

Budge, Ian, Ivor Crew, and David Farlie, eds. *Party Identification and Beyond*. New York: Wiley, 1976.

Burnham, Walter D. *Critical Elections and the Mainsprings of American Politics*. New York: Norton, 1970.

Burnham, Walter D. *The Current Crisis in American Politics*. New York: Oxford University Press, 1982.

Burnham, Walter D. "Theory and Voting Research: Some Reflections on Converse's "Change in the American Electorate" and "Rejoinder to 'Comments' by Philip Converse and Jerrold Rusk." *American Political Science Review* 68 (1974): 1002–23, 1050–57.

Caldeira, Tereza. "Electoral Struggles in a Neighborhood on the Periphery of São Paulo." *Politics and Society* 15 (Fall 1986).

Campbell, Angus, Philip Converse, Warren Miller, and Donald Stokes. *The American Voter*. New York: John Wiley, 1960.

Campbell, Jean. *Survey Research in the United States: Roots and Emergence 1890–1960*. Berkeley and Los Angeles: University of California Press, 1987.

Camargo, Aspasia, et al. *Artes da Política: Diálogo com Amaral Peixoto*. Rio de Janeiro: Nova Fronteira, 1986.

Cardoso, Fernando H. "Associated Dependent Development: Theoretical and Practical Implications." In *Authoritarian Brazil*, ed. Alfred Stepan. New Haven: Yale University Press, 1973.

Cardoso, Fernando H. *Autoritarismo e Democratização*. Rio de Janeiro: Paz e Terra, 1975.

Cardoso, Fernando H. *Dependency and Development in Latin America*. Berkeley and Los Angeles: University of California Press, 1979.

Cardoso, Fernando H. "Dos Governos Militares a Prudente-Campos Salles." In *História Geral da Civilização Brasileira*, ed. Sergio B. Holanda. São Paulo: Difel, 1973.

Cardoso, Fernando H. *O Modelo Político Brasileiro*. São Paulo: Difel, 1979.

Cardoso, Fernando H. "On the Characterization of Authoritarian Regimes in Latin America." In *The New Authoritarianism in Latin America*, ed. David Collier. Princeton: Princeton University Press, 1979.

Cardoso, Fernando H., and Bolivar Lamounier, eds. *Os Partidos e as Eleições no Brasil*. Rio de Janeiro: Paz e Terra, 1975.

Cardoso, Ruth C. L. "Movimentos Sociais Urbanos: Balanço Crítico." In *Sociedade e Política no Brasil Pós-1964*, ed. Bernardo Sorj and Maria H. T. Almeida. São Paulo: Brasiliense, 1984.

Carone, Edgard. *O Estado Novo*. São Paulo: Difel, 1976.

Carone, Edgard. *A Primeira República (Evolução Política)*. São Paulo: Difel, 1971.

Carone, Edgard. *A Primeira República (Instituições e Classes Sociais)*. São Paulo: Difel, 1970.

Carvalho, José M. "A Composição Social dos Partidos Políticos Imperiais." *Cadernos DCP* 2 (1974): 1–34.

Carvalho, José M. "Elites and State Building in Imperial Brazil." Ph.D diss., Stanford University, 1974.

Carvalho, José M. "Estudos de Poder Local no Brasil." *Revista Brasileira de Estudos Políticos* 25 (1968): 231–48.

Carvalho, José M. "Political Elites and State Building: The Case of Nineteenth-Century Brazil." *Comparative Studies in Society and History* 24 (July 1982): 378–99.

Castro Gomes, Angela, ed. *Regionalismo e Centralização Política: Partidos e Constituinte nos Anos 30.* Rio de Janeiro: Nova Fronteira, 1980.

Catterberg, Edgardo. *Argentina Confronts Politics: Political Culture and Public Opinion in the Argentine Transition to Democracy.* Boulder, Colo.: Lynne Rienner, 1991.

Cavalcanti, Themostocles, and Reisky Dubnic, eds. *Comportamento Eleitoral no Brasil.* Rio de Janeiro: Fundação Getulio Vargas, 1971.

Centro de Pesquisa e Documentação de História Contemporânea do Brasil (CPDOC). *A Revolução de 30.* Brasília: Editora da Universidade de Brasília, 1982.

Chacon, Vamireh. *História dos Partidos Brasileiros.* Brasília: Editora da Universidade de Brasília, 1981.

Chalmers, Douglas A. "Parties and Society in Latin America." In *Friends, Followers and Factions,* ed. Steffen W. Schmidt et al. Berkeley and Los Angeles: University of California Press, 1977.

Chalmers, Douglas. "The Politicized State in Latin America." In *Authoritarianism and Corporatism in Latin America,* ed. James Malloy. Pittsburgh: University of Pittsburgh Press, 1977.

Chalmers, Douglas, and Christopher Robinson. "Why Power Contenders Choose Liberalization Strategies." *International Studies Quarterly* 26 (1982): 3–36.

Chambers, William N., and Walter D. Burnham, eds. *The American Party Systems: Stages of Political Development.* New York: Oxford University Press, 1967.

Chilcote, Ronald H. *The Brazilian Communist Party.* New York: Oxford University Press, 1974.

Cohen, Youssef. "Democracy from Above: The Political Origins of Military Dictatorship in Brazil." *World Politics* 40 (1987): 30–54.

Cohen, Youssef. *The Manipulation of Consent: State and Working Class Consciousness in Brazil.* Pittsburgh: University of Pittsburgh Press, 1989.

Collier, Ruth, and David Collier, eds. *The New Authoritarianism in Latin America.* Princeton: Princeton University Press, 1979.

Colson, Frank. "The Destruction of a Revolution: Polity, Economy, and Society in Brazil, 1870–1891." Ph.D. diss., Princeton University, 1978.

Colson, Frank. "On Expectations—Perspectives on the Crisis of 1889 in Brazil." *Journal of Latin American Studies* 13 (1981).

Conniff, Michael. *Urban Politics in Brazil: The Rise of Populism, 1925–1945.* Pittsburgh: University of Pittsburgh Press, 1981.

Conniff, Michael, ed. *Latin American Populism in Comparative Perspective.* Albuquerque: University of New Mexico Press, 1982.

Conniff, Michael, and Frank McCann, eds. *Modern Brazil: Elites and Masses in Historical Perspective.* Lincoln: University of Nebraska Press, 1989.

Connoly, William. *The Terms of Political Discourse.* Princeton: Princeton University Press, 1974.

Conover, Pamela J., and John L. Sullivan, "Methodology in Voting Research." *Research in Micropolitics* 2 (19): 265–88.

Converse, Philip E. "Change in the American Universe." In *The Human Meaning of Social Change,* ed. Angus Campbell and Philip E. Converse. New York: Russell Sage Foundation.

Converse, Philip. "Comment on Burnham's 'Theory and Voting Research.' " *American Political Science Review* 68 (1974): 1024–27.

Converse, Philip E. "The Nature of Belief Systems in Mass Publics." In *Ideology and Consent,* ed. David Apter. New York: Free Press, 1964.

Converse, Philip E. "Of Time and Partisan Stability." *Comparative Political Studies* 2 (1969).

Coppedge, Michael. "Strong Parties and Lame Ducks: A Study of the Quality and Stability of Venezuelan Democracy." Ph.D. diss., Yale University, 1988.

Costa, Emília V. *Da Monarquia à República: Momentos Decisivos.* 3d ed. São Paulo: Brasiliense: 1985.

Costa, Octavio. "Governo e Comunicação Social." Prepared for delivery at the Escola Superior de Guerra (Superior War College, ESG), 1970.

Coutinho, Carlos N. *A Democracia Como Valor Universal.* Rio de Janeiro: Salamandra, 1984.

Daalder, Hans. "Parties, Elites, and Political Developments in Western Europe." In *Political Parties and Political Development,* ed. Joseph LaPalombara and Myron Weiner. Princeton: Princeton University Press, 1966.

Dahl, Robert. *Political Oppositions in Western Democracies.* New Haven: Yale University Press, 1966.

Dahl, Robert. *Polyarchy.* New Haven: Yale University Press, 1971.

Dahl, Robert. *A Preface to Economic Democracy.* Berkeley and Los Angeles: University of California Press, 1985.

Dahl, Robert. *Size and Democracy.* Berkeley and Los Angeles: University of California Press, 1973.

Dalton, Russell, et al. *Electoral Change in Advanced Industrial Democracies: Realignment or Dealignment?* Princeton: Princeton University Press, 1983.

Dassin, Joan. "Censorship in Brazil." *Index on Censorship.* London: Oxford University Press, 1979.

Deutsch, Karl W. *The Analysis of International Relations.* Englewood Cliffs, N.J.: Prentice-Hall, 1968.

Diniz, Eli. *Voto e Máquina Política: Patronagem e Clientelismo no Rio de Janeiro.* Rio de Janeiro: Paz e Terra, 1982.

Downs, Anthony. *An Economic Theory of Democracy.* New York: Harper, 1957.

Dreifuss, Rene. *A Conquista do Estado.* Petrópolis: Vozes, 1981.

Duarte, Nestor. *A Ordem Privada e a Organização Política Nacional.* São Paulo: Ed. Nacional, 1939.

Dudley, William. "Institutional Sources of Officer Discontent in the Brazilian Army, 1870–1889." *Hispanic American Historical Review* 45 (1975).

Durrel, Aldin, ed. *The Colonial Roots of Modern Brazil.* Berkeley and Los Angeles: University of California Press, 1973.

Duverger, Maurice. *Political Parties.* Cambridge: Metheun, 1954.

Erikson, Kenneth P. *The Brazilian Corporative State and Working Class Politics.* Berkeley, University of California Press, 1977.

Evans, Peter, et al. *Bringing the State Back In.* Cambridge: Cambridge University Press, 1985.

Faria, Vilmar. "As Eleições de 1974 em São Paulo: Uma Análise das Variações Inter-Regionais." In *Os Partidos e as Eleicoes no Brasil,* ed. Cardoso and Lamounier.

Faria, Vilmar. "Desenvolvimento, Urbanização, e Mudanças na Estrutura de Emprego: A Experiência Brasileira dos Últimos Trinta Anos." In *Sociedade e Política no Brasil Pós-1964,* ed. Bernardo Sorj and Maria H. T. Almeida. São Paulo: Brasiliense, 1984.

Faoro, Raimundo. *Os Donos do Poder.* Porto Alegre, Globo, 1958.

Fausto, Boris. *A Revolução de 30: Historiografia e História.* São Paulo: Brasiliense, 1970.

Fausto, Boris. "Pequenos Ensaios da História da República: 1889–1945." *Cadernos Cebrap* 10 (1972).

Fausto, Boris. *Trabalho Urbano e Conflito Social.* São Paulo: Difel, 1976.

Ferreira, Oliveiros. "Comportamento Eleitoral em São Paulo." *Revista Brasileira de Estudos Políticos* 8 (1960): 162–228.

Fiorina, Morris. *Retrospective Voting in American Elections.* New Haven: Yale University Press, 1981.

Fleischer, David, ed. *Os Partidos Políticos no Brasil.* Brasília: Editora da Universidade de Brasília, 1981.

Flynn, Peter. *Brazil: A Political Analysis.* Boulder: Westview Press, 1978.

Font, Mauricio. *Coffee, Contention, and Change in the Making of Modern Brazil.* Cambridge: Basil Blackwell, 1990.

Font, Mauricio. "Coffee Planters, Politics and Development in Brazil: An Alternative Scenario." *Latin American Research Review,* 22 (1987): 69–90.

Franco, Afonso A. M. *História e Teoria dos Partidos Políticos no Brasil.* 2d ed. São Paulo: Alfa Omega, 1974.

French, John. "Industrial Workers and the Origins of Populist Politics in the ABC Region of Greater São Paulo, Brazil, 1900–1950." Ph.D. diss., Princeton University, 1985.

French, John. "Workers and the Rise of Adhemarista Populism in São Paulo, Brazil 1945–1947." *Hispanic American Historical Review* 68 (February 1988): 1–43.

Fuchs, Esther, and Robert Shapiro. "Government Performance as a Basis for Machine Support." *Urban Affairs Quarterly* 18 (1983): 537–50.

Furtado, Celso. *The Economic Growth of Brazil: A Survey from Colonial to Modern Times.* Berkeley and Los Angeles: University of California Press, 1963.

Furtado, Celso. "Political Obstacles to Economic Growth in Brazil." In *The Politics of Conformity in Latin America*, ed. Claudio Veliz. New York: Oxford University Press, 1966.

Garreton, Manuel A. *The Chilean Political Process.* Boston: Unwin Hyman, 1988.

Garreton, Manuel A. *Dictaduras y Democratic ión.* Santiago: FLACSO, 1984.

Geddes, Barbara, and John Zaller, "Sources of Popular Support for Authoritarian Regimes." *American Journal of Political Science* 33 (1989): 317–47.

Germani, Gino. *Authoritarianism, Fascism, and National Populism.* New Brunswick, N.J.: Transaction Books, 1978.

Gillespie, Charles G. "Party Strategies and Redemocratization: Theoretical and Comparative Perspectives on the Uruguayan Case." Ph.D. diss., Yale University, 1987.

Goes, W. *O Brasil do General Geisel.* Rio de Janeiro: Nova Fronteira, 1978.

Golbery, G. do Couto e Silva, *Conjuntura Política Nacional—O Poder Ex- ecutivo e Geopolítico do Brazil.* Rio de Janeiro: José Olympio, 1981.

Graham, Richard. *Patronage and Politics in Nineteenth Century Brazil.* Stanford: Stanford University Press, 1990.

Grin, Guita. *Ideologia e Populismo.* São Paulo: T.A. Queiróz, 1979.

Hagopian, Frances. "The Politics of Oligarchy: The Persistence of Traditional Elites in Contemporary Brazil." Ph.D. diss., Massachusetts Institute of Technology, 1986.

Hartlyn, Jonathan. *The Politics of Coalition Rule in Colombia.* Cambridge: Cambridge University Press, 1988.

Haya de la Torre. Victor R. *El Anti-Imperialismo e el APRA.* Lima: Amauta, 1972.

Hays, Samuel. "Political Parties and the Community-Society Continuum." in *The American Party Systems: Stages of Political Development*, ed. William N. Chambers and Walter D. Burnham. New York: Oxford University Press, 1967.

Hermet, Guy, et al. *Elections Without a Choice.* New York: John Wiley, 1978.

Hilton, Stanley. "The Overthrow of Getulio Vargas in 1945: Intervention, Defense of Democracy, or Political Retribution?" *Hispanic American Historical Review* 67 (1987): 1–37.

Hippólito, Lucia. *PDS: De Raposas e Reformistas.* Rio de Janeiro: Paz e Terra, 1985.

Hirschman, Albert O. "The Turn to Authoritarianism in Latin America and the Search for Its Economic Determinants." In *The New Authoritarianism in Latin America*, ed. David Collier. Princeton: Princeton University Press, 1979.

Holanda, Sergio B., and Boris Fausto, eds. *História Geral da Civilização Brasileira.* 7 vols. São Paulo: Difel, 1973–1977.

Huntington, Samuel. *Political Order in Changing Societies.* New Haven: Yale University Press, 1968.

Inglehart, Ronald. "Aggregate Stability and Individual Level Flux in Mass Belief Systems: The Level of Analysis Paradox." *American Political Science Review* 79 (1985): 97–116.

Inglehart, Ronald. "The Changing Structure of Political Cleavages in Western Society." In *Electoral Change in Advanced Industrial Democracies: Realignment or Dealignment?*, ed. Russell Dalton et al. Princeton: Princeton University Press, 1983.

Inglehart, Ronald. *The Silent Revolution: Changing Values and Political Styles among Western Publics.* Princeton: Princeton University Press, 1977.

Jaguaribe, Helio, et al., eds. *Brasil, Sociedade Democrática.* Rio de Janeiro: José Olympio, 1985.

Kaufman, Robert. "Corporatism, Clientelism, and Partisan Conflict: A Study of Seven Latin American Countries." In *Authoritarianism and Corporatism in Latin America*, ed. James Malloy. Pittsburgh: University of Pittsburgh Press, 1977.

Keck, Margaret. "The New Union Movement in the Brazilian Transition to Democracy." In *Democratizing Brazil*, ed. Alfred Stepan. New York: Oxford University Press, 1989.

Keck, Margaret. *The Workers' Party and Democratization in Brazil.* New Haven: Yale University Press, 1992.

Key, V. O. *Public Opinion and American Democracy.* New York: Knopf, 1961.

Key, V. O. *The Responsible Electorate: Rationality in Presidential Voting, 1930–1960.* Cambridge: Harvard University Press, 1963.

Kinder, Donald. "Diversity and Complexity in American Public Opinion." In *Political Science: The State of the Discipline*, ed. Ada Finifter. Washington, D.C.: American Political Science Association, 1983.

Kinder, Donald. "Presidents, Prosperity, and Public Opinion." In *Public Opinion Quarterly* 45 (1981): 1–21.

Kinzo, Maria D. G. *An Opposition Party in an Authoritarian Regime: The Case of the MDB (Movimento Democrático Brasileiro) in Brazil, 1966–1979.* New York: St. Martins, 1989.

Kinzo, Maria D. G. *Representação Política e Sistema Eleitoral no Brasil.* São Paulo: Símbolo, 1980.

Kleppner, Paul. *The Cross of Culture: A Social Analysis of Midwestern Politics, 1850–1900.* New York: Free Press, 1970.

Kramer, G. H. "Short Term Fluctuations in United States Voting Behavior, 1864–1964." *American Political Science Review* 65 (1971): 131–43.

Krieger, Leonard. *The German Idea of Freedom.* New York: Columbia University Press, 1957.

Kugelmas, Eduardo. "Difícil Hegemonia: Um Estudo Sobre São Paulo na Primeira República." Ph.D. diss., Universidade de São Paulo, 1986.

Lafer, Celso. *O Sistema Político Brasileiro.* São Paulo: Perspectiva, 1975.

Lafer, Celso. *The Planning Process and the Political System in Brazil.* Ithaca, N.Y.: Cornell University Press, 1970.

Lamounier, Bolivar. "Authoritarian Brazil Revisited: The Impact of Elections on the Abertura." In *Democratizing Brazil,* ed. Alfred Stepan. New York: Oxford, 1989.

Lamounier, Bolivar. "Ideologia em Regimes Autoritários: Uma Resposta a Juan Linz." *Estudos Cebrap* 1974.

Lamounier, Bolivar. "Ideology and Authoritarian Regimes: Theoretical Perspectives and a Study of the Brazilian Case." Ph.D. diss., University of California, Los Angeles, 1974.

Lamounier, Bolivar. *1985: O Voto em São Paulo.* São Paulo: Idesp, Vol. 1, História Eleitoral. 1986.

Lamounier, Bolivar. "Opening Through Elections: Will the Brazilian Case Become a Paradigm?" *Government and Opposition* 19 (1984).

Lamounier, Bolivar. "Parlamentarismo ou Atenuação do Presidencialismo: Notas Sobre o Debate Brasileiro Recente." *Revista do Instituto de Estudos Brasileiros* No. 32-Especial, (1991) pp. 9–18.

Lamounier, Bolivar, ed. *Voto de Disconfiança.* Petrópolis: Vozes, 1980.

Lamounier, Bolivar, Franciso Weffort, Maria Victoria Benevides, eds. *Direito, Cidadania, e Participação.* São Paulo: Queiróz, 1981.

Lamounier, Bolivar, Alain Rouquie, and Jorge Schvarzer, eds. *Como Renascem as Democracias.* São Paulo, Brasiliense, 1985.

Lamounier, Bolivar, and Dieter Nohlen, eds., *Presidencialismo ou Parlamentarismo.* São Paulo: Loyola, 1993.

Lamounier, Bolivar, and Fernando H. Cardoso. "A Bibliografia de Ciência Política Sobre o Brasil (1949–1974)" *Dados* 18 (1978).

Lamounier, Bolivar, and Rachel Meneguello. *Partidos Políticos e Consolidação Democrática: O Caso Brasileiro.* São Paulo: Brasiliense, 1986.

Lane, Robert. *Political Ideology.* New York: Free Press, 1962.

LaPalombara, Joseph, and Myron Weiner, eds. *Political Parties and Political Development.* Princeton: Princeton University Press, 1966.

Leal, Victor N. *Coronelismo, Enxada, e Voto.* Rio de Janeiro: Forense, 1949.

Leff, Nathaniel H. *Economic Policy-Making and Development in Brazil: 1947–1964.* New York: Wiley and Sons. 1968.

Leite, Beatriz W. G. *O Senado nos Anos Finais do Império: 1870–1889.* Brasília: Imprensa do Senado, 1979.

Levine, Daniel H. *Conflict and Political Change in Venezuela.* Princeton: Princeton University Press, 1973.

Levine, Robert M. *Pernambuco and the Brazilian Federation, 1889–1937.* Stanford: Stanford University Press, 1977.

Lewis-Beck, Michael S. *Economics and Elections: The Major Western Democracies.* Ann Arbor: University of Michigan Press, 1988.

Lijphart, Arend. *Class and Religious Voting in the European Democracies.* Glascow, 1971.

Lijphart, Arend. *Parliamentary versus Presidential Government.* New York: Oxford University Press, 1992.

Lima, Oliveira. *O Império Brasileiro, 1822–1889.* 1927. Rpt. Brasília: Universidade de Brasília, 1986.

Linz, Juan. "An Authoritarian Regime: Spain." In *Cleavages, Ideologies and Party Systems*, ed. E. Allardt and Y. Littunen. Helsinki: Westermarken, 1964.

Linz, Juan. "Ecological Analysis and Survey Research." In *Social Ecology*, ed. M. Dogan and S. Rokkan. Cambridge: MIT Press, 1969.

Linz, Juan. "The Future of an Authoritarian Situation or the Institutionalization of an Authoritarian Regime: The Case of Brazil." In *Authoritarian Brazil*, ed. Alfred Stepan. New Haven: Yale University Press, 1973.

Linz, Juan. "The Transition from an Authoritarian Regime to Democracy in Spain: Some Thoughts for Brazilians." Unpublished MS, Yale University, 1983.

Linz, Juan. "The U.S. Constitution Abroad: The Failure of Presidentialism." Prepared for the annual meeting of the American Political Science Association, Chicago, 1987.

Linz, Juan, and Alfred Stepan, eds. *The Breakdown of Democratic Regimes, Latin America.* Baltimore: Johns Hopkins University Press, 1978.

Lipset, Seymour Martin. *Political Man: The Social Bases of Politics.* New York: Doubleday, 1960.

Lipset, Seymour M., and Stein Rokkan. *Party Systems and Voter Alignment.* New York: Free Press, 1967.

Love, Joseph. *Rio Grande do Sul and Brazilian Regionalism.* Stanford: Stanford University Press, 1971.

Love, Joseph. *São Paulo in the Brazilian Federation, 1889–1937.* Stanford: Stanford University Press, 1980.

Lowi, Theodore J. *The End of Liberalism*, 2d ed. New York: Norton, 1979.

Lowi, Theodore J. "Party, Policy, and Constitution in America." In Chambers, William N. and Walter D. Burnham. *The American Party Systems: Stages of Political Development.* New York: Oxford University Press, 1967.

Mainwaring, Scott. "Presidential Institutions in Latin America." *Comparative Politics* 23 (1990).

Mainwaring, Scott. "Political Parties and Democratization in Brazil and the Southern Cone." *Comparative Politics* 21 (1988): 91–120.

Mainwaring, Scott. "The Transition to Democracy in Brazil." Kellogg Institute, Working Paper No. 66.

Mainwaring, Scott, and Eduardo Viola. "New Social Movements, Political Culture, and Democracy: Brazil and Argentina in the 1980's." *Telos* 61 (Fall 1984).

Malloy, James. *The Politics of Social Security in Brazil.* Pittsburgh: University of Pittsburgh Press, 1979.

Malloy, James, ed. *Authoritarianism and Corporatism in Latin America.* Pittsburgh: University of Pittsburgh Press, 1977.

Malloy, James, and Mitchell A. Seligson., eds. *Authoritarians and Democrats: Regime Transition in Latin America.* Pittsburgh: University of Pittsburgh, 1987.

Marshall, T. H. *Citizenship and Social Class and Other Essays.* Cambridge: University Press, 1950.

Martins, Carlos E. *Capitalismo de Estado e Modelo Político no Brasil.* Rio de Janeiro, Graal. 1977.

Martins, Carlos E., and Maria H. Tavares. "Modus in Rebus—Partidos e Classes na Queda do Estado Novo." Unpublished MS. Universidade de São Paulo, 1973.

Maxwell, Kenneth. "The Generation of 1792 and the Downfall of the Luso-Brazilian Empire." In *The Colonial Roots of Modern Brazil,* ed. Aldin Durrel. Berkeley and Los Angeles: University of California Press, 1973.

McClosky, Herbert, and Arida Brill. *Dimensions of Tolerance: What Americans Believe about Civil Liberties.* New York: Russell Sage Foundation, 1983.

McClosky, Herbert, and James Zaller. *The American Ethos.* Cambridge: Harvard University Press, 1986.

McDonough, Peter, Samuel H. Barnes, and Antonio L. Piña. "The Growth of Democratic Legitmacy in Spain." *American Political Science Review* 80 (1986): 735–60.

Melo Franco, Afonso A. *História e Teoria do Partido Político no Direito Constitucional Brasileiro.* 2d ed. São Paulo: Alfa Omega, 1974.

Mello, João M. C. *O Capitalismo Tardio.* São Paulo: Brasiliense, 1982.

Mendes, Antonio, Jr. *O Movimento Estudantil no Brasil.* São Paulo, Brasiliense, 1982.

Meyer, Marlyse, and Maria L. Montes. *Redescobrindo o Brasil: A Festa na Política Brasileira.* São Paulo: T.A. Queiróz, 1985.

Miller, Warren E., and Donald E. Stokes. "Constituency Influence in Congress." *American Political Science Review* 57 (1963): 45–56.

Nabuco, Joaquim. *Um Estadista do Império*. 3 vols. São Paulo: Editora Nacional, 1936.

Neimi, Richard G., ed. *New Views of Children and Politics*. San Fransico: Jossey-Bass, 1974.

Nie, Norman H., Sidney Verba, and John Petrocik. *The Changing American Voter*. Cambridge: Harvard University Press, 1980.

Nogueira, Marco A. *As Desventuras do Liberalismo: Joaquim Nabuco, a Monarquia e a República*. São Paulo: Paz e Terra, 1984.

O'Donnell, Guillermo. *Modernization and Bureaurocratic Authoritarianism*. Berkeley: University of California Institute of International Studies, 1973.

O'Donnell, Guillermo. "Tensions in the Bureaucratic Authoritarian State and the Question of Democracy." In *The New Authoritarianism in Latin America*, ed. David Collier. Princeton: Princeton University Press, 1979.

O'Donnell, Guillermo, Philippe Schmitter, and Laurence Whitehead, Laurence, eds. *Transitions from Authoritarian Rule: Southern Europe and Latin America*. Baltimore: Johns Hopkins University Press, 1986.

Oliveira, Eliezer R. *As Forças Armadas*. Petrópolis: Editora Vozes, 1982.

Olson, Mancur. *The Logic of Collective Action: Public Goods and the Theory of Groups*. Cambridge: Harvard University Press, 1965.

Ostrogorski, M. I. *Democracy and the Organization of Political Parties in the United States and Great Britain*. Garden City, N.Y.: Doubleday, 1964.

Packenham, Robert. *Liberal America and the Third World*. Princeton: Princetin University Press, 1973.

Page, Benjamin. *Choices and Echoes in Presidential Elections*. Chicago: University of Chicago Press, 1978.

Page, Benjamin. "Presidents as Public Opinion Leaders: Some New Evidence." *Policy Studies Journal*. 12 (1984): 649–661.

Page, Benjamin, and Calvin Jones. "Reciprocal Effects of Policy Preferences, Party Loyalites, and the Vote." *American Political Science Review* 73 (1979): 1071–1089.

Page, Benjamin I., and Robert Y. Shapiro. *The Rational Public*. Chicago: University of Chicago Press, 1992.

Page, Benjamin, Robert Shapiro, and Glen Dempsey. "What Moves Public Opinion." *American Political Science Review* 81 (1987): 23–43.

Parayba, Maria A. "Abertura Social e Participação Política no Brasil: 1870–1920." *Dados* 7 (1970).

Pateman, Carol. *Participation and Democratic Theory*. Cambridge, Cambridge University Press, 1970.

Pierrucci, Antonio Flavio de Oliveira. "Democracia, Igreja, e Voto: O Envolvimento dos Padres de Paróquia de São Paulo nas Eleições de 1982." Ph.D. diss., Universidade de São Paulo, 1984.

Picaluga, Izabel F. *Partidos e Classes Sociais: A UDN na Guanabara*. Petrópolis: Vozes, 1980.

Pinheiro, Paulo S. *Trabalho e Política no Brasil.* Rio de Janiero: Paz e Terra, 1975.

Pitkin, Hanna. *The Concept of Representation.* Berkeley and Los Angeles: University of California Press, 1968.

Powell, G. Bingham. "Comparative Voting Behavior: Cleavages, Partisanship, and Accountability." *Research in Micropolitics* 2 (1987).

Prado, Caio, Jr. *A Evolução Política do Brasil.* 13th ed. São Paulo: Brasiliense, 1986.

Prado, Caio, Jr. *The Colonial Heritage of Modern Brazil.* Berkeley and Los Angeles: University of California Press, 1967.

Prado, Maria L. C. *A Democracia Ilustrada, O Partido Democrático de São Paulo, 1926–1934.* São Paulo: Ática, 1986.

Przeworski, Adam. "Democracy as a Contingent Outcome of Conflicts." Paper presented at the seminar "Issues on Democracy and Democratization: North and South," University of Notre Dame, November 14–16, 1983.

Queiróz, Maria I. P. "O Coronelismo numa Interpretação Sociológica." In *História Geral da Civilização Brasileira*, ed. Boris Fausto, 8:155–90.

Ramos, Plínio de A. *Os Partidos Paulistas e o Estado Novo.* Petrópolis: Vozes, 1980.

Reis, Elisa P. "The Agrarian Roots of Authoritarian Modernization in Brazil, 1880–1930." Ph.D. diss., Massachusetts Institute of Technology, 1980.

Reis, Fábio W. "Brasil: Estado e Sociedade em Perspectiva." *Cadernos do Departamento de Ciência Política* 2 (1974).

Reis, Fábio W. *Política e Racionalidade.* Belo Horizonte: Edições da Revista Brasileira de Estudos Políticos, 1984.

Reis, Fábio W., ed. *Os Partidos e o Regime.* São Paulo: Símbolo, 1978.

Reis, Fábio W., and Guillermo O'Donnell, eds. *A Democracia no Brasil: Dilemas e Perspectivas.* São Paulo: Vértice, 1988.

Rodriguez, Leôncio Martins. *Industrialização e Atitudes Operárias: Estudo de um Grupo de Trabalhadores.* São Paulo, Brasiliense, 1970.

Rokkan, Stein. *Citizens, Elections, and Parties.* New York: McKay, 1979.

Rose, Richard. *The Problem of Party Government.* New York: Macmillan, 1974.

Rouquie, Alain, et al., eds. *Como Renascem as Democracias.* São Paulo: Brasiliense, 1985.

Rua, Maria G. "O Comportamento Político de Eleitorado Rural: Uma Análise Comparada." M.A. thesis, Instituto Universitário de Pesquisas do Rio de Janeiro, 1984.

Rusk, Jerrold G. "Comment: The American Electoral Universe: Speculation and Evidence." *American Political Science Review* 68 (1974): 1028–49.

Sampaio, Regina. *Adhemar de Barros e o PSP.* São Paulo: Global, 1982.

Santos, Wanderley G. dos. "A Pós-Revolução Brasileira." In *Brasil: Sociedade Democrática*, ed. Hélgio Trindade. Rio de Janeiro: José Olympio, 1985.

Santos, Wanderley G. dos. "The Calculus of Conflict: Impasse in Brazil and the Crisis of 1964." Ph.D. diss., Stanford University, 1979.

Santos, Wanderley G. dos. *Cidadania e Justiça*. Rio de Janeiro: Campus, 1979.

Santos, Wanderley G. dos. *Ordem Burguesa e Liberalismo Político*. São Paulo, Duas Cidades, 1978.

Santos, Wanderley G. dos. *Poder e Política: Uma Crônica do Autoritarismo no Brasil*. São Paulo: Alfa Omega, 1979.

Sarles, Margaret J. "Maintaining Control Through Political Parties: the Brazilian Strategy." *Comparative Politics* 15 (1982): 41–72.

Sarles, Margaret J. "Political Parties in Authoritarian Brazil: 1964–1974." Ph.D. diss., Duke University, 1979.

Sartori, Giovanni. *A Teoria da Representação no Estado Representativo Moderno*. Belo Horizonte: Edicões da Revista de Estudos Políticos, 1962.

Sartori, Giovanni. "European Political Parties: The Case of Polarized Pluralism." In *Political Parties and Political Development*, ed. Joseph LaPalombara and Myron Weiner. Princeton: Princeton University Press, 1966.

Sartori, Giovanni. "From the Sociology of Politics to Political Sociology." In *Politics and the Social Sciences*, ed. Seymour M. Lipset. New York: Oxford University Press, 1969.

Sartori, Giovanni. *Parties and Party Systems*. Cambridge: Cambridge University Press, 1976.

Sartori, Giovanni. "Political Ideology and Mass Belief Systems." *American Political Science Review* 63 (1969): 398–411.

Sartori, Giovanni. "Representational Systems." In *International Encyclopedia of the Social Sciences*, vol. 13. New York: Macmillan and Free Press, 1968.

Sartori, Giovanni. *The Theory of Democracy Revisited*. Chatham, N.J.: Chatham House, 1987.

Sartori, Giovanni, and Giacommo Sani. "Polarization, Fragmentation, and Competition in Western Democracies." In *Western European Party Systems*, ed. Hans Daalder and Peter Maier. Beverly Hills: Sage, 1983.

Schattschneider, E. E. *Party Government*. New York: Rinehart, 1941.

Schattschneider, E. E. *The Semi-Sovereign People*. New York: Rinehart, 1960.

Schmitter, Philippe. *Interest Conflict and Political Change in Brazil*. Stanford: Stanford University Press, 1971.

Schneider, Ben. *Politics Within the State: Elite Bureaucrats and Industrial Policy in Authoritarian Brazil*. Pittsburgh: University of Pittsburgh Press, 1991.

Schneider, Ronald. *The Political System of Brazil*. New York: Columbia University Press, 1971.

Schultz, John Henry. "The Brazilian Army in Politics, 1850–1894." Ph.D. diss., Princeton University, 1973.

Schumpeter, Joseph S. *Capitalism, Socialism, and Democracy.* New York: Harper and Row, 1942.

Schwartz, Roberto. *Misplaced Ideas.* New York: Verso, 1992.

Schwartzman, Simon. *Bases do Autoritarismo Brasileiro.* Rio de Janeiro: Campus, 1982.

Seligson, Mitchell. "Political Culture and Democratization in Latin America." In *Latin American and Caribbean Contemporary Record,* vol. 7, ed. James Malloy and Eduardo Gamarra. New York: Holmes and Meier, 1989.

Serra, José, ed. *Reforma Política no Brasil, Parlamentarismo x Presidencialismo.* São Paulo: Siciliano, 1993.

Shapiro, Robert, and Bruce M. Conforto. "Presidential Performance, the Economy, and the Public's Evaluation of Economic Conditions." *Journal of Politics* 42 (1980): 49–80.

Shefter, Martin. "Party and Patronage: Germany, England, and Italy." *Politics and Society* 7 (1977): 403–51.

Shiveley, William P. "Party Identification, Party Choice, and Voting Stability: The Weimar Case." *American Political Science Review* 56 (1972).

Silva, Golbery do C. *Conjuntura Política Nacional: O Poder Executivo e Geopolítica do Brasil.* Rio de Janeior: José Olypio, 1981.

Simão, Aziz. "O Voto Operário em São Paulo." *Revista Brasileira de Estudos Políticos* 1 (1956): 130–41.

Singer, Paul. "A Política das Classes Dominantes." In *Política e Revolução Social no Brasil,* ed. Octavio Ianni. Rio de Janeiro: Civilização Brasileira, 1965.

Singer, Paul, and Vinicius C. Brandt, eds. *São Paulo: O Povo em Movimento* Petrópolis: Vozes/CEBRAP, 1980.

Skidmore, Thomas. "Brazil's Slow Road to Democratization: 1974–1985." In *Democratizing Brazil,* ed. Alfred Stepan. New York: Oxford University Press, 1989.

Skidmore, Thomas. *Politics in Brazil: An Experiment in Democracy.* Oxford: Oxford University Press, 1967.

Skidmore, Thomas. *The Politics of Military Rule in Brazil, 1964–1985.* New York: Oxford, 1988.

Smith, Eric. "The Levels of Conceptualization: False Measures of Ideological Sophistication." *APSR* 74 (1980): 685–96.

Soares, Glaucio D. *Sociedade e Política no Brasil.* São Paulo: Difel, 1973.

Soares, Glaucio D. "The Politics of Uneven Development: The Case of Brazil." In *Party Systems and Voter Alignment,* ed. Seymour M. Lipset and Stein Rokkan, 467–96. New York: Free Press, 1967.

Souza, Maria C. C. de. *Estado e Partidos Políticos no Brasil.* São Paulo: Alfa Omega, 1976.

Souza, Maria C. C. de. "O Processo Político-Partidário na Primeira República." In *Brasil em Perspectiva,* 14th ed., ed. Carlos G. Mota. São Paulo: Difel, 1984.

Souza, Maria T. R. "Concentração Industrial e Estrutura Partidária: O Processo Eleitoral no ABC, 1966–1982." Ph.D. diss., FFLCH, Universidade de São Paulo.

Spindel, Arnaldo. O P.C. na Gênese do Populismo. São Paulo: Símbolo, 1980.

Stanley, D. Changing Administrations. Washington D.C.: Brookings Institution, 1965.

Stein, Stanley. "Historiography of Brazil, 1808–1889." Hispanic American Historical Review 15 (1969).

Stepan, Alfred. The Military in Politics: Changing Patterns in Brazil. Princeton: Princeton University Press, 1971.

Stepan, Alfred. "Political Leadership and Regime Breakdown: Brazil." In The Breakdown of Democratic Regimes, Latin America, ed. Juan Linz and Alfred Stepan. Baltimore: Johns Hopkins University Press, 1978.

Stepan, Alfred. Rethinking Military Politics, Brazil and the Southern Cone. Princeton: Princeton University Press, 1988.

Stepan, Alfred. "State Power and the Strength of Civil Society in the Southern Cone of Latin America." In Bringing the State Back In, ed. Peter Evans et al., pp. 317–46. Cambridge: Cambridge University Press, 1985.

Stepan, Alfred, ed. Authoritarian Brazil. New Haven: Yale University Press, 1973.

Stepan, Alfred, ed. Democratizing Brazil. New York: Oxford University Press, 1989.

Stinchcombe, Arthur. Constructing Social Theory. New York: Harcourt Brace, 1968.

Sullivan, John, James Pireson, and George Marcus. Political Tolerance and American Democracy. Chicago: University of Chicago Press, 1982.

Tavares, Maria C. D. "Rise and Decline of Import Substitution in Brazil." Economic Bulletin from Latin America 9 (1964): 1–65.

Trindade, Hélgio. "Bases da Democracia Brasileira: Lógica Liberal e Práxis Autoritária: 1822–1945." In Como Renascem as Democracias, ed. Alain Rouquie et al. São Paulo: Brasiliense: 1985.

Trindade, Hélgio. O Integralismo: O Fascismo Brasileiro na Década de 30. São Paulo: Difel, 1974.

Universidade de Brasília. A Revolução de 1930. International Conference. Brasília: Editora da Universidade de Brasília, 1982.

Universidade Federal do Rio Grande do Sul. Simpósio Sobre a Revolução de 1930. Porto Alegre: 1982.

Uroc'ocheia, Fernando. O Minotauro Imperial: A Burocratização do Estado Brasileiro no Século XIX. São Paulo: Difel, 1981.

Valenzuela, Arturo. The Breakdown of Democratic Regimes: Chile. Baltimore: Johns Hopkins University Press, 1978.

Valenzuela, J. Samuel, and Arturo Valenzuela. "Party Oppositions Under the Chilean Authoritarian Regime." In Military Rule in Chile: Dicta-

torship and Oppositions. Baltimore: Johns Hopkins University Press, 1986.

Verba, Sidney, Norman H. Nie, and Jae-on Kim. *Participation and Political Equality: A Seven Nation Comparison.* Chicago: University of Chicago Press, 1978.

Vianna, Oliveira. *Instituições Políticas Brasileiras.* Rio de Janeiro: José Olympio, 1951.

Vianna, Oliveira. *O Ocaso do Império.* São Paulo: Companhia da Editora Nacional, 1950.

Vianna, Oliveira. *Problemas da Política Objetiva,* 2d ed. São Paulo: Companhia Editora Nacional, 1947.

Von Mettenheim, Kurt. "The Brazilian Voter in Democratic Transition, 1974–1982." *Comparative Politics* 23 (1990): 23–44.

Von Mettenheim, Kurt. "Media-State Relations in Brazil, 1955–1980." Unpublished MS, Columbia University, 1982.

Weber, Max. *Economy and Society.* Berkeley and Los Angeles: University of California Press, 1978.

Weber, Max. *From Max Weber: Essays in Sociology,* ed. Hans Gerth and C. Wright Mills. New York: Oxford University Press, 1946.

Weffort, Francisco. *O Populismo na Política Brasileira.* Rio de Janeiro: Paz e Terra, 1978.

Weffort, Francisco. "Origens do Sindicalismo Populista no Brasil (A Conjuntura Pós-Guerra)." *Estudos Cebrap* 4 (1973).

Weffort, Francisco. *Porquê Democracia.* São Paulo: Brasiliense, 1985.

Weffort, Francisco. "Raízes do Populismo em São Paulo." *Revista de Civilização Brasileira* 2 (1965).

Weffort, Francisco. "State and Mass in Brazil." In *Masses in Latin America,* ed. Irving L. Horowitz. New York: Oxford, 1970.

Weffort, Francisco. "Why Democracy?" *Democratizing Brazil.* New York: Oxford University Press, 1989.

Weissberg, Robert. "Collective vs. Dyadic Representation in Congress." *American Political Science Review* 72 (1978): 535–47.

Werner, Altman, ed. *El Populismo en América Latina.* Mexico City: Siglo XXI, 1983.

Weyland, Kurt. "The Rise and Fall of President Collor and Its impact on Brazilian Democracy." *Journal of Interamerican Studies and World Affairs* 35 (1993): 1–37.

Wiarda, Howard, ed. *Politics and Social Change in Latin America: The Distinct Tradition.* Amherst: University of Massachusetts Press, 1974.

Wirth, John. *Minas Gerais in the Brazilian Federation, 1889–1937.* Stanford: Stanford University Press, 1977.

Index